Helping?

Gillian Berry

Helping?

A Search to Understand Healing from an Indigenous African-Centered Perspective

Springer

Gillian Berry
Mount Pearl, NL, Canada

ISBN 978-3-031-88585-3 ISBN 978-3-031-88586-0 (eBook)
https://doi.org/10.1007/978-3-031-88586-0

This Springer imprint is published by the registered company Springer Nature Switzerland AG
The registered company address is: Gewerbestrasse 11, 6330 Cham, Switzerland

Birds born in a cage think flying is an illness.—Alejandro Jodorowsky

Foreword

When I read the final draft of *Helping?: A Search to Understand Healing from an Indigenous African-Centered Perspective*, I knew immediately that this was something different. It offers a special opportunity to understand healing in a new way. In passionate, eloquent, and skillful prose, Gillian shares poignant and stark stories about growing up and growing into a powerful and caring healing professional. These stories invited me to explore how I might become more open to healing, both in my own healing journey and in the work I do as a healing "professional." I believe this is also the opportunity she offers to you, her future readers.

Gillian's analysis of the shortcomings of Western approaches to healing lands on so many thoughtful and moving themes. Cradled lovingly between those heartfelt stories about how she grew into her mission as a healer, Gillian provides an account of why Western mental health care continues to fail so many people. But it is those stories, and the unfolding life they document and express, that truly invite us to explore the unexpected, to think and feel in new ways, and to connect more fully with our most vital (and often elusive) ways of being. Because she is willing to interrogate her own life, Gillian is able to pose frightening but essential questions that are too often avoided, such as when she asks herself whether, as a professional healthcare provider, she has actually done more harm than good. This fearless exploration of what it means to heal and to help invites readers to examine their own fears, biases, and preconceptions, and empowers us all to search for deeper truths.

It is rare to encounter a book like this one, which is both intriguing and inspiring, and which encourages us to make such questions a part of our everyday lives. For me, despite—or maybe because of—my own experience in the field of psychology and healing, including the writing of my own books, it's not always easy to explore new ways of being. There are already so many solutions, practices, theories, and ways of being available, and some of them have seemed to work for me—at times really well. Why risk change when the familiar is so comfortable and comforting? Even when the familiar path is not so fruitful, the familiar remains attractive simply by virtue of being predictable. But in quiet moments of self-reflection or moments of forced re-examination, I feel the tide changing. Defenses go down, the often-troubling unease of the unpredictable emerges, and real change becomes possible. This is where Gillian speaks to us.

Through her courageous willingness to question, she invites us to wake up, open our eyes, and trust our own inner strength to meet and greet the unexpected. She does not guarantee anything, but she offers the hope that, as a result of this new vision, we might begin to see—actually see—and so begin new paths toward healing.

I received my PhD in Clinical Psychology from Harvard in the 1960s. Despite my questioning and skepticism about that training, it did teach me what mainstream Western psychology is about: and I learned that Western psychology fails to deal with real and actual healing as it pursues one version after another of an imperialistic, Eurocentric approach to life issues. Out of conviction that there was something more to be learned, I set out on what has become a more than 50-year journey toward a different kind of learning and healing. By spending different periods of time living and working with Indigenous healers to learn about Indigenous approaches to individual, community, and planetary health—all of which are connected—I came to realize that values stressed by those Indigenous healers, such as respect, honesty, humility, vulnerability, and service, are the foundations of healing. I also came to understand that spirituality, and especially the spirituality of everyday life, is the very source of healing energy. This journey has taught me to recognize companions along the way, fellow-seekers of strength of understanding from Indigenous perspectives—and Gillian is one of them. Her story of moving from a thorough exposure to the Western approach to healing to the realization that Indigenous traditions offer much that we can learn from today reminded me of my own.

Reading Gillian's book released a memory I have of working with Ratu Noa, an Indigenous Fijian healer I was apprenticed to for several years while living in Fiji. I once asked him how I should treat his teachings when I returned to my home. "You must decide what is meant to be shared and what is meant to stay only in your special work," he said, "but above all, tell only what you know, only what has become part of your actual life—and no more . . . and no less."

In that spirit, I will speak about the gifts of healing Gillian offers in this book—telling only what I know, "no more…and no less." As a Black woman growing up and working in the often-crushing environments of England and America, she teaches about vulnerability (which allows us to be open to these new ways of being) and hard work, courage, and a grounding in the spiritual (which allows us to cultivate these new ways into actions in our daily lives). As we reflect on our life stories, expressed in the realities of everyday life, we can learn to move beyond "helping" into the profound depths of "healing." And we can understand our life journey as a vehicle for learning, transforming into our healing journey, a continuing challenge awaiting our continuing commitment.

The book you have before you is a gift, given with heart, waiting to be received with heart. That exchange can bring wonderful changes to our lives.

Professor Emeritus, First Nations University of Canada
Saskatoon, SK, Canada

Richard Katz

Introduction: Starting Point: Latisha

> The Black Girl, a fine creature, whose satin skin and shining muscles made the white Missionary folk seem like ashen ghosts by contrast, was an interesting but unsatisfactory convert; for instead of taking Christianity with sweet docility exactly as it was administered to her, she met it with unexpected interrogative reactions which forced her teacher to improvise doctrinal replies and invent evidence on the spur of the moment ... (Shaw, 1932, p. 8)

The First Step

"I want to help people." These were the first words on my application to study clinical social work. After seeing them in print, I decided they would not impress the college admissions officer, so I spent the next couple of hours trying to figure out another catchy opening sentence. The many cups of coffee and countless games of solitaire I played did nothing to increase my creativity, so I admitted defeat and reluctantly left my opening statement as it was. It *was* the reason I wanted to study clinical social work, after all, and I didn't know how else to say it.

I submitted my application and held on dearly to one of my late mother's favorite sayings "What is for you, is for you." Six stress-filled weeks later, I finally received what I had hoped for—a letter of acceptance into the Master's in Social Work program. I was so happy. My life is on track, I thought to myself, and when the course was over, I would be a qualified "professional helper" with a license to practice. I'd be earning a paycheck for doing something I loved. My acceptance into the program was a dream come true. However, the excitement about going back to school was soon overshadowed by my imposter syndrome, which dominated my thoughts. Would I be good enough? Would I truly be helping? Did I really have anything to offer? Secretly, I was scared and extremely nervous at the thought of being let loose on unsuspecting clients. I resolved that my secret thoughts were going to remain secret. No one needed to know my vulnerability. I became best friends with the phrase "fake it till you make it!"

The first 4 weeks of classes came and went far too quickly. Having covered basic social work theories, techniques, ethics, and professional expectations, my classmates and I were sent off into the field to start our placements. Did I feel prepared? Absolutely not. It felt like I was being thrown into the deep end of the pool by those who just assumed I knew how to swim. "Everyone feels the same way when they first start" was the mantra I heard from my professors, supervisors, and colleagues. Despite my nervousness, I held on tightly to my chosen theoretical perspective ("person-centered," because it seemed so simple), as well as to my commitment to making a real difference. I romanticized my role as one in which I was figuratively flying in on my magic carpet to fix other people's problems. The stark reality of the helping profession soon shattered my idealized views about saving the poor and needy, and, though I didn't know it at the time, it would change the direction of my life forever.

I interned at a domestic violence shelter where one of my responsibilities was to "counsel" the residents. One of the conditions for being in the shelter was to attend individual psychotherapy sessions once a week. Most residents hated the forced requirement and went half-heartedly. Latisha (not her real name of course), who had been living in the shelter for about 8 months, was renowned for being "difficult." However, when she was assigned to me, she enthusiastically came to all our arranged sessions. I learned pretty quickly that she was pleased to be assigned to a Black woman counselor. I met her every other day for the prescribed 50-minute sessions, in which we looked at issues with her biological family, intimate relationships, and the physical abuse that had led to her being at the shelter. I was excited to work with Latisha. It was clear she trusted me, and she made me feel like I was actually doing what I had signed up to do. I genuinely believed I was "helping" by creating an environment where she could talk about what was really going on for her. I would then do an assessment and pass it on to the "qualified" professional who would do the analysis and develop a treatment plan. I strived to be creative with the development of her ecomap, time chart, and genogram.

"Hi, Gill!" said Latisha excitedly when she arrived, on time as usual. "Oh, I have so much to tell you. I resisted the urge to call my ex last night."

"I am so proud of you," I said, happy that my strengths-based perspective was being put to good use. "You have so many examples of making positive changes in your life. Let's start to focus on those things today."

I wanted to make sure she realized that she had the skills to keep away from the abusive relationship that had put her in the hospital for nearly a week. Latisha happily retold key aspects from her life, and I dutifully recorded them in her case notes. I quickly got a reputation of being too "detailed," but I wanted to make sure the "qualified" person reading my notes had the relevant information they needed to develop the most appropriate treatment plan for her.

When I showed my supervisor all the notes, she was quick to point this out. "This is too much detail, way too much," she said. I resisted the urge to ask how a proper assessment could be done without such information. In my naivety, I did not realize that there was a strong likelihood that no one would ever review my notes, except perhaps another enthusiastic intern or member of the legal profession.

My white supervisor liked to be nice, supportive, and encouraging, and even the hint of saying something that could be perceived as critical was out of character for her. Our supervisory sessions were normally held at a local restaurant or coffee shop, where she usually went above and beyond to make me comfortable (especially by picking up the bill). Despite the relaxed atmosphere of our supervisory sessions, and her gentle, supportive approach, I did not feel comfortable telling her what was really going on in my mind. Our first session together had come with the expectation that I would willingly share my life story, which included the traumas related to being a Black woman in an oppressive society. I formed the impression, rightly or wrongly, that it would be a notch on her belt to say she had a Black friend, and that she was motivated by the desire to "obtain information for her research project" (I had heard she did the same thing to another Black student in the previous year). So, I did not feel I would be understood, and chose to respond superficially to her exploratory questions, choosing to struggle with my assigned cases on my own.

On this occasion, however, seeing my facial expression may have made my supervisor follow up quickly with constructive feedback about my notes.

"Try to just note the key points; a lot of people will have access to your documentation. I am sure you understand the need for privacy." She was referring, of course, to my inclusion of references to her many abortions, her traumatic childhood (which included incest and sexual abuse), and her years living on the streets.

"Yes, of course, that makes sense," I quickly responded. I didn't need to be told twice about not putting Latisha's business out there.

I knew I didn't know how to document my sessions properly. On a deeper level, I knew it was because I wanted the person who eventually did read my notes to have all the information they would need to make a decision about what to do with all the painful information my client was sharing. On an even deeper level, being brutally honest, I didn't trust my supervisor. I didn't feel she would understand my concerns, or that she could help me unravel the struggle I was facing: namely, that my client actually believed me when I said I could help her, even though I didn't think I could.

In other ways, though, working with Latisha made me feel that I didn't have to fake it any more. We were both so invested in the process that time seemed to stop when we met. I got the sense that as a result of our work together, the physical abuse she had suffered, being homeless, and living in her car seemed far in the past, and this made me feel hopeful both for her future and for my professional career.

So, I continued to listen attentively, offering advice when I thought it was appropriate, and consciously giving exaggerated head nods to show I was listening and to demonstrate my supportive, caring nature. I convinced myself that her life was going to get back on track because of "our" work together. After one particular session, I remember feeling particularly optimistic. Things were going well, and if I could have, I would have patted myself on the back for a job well done. I was unaware that it would be our last meeting.

I arrived home from my placement that evening to a frantic call from my family saying that my sister had fallen seriously ill while on vacation. They had booked me on a flight scheduled to leave a few hours later. Within minutes, I had packed a small bag and was off to my hometown to be by her side. Work was the last thing on my mind, but I vaguely remember asking someone to tell the shelter I wouldn't be coming in the next day, and was not sure when I would be back. I later found out they had forgotten to pass this on. Thankfully, my sister recovered, and I returned to my internship about 4 weeks later. It was then that I learned Latisha had been evicted soon after I left. She had had "a breakdown" and destroyed the room she had been staying in. Workers had heard that she returned to the welcoming arms of her abusive partner, primarily because she was without financial or family support. I never saw or heard from her again.

My colleagues at the shelter were supportive of my developing clinical skills, and tried to cheer me up when they saw me looking sad and confused. "You can't change anyone, except yourself," they reminded me. "You shouldn't take it personally," they said. "You are not responsible for your client's actions." They told me that it can take at least eight times before someone in an abusive relationship finally leaves, and perhaps Latisha was not yet ready. They eventually seemed satisfied to conclude that Latisha was unwilling to receive the "help" I was offering. But their supportive efforts were lost on me. Although I knew their words had some merit, the real problem was that my idealistic bubble had burst. The cold light of reality was shining through, and I didn't like how it felt. It had forced me to face the questions I wanted to avoid—had my "help" contributed to Latisha's breakdown and led her to return to a potentially life-threatening situation? Could I live with myself, knowing that my "interventions" into people's lives could have the opposite of the desired effect? I could no longer think of "helping" as a nice, safe, or comfortable profession. It was serious, and I needed to take it seriously.

This incident challenged me to think about what it was I was doing under the label of "helping." As the agency I worked at relied heavily on the work of interns to ensure its day-to-day operations, I knew they were not particularly concerned about whether I would develop into an *effective* helper. I would not be judged on the results of my interventions. I was simply expected to use my own judgment and provide care in the way that I was told was right.

I've since come to understand that this attitude mirrored the way wives of the late-nineteenth-century philanthropists laid the foundation for the formalization of the helping profession as it exists today (Global Institute of Social Work, 2022). Having assumed that their lifestyle was optimal, they saw it as their role to teach *their* values of hard work and thrift to individuals and families so as to enable them to conform to normative social standards. Despite the passing of time, I concluded that I was expected to do the same as those early "friendly helpers." But something didn't sit right with me: I wanted to know what I could have done differently to achieve a different outcome for Latisha. I genuinely wanted my clinical interventions to have that happy Hollywood ending—why should I desire anything less? I expect, no, *demand* that my doctor, my dentist, the person who does my nails or hair, or even the person who fixes my coffee in the morning get it right every single time. I wanted to offer the same quality service for those I served. With Latisha, I had followed, to the letter (and without thought), the theoretical perspective presented to me. I trusted that research had been done and had proven positive outcomes. I truly believed that my work was engaging, non-judgmental, and genuine—that, in other words, I had done the "right" thing.

As a result, I began to question whether this outcome came about because I was new to the helping profession. Did Latisha feel abandoned because I had left so suddenly? Maybe I had let her down, and if so, how? Had my interactions triggered her destructive actions? Had I led her to believe I was more than just her key worker? Was I being too hard on myself, or was I simply being naive about what it means to work with the general public? Where did I go wrong in the use of theory? Why didn't it work? Simply put, I wanted to know how a helper effectively helps. I had many sleepless nights as a result of this incident, and realized pretty quickly that my conscience was forcing me to examine and question my practice. I resolved then to begin a search to find answers for my many questions. This book is a result of that search.

About the Book

Entering into the helping profession as a student of color during the 1980s was like answering a conscription call or being drafted into the military. Academic and support programs, recognizing their lack of diversity, were proactive in prioritizing our admission. Although I intellectually understood that having more helping professionals of color would benefit clients, I could not deny a sense of unease that the pigmentation of my skin was a primary criterion for my admission. The novelty of being a minority student wore off pretty quickly when my fellow students of color and I realized that our professional development needs were not being recognized or met. We were validated for sharing the "minority/Black" perspective as we understood it, but we were also expected to conform to recognized theories in our papers, exams, and practice if we were to meet the competencies of the profession.

This push for visible diversity and ideological conformity left me with a lot of questions. Who am I as a professional helper? What is different about the counseling I provide as a person of color? What is the "Black" perspective that I am expected to bring to my practice? How is it applied? Is it applicable for all clients, regardless of their color? When these questions went unanswered, my fellow students of color and I took up our academic program's invitation to help fix the problem. We were thanked for sharing our concerns related to poor supervision, inappropriateness of recognized theories, and the need for more Black professors on staff. But the philosophical points behind our questions went unaddressed, and we left with degrees and certifying certificates in hand, unprepared for the reality we were to face.

Forty years later, this problem still exists. While the helping professions talk a lot about diversity and decolonization, there remains an unwillingness to engage with the deep questions around what it means to "help." Do our training programs produce effective helpers? Do our professional interventions actually work? If so, are they applicable to everyone, and do they need to look the same in every community? Are the helping methods we use capable of meeting the huge amount of need that currently exists? Is helping actually…helpful?

At the start of my journey, I naïvely assumed that what I had been taught at graduate school about helping was true—after all, it was backed by "evidence-based" research; recognized and legitimized by government policies and procedures; required for academic, accreditation, or licensing purposes; and accepted by health, educational, and legal systems. As I entered practice, however, my experiences led me to start asking uncomfortable questions. These questions led to other questions, and I began to realize that what I had been taught was *the* concept of helping was merely *a* concept of helping. If I wanted to understand what it meant to be a helper, I would need to look beyond the confines of the Western professional helping tradition.

This book is the result of my journey. It is an attempt to conceptualize an Indigenous African-centered philosophical perspective on helping, and to explore what this perspective looks like in practice. In writing it, I have attempted to bring together two different ways of knowing—the analytic approach to knowledge typified by Western academia and the introspective, spiritual, story-telling approach honored by Indigenous cultures. The book takes its structure from George Bernard Shaw's *The Adventures of the Black Girl in Her Search for God*, and each chapter consists of academic argument followed by personal narrative. An Indigenous African-centered approach does not pretend to be an objective view from nowhere; it acknowledges that everything we believe, think, feel, and know arises from the unique circumstances of our own lives. This book is also, therefore, the story of my own professional, intellectual, and spiritual development.

For this reason, readers who are looking for a straightforward definition of "helping" and a clear, actionable list of successful helping methodologies backed by clinical trials will be disappointed. This book is written to take you on a journey toward an understanding of what it means to be an effective professional helper—or, better yet, a healer. I know that in a society obsessed with technical fixes, efficient solutions, and "life-hacks," this is a counter-intuitive approach. If you embark on this journey, you will need to open yourself up to new ideas and ways of seeing, just as I did. Like me, you will need to confront painful and difficult truths. At times, you might wonder how anything that I am talking about is relevant to your own life and work. But an Indigenous African-centered philosophy understands that transformation happens during the journey, not when you arrive at the destination. And if you want to be transformed, this is a book for you.

Contents

Part I
Seeing Things Differently

Chapter 1
The African Forest: The Road Map

One day back in the 1990s, I found myself working behind a Women's Health Conference booth. It was cold and rainy, and as a result the conference was not well-attended. The work was boring, but as we booth attendees had committed ourselves to staying, we stayed. Wondering how to pass the time, a friend of a friend approached me out of the blue and handed me a small book. "I think you might find this little story interesting," she said, before walking away. It was a copy of George Bernard Shaw's 1932 novella *The Adventures of a Black Girl in Her Search for God*, and by the time she returned a couple of hours later, I had finished reading it. That little book made an unforgettable impression on me. I immediately saw my own search for understanding and professional development reflected in the Black Girl's adventures. Like the Black Girl, I had encountered "missionaries" who believed they had found the one universal truth, and like the Black Girl I had trusted their authoritative knowledge and experience—albeit questioningly. Like the Black Girl, "instead of taking with sweet docility exactly as it was administered," I decided to seek my own answers to the questions I was asking.

The Adventures of the Black Girl in Her Search for God tells the story of an African girl who is introduced to Christianity by a white Missionary, and who then decides to take literally the Missionary's assertion of "seek and ye shall find." It unfolds through a series of encounters in which the Black Girl questions the central paradigms of Western thought and liberates herself from them one by one, ultimately liberating herself from the constraints of paradigmatic thinking in general. She is guided in her quest by a skeptical, questioning attitude, but she is not a cynic; she takes everything she is told seriously, but then puts it to the test. What appears to be naivety is actually an innocence and innate good sense which enables her to see through the inconsistencies and hypocrisies of the various figures she encounters in her quest. Although Shaw's story is open to many different interpretations, and has been criticized as reactionary and patriarchal, I will use it as a framework for examining my own journey in search of what constitutes "helping."

When I first began to think about writing this book, I felt overwhelmed by the multidimensional nature of what I was trying to capture. For a long time, I could not

G. Berry, *Helping?*, https://doi.org/10.1007/978-3-031-88586-0_1

see how my ideas could be brought together and presented coherently. Shaw's story, which was initially just a paragraph in my original draft, grew to provide the entire structure of the book, symbolically translating the development of my thinking into a parallel series of encounters. My integrational use of the story aims to illustrate an Indigenous African-centered perspective in a manner that is itself holistic, multidimensional, and interactive.

In the novella, the encounters the Black Girl experiences, and the lessons she takes from them, are understood as being divinely guided. As she goes in search of God, she is unaware that God is within her all the time. Although she herself remains unconscious of this until the encounter which proves to be the turning point in her search, it is her congruence with this lived spirituality that enables the Black Girl to keep an open mind toward the information she receives, while at the same time providing her with "an instinctive good sense" (Holroyd, 1991, p. 280) and a solid foundation from which to question, debate, and challenge the various characters she encounters in the African forest. As I am interpreting the fundamental process of helping to be one in which an individual questions and determines their own life purpose, Shaw's narrative captures the essence of my personal search.

Shaw and the Black Girl

George Bernard Shaw was one of the twentieth century's most prominent and influential playwrights. As a result of his wit, satire, and social commentary, he was awarded the Nobel Prize for Literature in 1925. He was a politically engaged and even revolutionary writer, and his purpose in writing *The Adventures of the Black Girl in Her Search for God* was mainly to satirize formalized religion. He regarded all formalized religions as collections of inconsistencies and hypocrisies that survive only because most people do not actually test their assertions. For Shaw's purposes, the Black Girl is a literary device in the tradition of Voltaire's Candide and Swift's Gulliver: her honest skepticism and literal-mindedness are a way for Shaw to critique dogmatic religious beliefs by looking at them through the eyes of an innocent, honest outsider (Brown, 1970), thereby exposing their moral and logical failings.

As a radical writer who wanted to change the world, Shaw saw his pen as a sword in a struggle that was more ethical than aesthetic (Bentley, 1967, p. 133). After his wife fell ill while on holiday in South Africa, he wrote *The Adventures of the Black Girl in Her Search for God* in only 17 days. The story provides not only a satirical interpretation of formalized religion, but also offers explicit suggestions for "how to break from the molds of sexism, racist imperialism, and capitalist deadlock" (Davis, 1994). Five years previously, Shaw had begun a correspondence with the Missionary Mabel Shaw, who lived in what was then Northern Rhodesia, and he noted that "she makes it clear that a Negro girl is much less of a savage than an average post-war flapper" (Holroyd, 1991, p. 278). Shaw also intended this story to cause a reaction in white supremacist South Africa (Brown, 1970).

While Shaw was deeply critical of religion, his work was not an attack on spirituality. On the contrary, he believed strongly in the reality of the spiritual dimension and in the need for people to live their lives in harmony with it. An Indigenous African-centered perspective shares such a belief. Shaw's interpretation of spirituality involved a feeling that reality is an extension of God. Life is governed by the desire to understand, respect, and be in harmony with what Shaw called the "Life Force," which he believed guided the evolution and development of human beings toward ever-higher levels of awareness. He loathed formalized religions because he felt that they replace spirituality with dogmas, theories, and regulations, which distort the Life Force and lead people away from their true spiritual awareness.

Shaw's novella can, therefore, be understood as integrating rejected forms of wisdom not normally considered part of political power and scientific knowledge (Nyamnjoh, 1999). The Black Girl is prompted to make decisions about her course of action based on her subjective experiences, bringing into practice a research methodology which is creative and flexible, and which attempts to provide an accurate picture of what is being observed. This book attempts to mirror this methodology. In determining its findings and operating with such guidance, one accepts one's inability to predict or control an event. Instead, faith leads.

For my purposes, the Black Girl's skeptical quest parallels my own experience of encountering and "trying on" various Eurocentric helping models in an attempt to live more satisfyingly. The dogmas and forms which Shaw denounced in established religion are paralleled by the theories and models of helping I encountered. In using Shaw's book to organize my own, I have chosen to interpret each of the Black Girl's encounters in relation to the fundamental characteristics of the main Eurocentric approaches to professionalized helping. Since Eurocentric helping has its roots deep in Western Judeo-Christian religious traditions, and therefore shares the same basic paradigms and ways of thought, this comparison is not as fanciful as it might seem at first (Delaney & DiClemente, 2005; O'Grady & Slife, 2017). Most of the pretentious and oppressive religious doctrines which Shaw attacks in *The Adventures of the Black Girl in Her Search for God* have literal parallels in the helping profession, which has always been a close (if sometimes disguised) relation of mainstream Judeo-Christian thought. Shaw's story is essentially a satire on the pretensions to universalism and authority of this ideological tradition. He focuses on religion because, for him, it provided the clearest and most harmful examples of these pretensions. I argue that the same universalism and authoritarianism dominate Western counseling "dogma," and prove equally hollow when put to the test.

However, it must be said that like many in that specific period in history, Shaw expressed racist views toward certain ethnic groups, and was a strong advocate for eugenics. Such views were rightly considered unacceptable then, and they continue to be unacceptable today. I accept the view that Shaw, despite his reputation as a progressive thinker, makes use of the racial stereotype of Black infantilism/innocence. The Black Girl is "lifted straight out of her native tribal fetichism" (p. 74). She is violent (always ready to resort to her knobkerry), highly emotional (giving priority to emotional interpretations before internalizing knowledge and making a decision), presented as a sexual object (depicted in John Farleigh's engravings of the characters in Shaw's novella as voluptuously naked), as accepting the gendered role of domestication (marrying the Irishman and becoming a "conventional" wife), and as representing a nostalgic view of the colonial romantic ideal that envied the "free" nature of Africans.

So why, when aiming to illustrate an Indigenous perspective, choose a novella written by an author who held such problematic views? Why give such precedence to the words of a white man from a period of time and a social climate in which it was the norm to enact inhumane policies toward people who were categorized as being different, subhuman, and dispensable?

Using Shaw's story to provide a structural framework for this book is an attempt to symbolically demonstrate my understanding of an Indigenous African-centered philosophy in action. Shaw's novella came to me and had an impact on my life, and so I have chosen to use it—despite its author's shortcomings. The use of the story aims to illustrate congruence between the written word and the symbolic imagery of both my personal search for understanding and that of an Indigenous African-centered perspective on helping. I interpret the story as the account of a paradigm shift, illustrating the multidimensional forces that influence such a journey both subjectively and objectively. I believe it demonstrates how an Indigenous African-centered perspective or worldview impacts behavior and enables the Black Girl to navigate her encounters with wisdom, initiative, and intelligence, and I argue that this can also be extended to my reality and that of others.

An Indigenous African-centered perspective on helping is restorative, and offers a corrective measure to the psychological legacy of oppression, just as Shaw was motivated to offer a corrective solution to the "race" problem in South Africa in 1932 by writing his story. Considering it necessary in this postmodern age to undertake corrective measures to redress inequalities and oppressive practices, I see the critical examination of an Indigenous perspective as an attempt to validate this alternative cultural paradigm in the facilitation of a process that will enable people to live more satisfyingly.

Shaw's story aims to highlight the post-colonial journey of colonized people, in which exploration is a necessary part, indicating that the journey is still in progress. Davis (1994) points out that "when parted from her do-gooder converter, the Black Girl finds the Missionary's influence quickly waning" (p. 127), and the encounters of the Black Girl imitate the evolution of change undergone by post-colonized people, whereby they begin to value and acknowledge alternative ways of interpreting knowledge to those of the former colonizer. Such a position provides the liberational approach necessary to the process of healing and the development of anti-oppressive practices. The Black Girl finds that the more she travels, the more she relies on her intrinsic worldview, or intuitive common sense, allowing her to navigate her way through the myriad of influences within the forest.

The Black Girl's Adventures

Since this book follows the plot of Shaw's, it will be helpful to spend a little time exploring each of the episodes in the novella, and how I see them being relevant for my critique of the helping profession. Outlined below or the key episodes in the story.

The Missionary

The novella opens with the Black Girl's initial encounter with a Western authority figure. This is the Missionary, "an odd little body" (Shaw, 1932, p. 7) with a self-indulgent and unhealthy love of suffering. She is a kind of psychopath, a "coquette and a jilt," as her cousin calls her, who deliberately falls in love with clergymen, becoming "engaged to six of them in succession." However, "when it came to the point she always broke it off; for these love affairs, full at first of ecstatic happiness and hope, somehow became unreal and eluded her in the end." In one case, her rejection results in the suicide of her suitor, which provides the Missionary with "an extraordinary joy" and leads her to go to Africa in order to wallow in a region where, as she sees it, "intense suffering became transcendent rapture." Thus, she goes to Africa to devote herself to saving others' souls—despite the obvious fact that her own soul is hardly in a healthy state.

Upon her arrival, the Missionary approaches her work with the arrogance of the typical Western colonialist in Africa (Rodogno, 2020). She assumes that the "natives' ' are spiritually ignorant and that, as an enlightened European, her assumptions and ideas are universally applicable. She assumes the right to present herself as an authority figure with the power to enlighten and "save" Africans. Ignoring any possible validity of the Black Girl's own philosophical or spiritual foundations, the Missionary preaches the benefits of her own faith and understanding of God. In this way, she illustrates the universalistic and authoritarian approach of Eurocentric ideology, which has been as characteristic of the development and promotion of professionalized helping theories as it has been of Christianity. The helping profession is rooted in the authoritarian and universalistic European philosophical tradition and, like the Missionary, is either unaware of or consciously ignores the validity of any philosophical perspective contextualized by the cultural experiences of Africa—while confidently proclaiming its own universal applicability.

Historically, this perspective (supported by the political dominance of Europe's universalism and authoritarianism) has generally been imposed on non-Europeans, leaving many feeling physically and/or psychologically obligated to accept the perspective. This has often resulted in a response of conflicted acceptance on the part of non-Europeans. Despite the efforts that have been made to address cultural needs within the helping profession, acceptance of diversity, equity, and inclusion theories on the part of colonized people is often motivated by self-interest—for example, the need to get or keep a job, or to get ahead in the system. But this acceptance is usually only partial, and often involves painful compromises or humiliation. It almost always clashes with their own deeply rooted (though often unacknowledged) cultural and philosophical values.

Shaw's Black Girl, however, is different. She listens to what the Missionary has to say, but "instead of taking Christianity with sweet docility exactly as it was administered to her, she met it with unexpected interrogative reactions" (Shaw, 1932, p. 30). Her adventures begin when she asks, logically enough, "Where is God?"—a question the Missionary is unable to answer. The Missionary's conventional response, "He has said 'Seek and ye shall find me,' " is intended to disguise her own ignorance, but the Black Girl takes the proverb literally and promptly sets off into the African forest in search of God. In doing so, she not only calls the Missionary's bluff, exposing the Missionary's pretension to authority as a fraud, but she also enacts one of the core elements of an Indigenous African-centered perspective, which requires one to question and test assertions using one's own inner light. The Missionary embodies the universalist and authoritarian assumptions of Western thought in general, and of Western helping models in particular, while the Black Girl typifies the skeptical and questioning response, and the reliance on spiritual insight—these being the only tools for people in general to liberate themselves from the position of conflicted acceptance.

The African Forest

The African forest is the context in which the Black Girl is raised, and I interpret it as the Indigenous African-centered philosophy or worldview through which the world is seen and understood, and which is culturally expressed by the nuances of life on the African continent. It is this environment that has shaped and sustains the Black Girl in her search for the truth, and provides context regardless of race or where she is in the world. The Black Girl, though perhaps unaware of this herself, is operating from within this perspective. The same perspective, with its multidimensional, holistic, and interactive nature, also provides the methodology for my own search for understanding.

Gods of Oppression: The Lord of Hosts and the Nailer

The first creature the Black Girl encounters after leaving the Missionary is a mamba, one of the few poisonous snakes that will attack a person if crossed (Shaw, 1932, p. 9). However, having been told by the Missionary that God commands us not to kill, she befriends the snake and asks it to take her to the God that made it. The mamba leads her to an aristocratic-looking white man with "an imposing beard and luxuriant wavy hair, both as white as isinglass, and a ruthlessly severe expression"

(p. 31). This turns out to be the Old Testament Lord of Hosts, who, instead of being the God of Love the Missionary preached about, is a menacing, egotistical figure. He immediately kills the snake with his scepter and demands that the Black Girl bow down to him and prove her devotion through a sacrifice.

The Black Girl rejects this God with contempt, but when she goes to strike him down with her knobkerry, he vanishes. Shaw is satirizing the contradictions between Christian conceptions of God, and also implying that the Old Testament God is a fantasy. The Lord of Hosts is an authoritarian figure who demands obedience, but he vanishes if defied. I take him as an embodiment of the authoritarianism of Western thought and a symbol of the sacrifices this tradition demands. Like the authority of the Lord of Hosts, the authority of the tradition is self-styled, bogus, and vanishes if challenged.

The Black Girl then meets another snake, a rattlesnake this time, and once more asks to be taken to the God who made him: "You are not so ill-natured as the mamba. You give warning and go quietly about your business if we go quietly about ours. Your God must be nicer than the mamba's God" (Shaw, 1932: 11). The rattlesnake's God is another old white man with a beard and long hair, but instead of being an authoritarian figure he appears "kindly." He is a scholar, and sits at a table covered with manuscripts. However, "his turned up mustaches and eyebrows expressed a self-satisfied cunning which the Black Girl thought silly" (p. 11). This God, who says he is "a Nailer at arguing," demands not sacrifice and obedience, but criticism and debate. He is not really interested in "truth," but only in argument for its own sake. "Throw something in my teeth," he says, "so that I can argue about it." He appears to invite dissent and to encourage discussion and freedom of thought, but it is all an illusion. The Black Girl refuses to get bogged down in empty arguments and theories and therefore rejects Nailer as well.

Shaw uses Nailer to satirize the God presented in the Biblical *Book of Job*, and through him what Shaw sees as the element of sadomasochism in the Christian concept of God. For me, Nailer embodies the tendency in the helping profession to focus on theories and arguments for their own sake, and to use these to create a self-serving illusion that there is freedom of thought and debate within the field—meanwhile sustaining the oppressive status quo.

Koheleth the Greek Scholar

The next figure the Black Girl encounters is not a God but a "good looking clean shaven white young man in a Greek tunic" (Shaw, 1932, p. 14). Koheleth is a Greek philosopher who is also "Ecclesiastes the preacher," in other words, the author of the famous biblical wisdom book that advocates taking the world as it comes and being content with that. For Koheleth, everything is vanity, and there is little point in the Black Girl's quest or in anything else: "My counsel to you is to do all the work that comes to you as well as you can, and so fill up with use and honor the days that remain to you before the inevitable end" (p. 14). Koheleth's materialistic reply puzzles the Black Girl, but, in the spirit of the discipline of philosophy, their discussion proves to be a turning point in her thinking, enabling her to reason that "to know God is to be God" (p. 16). I interpret this encounter as mirroring my own discovery of Indigenous African-centered philosophy, a tradition that acknowledges that a worldview coming from within the Africa continent is fundamentally different in origin, content, and direction as compared to the Western philosophical tradition. Indigenous African-centered philosophers, like the Black Girl, began to "look inward" toward an Indigenous African philosophical tradition.

The Myop

After an encounter with a cowardly lion and a bad-tempered prophet called Micah, the Black Girl meets the Myop, a representative of Western science who tries to persuade her that all her fears and hopes are "only fancies" (Shaw, 1932, p. 20). The Myop attempts to prove that everything in life can be explained in terms of "conditioned reflex" (p. 20), but the 25 years he has devoted to cruel research on dogs turns out only to reveal something the Black Girl realizes she could have told him in 25 seconds. She demonstrates the short-sighted arrogance of his approach by revealing that he has been sitting on a crocodile and not the rough old log he had taken it to be. The Myop is representative of the short-sightedness and narrow materialism of the modern Western scientification of knowledge.

The Myop denies the existence of God and spirituality because they cannot be scientifically proven, yet he cannot see that his own experiments are both cruel and pointless. The Black Girl, by frightening him up a tree and down again, demonstrates that her instinctive good sense is more powerful than his scientific rationality. She demonstrates that there are alternative ways of eliciting information far more effective than his scientific methods. The Myop, who is motivated only by the egotistic goal of gaining the admiration of "the whole scientific world" (p. 20), is not interested in wisdom but only in the acquisition of knowledge for its own sake. However, the Black Girl's position of agency, the ability to recognize that her actions are not subject to another's control, empowers her to reject his limiting and oppressive epistemology. I interpret this encounter as reflecting the oppressive nature of Western science. By ignoring the cruelty of its experiments, such scholarship has produced inaccurate or irrelevant findings. An alternative perception of knowledge can be gained when we approach these questions from a position of agency.

The Cathedral Carriers

After a brief encounter with a Roman soldier, who appears to symbolize South African racism, and a conversation with a Jesus figure whom Shaw calls "the conjurer," the Black Girl encounters a series of bizarre figures carrying paper cathedrals on their backs and fighting with one another over points of religious doctrine. They each claim to represent "the true Church" (Shaw, 1932, p. 30), and each tries to convert the Black Girl, but she instinctively keeps away from them all.

For Shaw, the Cathedral Carriers symbolize the confusion inherent in organized religion and the tendency of churches to substitute forms and doctrines—the external trappings of faith—for true, inwardly lived spirituality. In my own journey, the Cathedral Carriers represent the fact that most counseling approaches provide only an illusion of helping. They substitute empty theories and models for real engagement with human beings, and therefore constitute what Na'im Akbar called an "artificial humanism" (Akbar, 1984). They substitute a pseudoscientific approach for spirituality and, therefore, lose sight of the need for congruence between practice and the inner self. It is because the Black Girl is congruent, self-aware, and in praxis with herself that she is able to instantly recognize the Cathedral Carriers' lack of authenticity and keep away from them.

The Black Girl

As the Black Girl encounters various characters in her search for the truth about God, she has opportunities to explore and measure her own values. She critically evaluates the information she is offered and uses it to influence the course of her journey. It becomes clear that the Missionary, far from instilling an understanding of God, has not prepared her for the encounters she faces on her journey. The Bible she takes with her for guidance soon disintegrates, and the Black Girl falls back on her own resources. Finally, after encounters with the caravan of the curious, a Muslim, and a Jew, the Black Girl is diverted from her search when she meets an old philosopher and agrees with his advice that "God is at your elbow, and he has been there all the time" (p. 54). Reasoning that to "cultivate her own garden" means to marry and have children, she coerces the racist "red-bearded, potato-digging Irishman" (who had come by faith to dig the garden of the old philosopher) into marrying her. The Black Girl then settles down to manage him and their "charmingly coffee coloured children." However, she "often returns to the thoughts of her journey" (p. 58).

The Black Girl and Me

The profession of helping is concerned with self-discovery and exploration, and so I feel it is essential to incorporate my personal experiences into my investigation. My specific personal history is an aid in my process of discovery because it emphasizes that it *is* my specific experience that is under investigation. From an Indigenous African-centered perspective, our own interpretations of our own experiences are central to understanding the world around us, and so throughout this book I will weave personal stories into my academic analysis.

I was raised in an extended family environment in which discussions were constantly held whenever personal problems arose. Whatever the source, whether on the spiritual or "earthly" level, conscious or unconscious, a problem had to be confronted and addressed. Guidance from a deity was sought through prayer and meditation, or through spiritual advice and the use of proverbs or wise sayings, as well as passages from the Bible. However, belief in these methods of personal problem-solving was devalued when my siblings and I were discouraged from talking and practicing them outside the family and community network.

As a child growing up in South London during the 1960s, I remember being patted on the head at age six, in a manner similar to a pet animal. I also overheard, during a family outing, a conversation about how South Africa's practice of apartheid was the best method for dealing with "these people"—the people having this conversation were referring to me and my family. I remember being told about the National Front (a far-right political party active in Britain at the time) which advocated the repatriation of non-white people from the British Isles. It was said that their regular Saturday march had been headed by a flag bearer who was a local doctor. These and other such incidents led me to conclude that the pigmentation of my skin meant I was somehow different from what was considered the "norm," and that I would be tolerated only if I stayed in the place allocated for me and my kind. I understood that those in authority—government representatives, physicians, teachers, and other community leaders—shared these views and opinions, and therefore could not be trusted.

My early formal education meant I was acculturated into a Western worldview. I had many "Janet and John books" which promoted what was "normal" and, by omission, what was not. My parents' way of coping with all of this was to teach me that the ruling classes had the right to develop whatever systems they chose—just as we had the right to create our own system and not take what they said personally. Coming home from a math class explaining to my mother that I didn't understand what I was supposed to be learning, she matter-of-factly stated: "Why would you expect them to teach you?" By asking me these probing questions, she made me think and question what I was doing. In our household, we didn't run away from problems—we were taught to face them and deal with them. But I was straddling two worlds. I made what I considered to be the conscious choice to seek the guidance of my teachers and doctors, who were all white. My education taught me that their helping theories and methodologies were scientific, and as such had been proven to be effective for all people. By inference, I considered what my elders did to be unscientific or, to use a common term from this period, "mumbo jumbo."

Reflecting on my early encounters with "formalized" therapy, I realize how complicated my attitude toward the helping profession was, even then. In hindsight, I think that despite acknowledging all the personal and institutional oppression, I made a conscious choice to prefer the approach of the counselors, doctors, and teachers over that of my extended family. I felt safe and secure in the knowledge that these professionals did not really know me, did not care to know me, and in their interactions with me basically seemed afraid that their limited knowledge about "me and my kind" would be exposed. I had the power to choose what I revealed or didn't reveal, and I knew better than to show them the real or whole me. My family, on the other hand, would see right through me, and so by choosing the counselors, I could avoid being confronted with truths I did not want to face. The parables, sayings, and words of wisdom were relayed in a manner I clearly understood, and they spoke to something deep within me. This, coupled with the expectation that I would "do the right thing," put pressure on me to change, to move, to address the problem.

I vividly remember how uncomfortable it felt to be called to account in this way. Such was the pain of these "discussions" that, although I was never physically chastised as a child, there were many occasions when I might have preferred that to the challenging words about my "misbehavior"—and the expectation that I would undergo difficult transformation as a result. So, I opted for what I considered the easier choice, the one I perceived would allow me to become other than myself. When I got to the point in life when I actually had the choice, I chose the method of counseling I interpreted as involving the fewest expectations and the least pressure, the method that left the choice of change entirely up to me. In this way, I could escape my responsibility to move, to take action, to transform—which was always the expectation when receiving counsel within the extended family. I could wallow in emotional support, appreciate and value being listened to, and expect to be agreed with regardless of whether my actions were inappropriate. Looking back, I realize that professional helping provided a framework for me *not* to grow.

At the start of my career in the helping profession, I specialized in the area of person-centered counseling. This was not a cynical choice: I really believed in the achievable objectives of this theory. Naively, I thought that by offering clients the core conditions of empathy, genuineness, and acceptance of the model, I could facilitate a process that would result in a more satisfying life for the person being counseled. However, my commitment to facilitating this helping process meant that I had to acknowledge the reality of what I was being presented with in my work as a professional helper. Take the case of Mr. E, a Black person, who saw the reflection of a white person when he looked in the mirror. Or Ms. M, who wanted to understand why, when she pretended to be "sane," she was subsequently released from hospital under the British Mental Health Act. Or Mr. C, who just wanted some designer clothes and a car in order to have a sense of belonging and to feel good about himself. I was truly horrified when I heard that a client had been in therapy for nearly 10 years before she felt comfortable enough to admit to her therapist that she had had an abortion when she was 16 years old. These and many other professional experiences made me feel ill-equipped for the facilitative role.

My commitment to the profession meant that I became motivated to seek a methodology which would equip me for the reality of the community in which I was expected to work. Despite my belief that I had the therapeutic tools to operate empathically, to be accepting and genuine, I had to admit to myself that it felt like I was merely providing a cushion, a sticking plaster over a gaping gash. I was a listening ear, rather than the facilitator of a process that could help clients live more satisfyingly. I questioned and reviewed my professional skills, theories, and practice, and was forced to conclude that the recognized theories and methodologies of professional helping that had dominated my training were inadequate. I would need to go beyond the boundaries I had originally envisaged if I wanted to grow as a helper. I felt that race was an issue for the white clients I counseled, while for Black clients there was either toleration coupled with suspicion or lack of trust. Some saw me as a "conformist" or an "Auntie Tomess" (the feminine equivalent of an "Uncle Tom"), believing I had sold out and become a member of a racist, oppressive system (Burkett, 2017).

I wanted to understand why Black clients in particular did not trust this formalized process of counseling. Did some of them also share my feelings of holding something back, of not wanting to truly be understood? Did their apparent satisfaction with the opportunity to talk and be heard conceal a reluctance to follow the process to its conclusion, to develop their potential and change their reality? My feelings had left me wanting to go deeper, to figure out whether the helping relationship was actually capable of delivering the sense of well-being it promised.

Even as I trained to become a professional helper, I had never forgotten, and had returned time and again, to memories of my late grandfather. Out of all my family members, he was the one who best practiced the method of counseling admired by my family. And although he died when I was very young, the "back-home stories" brought him to life. In the words of my grandmother, "nuff, nuff people used to crowd the house on a night to com talk to em." He had no appointment system, no assessment sessions, no written documentation, and he charged no money. People chose to wait in line to talk to him. They repaid him for his time and counsel with gifts of food, with positive changes in their behavior—or hid when they saw him coming to avoid the menacing glares he gave them because they had not acted on his advice. He had gained the respect of the community. He was known for his political work, his fight for justice, and for how he provided for his ten children and wife. He had the reputation of living an honorable and spiritual life. The people who came shared issues with him that ranged from the behavioral problems of children to the marital problems of the headmistress. My grandfather never hid the fact that the wisdom he used was rooted in his belief in God.

The question of paramount importance to me was whether just being, living, and following the practice of my grandfather and those who practiced as he did, could supply the missing sense of wholeness. So, I dared to go against my professional training when the answers it provided did not satisfy my concerns. Unsure of how else to move forward, I felt obligated to revisit the helping methods I learned about during my childhood.

I have come to understand that my grandfather's approach to healing was essentially an Indigenous African-centered one, which grew out of a common understanding of beliefs, values, and assumptions that shape an individual's or a collective's perception of the universe, their place in it, and the nature of reality. Although this worldview is expressed differently in different Indigenous communities, they all share a belief that the universe is a complex system of interconnected parts that cannot be fully understood in isolation. This interconnected ecosystem recognizes order, structure, and/or purpose in the known world and assumes the existence of a God-figure(s), higher force(s), or creative energy(ies). This is in contrast to formalized religions, which may embody spiritual elements but are defined more by organizational, bureaucratic, and instrumental requirements (e.g., specific doctrines, rituals, and traditions), as well as by the drive to perpetuate themselves. An Indigenous African-centered perspective is governed by a desire to understand, respect, and be in harmony with this interconnected material/spiritual ecosystem (which may also include, for example, specific doctrines, rituals, and traditions).

From this perspective, oral history, parables, proverbs, and fables are methods of learning, preserving, and transmitting knowledge—as are personal experiences, dreams, memories, and traditions, each of which can provide moral and ethical lessons. Individuals are encouraged to take an introspective look at their own thoughts, emotions, motivations, and desires in order to find inner peace, develop wisdom, and cultivate a harmonious relationship with the world around them. It is understood that everyone is on their own unique journey, including the helper themselves. A helper who has focused on their own self-improvement and self-awareness can better equip themselves to support and assist others in a more meaningful and effective manner, having recognized that helping someone means supporting them to discover and learn for themselves. This is the kind of worldview my grandfather had, and when I talk about an Indigenous African-centered approach or philosophy, this is what I mean.

Having been socialized in an English paradigm meant I was raised in an environment where Shaw's and other "canonical" literary works were promoted above other texts. This made it more likely that I would read a copy of this text and identify its subtle innuendos and culturally specific, "witty" caricatures than I would if presented with, for example, an equivalent African or Asian literary text. Other, similar, stories describe searches for meaning and purpose in life, including *Siddhartha*, written by the German novelist Hermann Hess in 1922, or the 1988 novel, *The Alchemist* by Paulo Coelho, which also saw the protagonist navigating complex challenges, making difficult choices, and having to learn from both successes and failures. Could I have used these texts to avoid controversy? Possibly. But it was Shaw's story that caught my attention at a specific time in my life and enabled me to address a dilemma from a culturally specific perspective. As Shaw used the Black Girl as a vehicle for his critique of Western civilization, so I want to use this story as a vehicle for highlighting the search to find the resolution to personal distress, or "peace," which professional helping promises.

In the light of these comparisons, I intend to take an exploratory and observational approach to the journey of discovery undertaken by the Black Girl on her journey in search of God. The aim is to show the dynamic interplay of culture and purpose and to offer an analysis and understanding of what operating from an Indigenous African-centered philosophy looks like when applied to the concept of helping. In using Shaw's story to provide a structural framework for this book, the text is not analyzed but treated as a discursive resource to demonstrate the application of an Indigenous African-centered perspective. Its main themes—spirituality, skepticism about dominant narratives, openness to learning, personal exploration, cultural applicability, and an anti-oppressive stance—enable the Black Girl's search for understanding. Ultimately, her journey leads to the development of her agency. This mirrors my own story, and hopefully that of readers as well. In addition to tangibly demonstrating the holistic, multidimensional, and interconnected principles of an Indigenous African-centered perspective on helping, the goal of this book is to encourage readers to be in harmony with life, to have the ability to negotiate their experiences, and to provide the resources to live more satisfyingly.

Chapter 2
The Missionary: Universalism and Authority

> *The Missionary was a small white woman, not yet thirty: an odd little body who had found no satisfaction for her soul with her very respectable and fairly well-to-do family in her native England, and had settled down in the African forest to teach little African children to love Christ and adore the Cross.*
> *(Shaw, 1932, p. 7)*

Mabel Shaw (1888–1973) was at one time the most renowned female missionary in Africa. Heading the London Missionary Society's Girls Boarding School in Mbereshi from 1915–1940, in what was then Northern Rhodesia, she had a lengthy correspondence with George Bernard Shaw and became the inspiration for the character of the Missionary in his story. In the signed first edition copy he sent to her, he wrote "it was you who set me thinking about the contact of black minds with white religions in the African forest which your descriptions brought so vividly before my imagination" (Christie's, 1995). Just as the Missionary in Shaw's story traveled to Africa to teach Christianity, so too have Western models of helping been "exported" to Africa and other continents around the world. They are being taught as an authoritative "science" and have monopolized the perception of how people are helped (Katz & Murphy-Shigematsu, 2012).

Two main assumptions evident from the above quote set the scene for the story and arguments of this chapter. First, the Christian doctrine is presented to the Black Girl in Shaw's story as a universal concept. Second, the Missionary is regarded as an authority, despite having a limited understanding of herself or the doctrinal matters she imparts. A Western approach to helping adopts a similarly universalist perspective, and the helper and the profession of helping are regarded as authorities *despite* the lack of agreement about what exactly constitutes "helping." My experiences at Zambia's Kara Counselling Center, Chinamon Mental Hospital, and the Counselling Center at the University of Zambia, shared in the second half of the chapter, illustrate these issues.

G. Berry, *Helping?*, https://doi.org/10.1007/978-3-031-88586-0_2

Leading the Way

The Western approach to professional "helping" (counseling, therapy, psychotherapy, etc.) has gained significant recognition internationally, with the World Health Organization recommending it as an essential process to aid and support medical services (World Health Organization, 2022). This approach has its foundations in a universal concept of humanity, and helping, as an applied discipline, draws theoretically from the study of human behavior shared by numerous academic disciplines, all of which attempt to understand and interpret human behavior. Nevertheless, psychology has remained the dominant influence on the helping profession and distinguishes itself from sociology, anthropology, political science, and statistics by concerning itself with the hows and whys of human behavior and thought. From such knowledge, a helper has the ability to understand basic "norms" of human behavior. To ascertain such normative standards in human behavior, psychology relies on the "scientific" method: "careful, systematic observation; attempting to explain what has been observed by developing theories; making new predictions based on those theories; and then systematically testing those predictions through additional observations and experiments to determine whether they are correct" (Morris & Maistro, 1998, p. 8). This process aims to promote objectivity and consistency in the gathering and interpretation of information, leading to the establishment of scientific truths.

And yet if we look at the roots of the discipline of modern psychology, we find that they are anything but universal. They originate in a particular time and particular places, namely, nineteenth-century Europe and the United States. As a discipline evolving in the context of a Western worldview infected by racism and social Darwinism, psychology was an important contributor to those ideas (Winston, 2020). In particular, it searched for and magnified the existence of racially distinct mental abilities and character traits among the peoples of the world. The zeal and zest of psychologists reinforced prevailing Western mythologies of racial superiority, while its reliance on the scientific method led its practitioners to conclude that human behavior per se was being examined. This latter assumption, as Robinson (2009) argues, is based on an assumption that people are fundamentally the same everywhere.

> In order to explain "universal human phenomena," white psychologists established a normative standard of behavior against which all other cultural groups were to be measured. What appeared as normal or abnormal was always in comparison to how closely a specific thought or behavior corresponded to that of white people. Hence, normality is established on a model of that of white, middle-class, Caucasian males of European descent. (p. 12)

From its anthropological beginnings, the study of human groups meant comparing everyone to the standards laid down by West. Anthropology provided psychology with the racial systems needed to justify intellectually the existence of racial difference among human beings (Winston, 2020).

Psychology did not, therefore, take a cultural relativist position, seeing the beliefs and practices of other human groups as having equal and intrinsic value, but rather assumed that Western cultural norms and practices were superior, as a result of its colonial history and subsequent economic and political dominance in world affairs. Having evolved from such an environment, when psychology deigned to study minority groups it was generally from a white, male middle-class perspective. What followed was a marrying of science and ideology in subtle ways and for hegemonic purposes. Western scholars in the helping professions believe they are engaged in neutral forms of research, but in fact they are exponents of a particular ideological worldview (Nyamnjoh, 2000), one they have spread across the globe. History provides incontestable evidence of the manipulative ability of academic research to prove and perpetuate the dominance of one race over another. For example, at the beginning of the last century, theologians influenced by political, economic, ideological, and philosophical power debated whether African people had souls, psychologists "proved" that Africans were genetically mentally inferior, anthropologists labeled Africans as "primitive," historians argued that Africans had no history, and biologists even debated the fundamental humanity of Africans (Browder, 1992).

However, despite a very strong commitment in recent years to "decolonize," "revise," "critically analyze," or otherwise infuse social justice principles into helping models, psychology has not been able to completely divorce itself from the legacy of Western cultural supremacy. This legacy continues subtly to influence its practice today, as will be discussed in the following pages.

The Legacy of Colonialism

The roots of cultural supremacy lie in colonialism, the "exploitation by a foreign society and its agents who occupied the dependency to serve its own interests, not that of the subject people" (Fieldhouse, 1988, p. 7). Boahen (1987) concludes that, despite having a military advantage, Europeans were only able to achieve their colonial conquest of Africa primarily through propaganda. According to Clarke (1991), this propaganda centered on the idea that the non-European world was in darkness "awaiting the light of the European to provide culture and civilization by imposing a European concept of God and seeing the European as a civiliser" (Clarke, 1991, p. 323).

Initially, Europeans did not necessarily see Africans as inferior. The European explorers who cautiously sailed around the coast of Africa in the fifteenth century came into contact with Africans whose way of life appeared strange, but they did not necessarily conclude that they were inferior (Killingray, 1973). However, this attitude changed rapidly to one that regarded Africa as "the dark continent," a mysterious and savage place inhabited by backward and superstitious people ripe for exploitation, evangelization, and conquest. This resulted in important psychological consequences for both the conquerors and the conquered (Christian, 2019).

Cultural Supremacy

Focusing on the Central African region, Cairns (1965) stated that "the early pioneers saw little of virtue in African culture, their observations, usually biased, frequently contradictory, and often simply wrong, are replete with danger to the uncritical research worker" (pg. xii). Examining the attitude and reactions of the early British pioneers in Central Africa, so accurately dramatized by Shaw's depiction of the missionary who "converts" the Black Girl, we see that the pioneers saw themselves as morally, spiritually, and technologically superior, as giants among pygmies, dwarfing the Africans among whom their activities were carried out. With their assumed universality, as Bar-On (1999) argues, the missionaries promulgated values that were essentially alien to Africa and that sought to remake Africa's people in their own image. The adoption of Western culture by Africans was, then, no accident. European imperialism deliberately set out to "Europeanize" Africans, and in this the role of missionaries was crucial.

As Cairns (1965) highlights, the large missionary element among the early pioneers of imperialism functioned basically as "transmitters of western civilization." Missionary publications—torn between the demands of truth, the propaganda necessities of the cause, and sentiments of fidelity for the martyrs who had passed on to their reward—distorted cultural contact into a one-way flow of benevolence. Similarly, in travel books, the only constant amidst ever-changing scenes are the dauntless explorers, surmounting hardships and overcoming human and climatic obstacles by the force of their iron will. Evidence of a glorious African past never causes the travelers to tarry and reflect on their own insignificance when confronted with the achievements of an alien culture; on the contrary, the picture of African life presented to the readers of these travel books is Hobbesian in its harshness and primeval in the domination of nature over man. In these European accounts, individual Africans rarely emerge from the mass as distinct personalities; they appear rather as objects of salvation, obstacles to rapid travel or as faithful followers, relegated to a secondary position. Not surprisingly, by the end of the nineteenth century, with Europe effectively controlling most of the land and peoples of the earth (Christian, 2019), the Missionary "saw himself not only as a member of a superior race possessed of an advanced culture, but also and more importantly, as adherent of a cause commanded by God and backed by divine assurance of success" (Cairns, 1965 p. 154). Cairns argues that nineteenth-century Europeans had the confident belief that their technological achievements should, in the name of "civilization" and progress, be imposed on Africans—by force, if necessary.

One of these supposed "civilizers" was a man named Sir Harry Johnson, sometimes described as among the most sophisticated of the builders of European empires in Africa (Ajayi, quoted in Boahen, 1990). Johnson did not share the romantic illusions of many of his contemporaries, particularly those military leaders of "punitive expeditions" who looked upon themselves as new conquistadors in the posture of Gods destined to exterminate a backward, decadent people in order to clear the ground for an entirely new civilization. Nevertheless, he shared the

Victorian belief that Europeans were not like other men, and that of all humanity, it was "the white skinned sub-species which alone had evolved beauty of facial features and originality of invention in thought and deed" (p. 497).

Johnson held the belief that, in tropical areas, where the climate and the prevalent diseases discouraged large-scale European settlement, the presence of Africans could not be ignored. But this did not destroy his belief that European rule in Africa would have permanent racial and demographic results. It was possible, he said, that science might "annul the unhealthy effects of a tropical climate" or "a disease may break out which destroys the Negro and leaves the white man standing" (p. 498). He had no doubt that, as in parts of Asia and South America, the eventual outcome of the colonization of Africa by alien people would be a compromise—a dark-skinned race with a white man's features and a white man's brain.

Cultural Inferiority

For the African on the receiving end of such assumed superiority, the psychological effect was devastating.

> The whiteman strove with might and main to despoil the black man on his own continent, of his own continent, strove to keep him down lest he should rise and become a rival. And to make this new implacable thraldom more complete, they decided to enslave his soul, to inculcate into his mind, through raillery and contempt, the idea that he was inherently despicable and inferior and that all excellence, all nobility, all that is beautiful and sublime was white. And thus they were able to make him detest himself and the works of his hands. (Fonlon, 1967, p. 20)

So totally overwhelming was European power that African political, economic, religious, psychological, and ideological systems—the whole traditional way of life—were unquestionably affected. The colonial regimes used their sovereignty to ruthlessly suppress practices that were considered incompatible with the cultural traditions of Western society. Boahen (1987) describes, for example, the colonial rule campaign against polygamous marriage customs, which worked to promote the individualistic and exclusively patrilineal approach of the Western world. Traditional African institutions that had their roots in village and rural life had to be transformed and adapted for urban living patterns. The French and Portuguese conferred certain citizenship and legal rights on those who managed to pass an acculturation test, and these Africans became known as *evolués*, or *assimilados* and *naos indigenas*, respectively. It seems logical to surmise that people's confidence in the old gods and the old social order waned as a result.

To be a "civilized" African was to behave, dress, and speak like a European. After all, Africans had been educated in European schools, beginning with the mission schools, and were therefore trained to uphold European values and to perpetuate European control—for the purpose of any educational system is to perpetuate the society that created it. The "non-*evolué*" or "uncivilized" African was "unsaved," "uneducated,' "'primitive," and non-Christian and, therefore, "a usable chattel for mines and farms"—so thought the Europeans and their "civilized" Africans. Missionary Christianity stripped colonized non-Europeans of everything, and in this psychologically insecure state, the African people could be immersed in the ideology of the Western order. Many Africans themselves will speak of the "blessings'' of Christianity, because they are sold on the "ideology of progress" to which its European adherents subscribe (Ani, 2000, p. 187). For Ani, then, "Christianity" is a configuration of values, attitudes, and behaviors that are inseparable from the history of Europe. Unfortunately for non-European people, "real" European Christians do exist and have existed in large enough numbers to have successfully imposed their own brand of European cultural nationalism wherever they have ventured, inevitably backed with the armed might of the West (p. 192).

As a result of this violent process, Western culture became regarded as "the culmination of all human progress, a model to be followed without equivocation or reservation" (Nyamnjoh, 2000, p. 7, quoting Ajayi 1966, p. 606). The perpetuation of Western cultures as the standard of measure not only devalues African culture in the eyes of Africans, it infantilizes and disempowers them by forcing them to learn afresh, under the guidance of condescending and overbearing Western overlords, new ways of seeing, doing and being. Ndlovu-Gatsheni (2015) cites Ngugi wa Thiong'o as saying:

> The biggest weapon wielded and actually daily unleashed by imperialism against that collective defiance is the cultural bomb. The effect of a cultural bomb is to annihilate a people's belief in their names, in their languages, in their environment, in their heritage of struggle, in their unity, in their capacities and ultimately in themselves. It makes them see their past as one wasteland of non-achievement and it makes them want to distance themselves from that wasteland. It makes them want to identify with that which is furthest removed from themselves; for instance, with other people's languages rather than their own. It makes them identify with that which is decadent and reactionary, all those forces which would stop their own springs of life. It even plants serious doubt about the moral rightness of struggle. Possibilities of triumph or victory are seen as remote, ridiculous dreams. The intended results are despair, despondency and a collective death-wish. Amidst this wasteland which it has created, imperialism presents itself as the cure and demands that the dependent sing hymns of praise with the constant refrain: "Theft is holy." Indeed, this refrain sums up the new creed of neo-colonial bourgeoisie in many 'independent' African states. (p. 488)

The Scientification of Helping

With the emergence of the scientific method in seventeenth-century Europe, the pursuit of "scientific truth" challenged the prevailing perspectives of earlier ages, when religious and/or spiritual reasoning had provided answers to scholarly questions about human behavior and thought. Helping, due to its origins in the Judeo-Christian religious and spiritual traditions, with diagnoses and methods of treatments rooted in a theoretical interpretation provided by religious scriptures, faced initial difficulties in achieving scientific respectability (Delaney & DiClemente, 2005; O'Grady & Slife, 2017).

However, by shedding overt religious connotations while holding onto promises that "man can be made whole, can transcend his cultural mold, and can be captain of his fate," counseling became humanism's answer to Christian charity (Bolger, 1982, p. 10). Helping developed "out of the decay of religion and its replacement by faith in technology and the perfectibility of man," and was married to Western science and Western religion (Bolger, 1982, p. 9). This dualism has led to counselors being regarded as secular priests, mandated to obtain for their clients a state of unspecified virtue, even a state of grace—or at least a return to the virtues of the community. Halmos (1967) describes this as follows:

> practitioners of counselling have a common origin and a common aim: their common ancestor is the giver of spiritual solace and their common aim is health, sanity, a state of unspecified virtue, even a state of grace, or merely a return to the virtues of the community, adjustment. (p. 2)

He continues:

> on the whole the counselors are frankly and humbly agnostic, and for this reason, their much-restrained piety is plausible and acceptable in the skeptical age in which they have to work, yet they use a language of reverence, and even a theological language and imagery as if they could not do their job effectively without their evocative power. (p. 6)

Helping, like other sciences, established a paradigm or shared ideology, defining what it means to be a helper or to do research in counseling, while legitimating counseling as a profession in its own right (Dryden et al., 1989). Embracing the "rules and canon of scientific method," counseling has been constructed as a sub-branch of applied psychology or as a discipline allied to medicine, uncritically adopting their methods of knowing (McLeod, 2017). In other words, counseling evolved from an attempt to explain the world through a priori assumptions, an approach that sees counselors as operating within "correct" or clear frameworks for undertaking a counseling session (e.g., behaviorism, psychoanalysis) (Kuhn, 2012).

Underpinning this process was a deep-seated faith in Positivism, a philosophical system that holds that every rationally justifiable assertion can be scientifically verified or is capable of logical or mathematical proof, and which rejects metaphysics and theism. Although positivism was once (and in some academic circles continues to be) considered the highest level of human thought, the rise of post-positivism in the late twentieth century produced a paradigm shift in the understanding of scientific knowledge (Angers, 2011). However, while Positivism is no longer the default philosophical worldview in the social sciences, many of its underlying assumptions are still present: human biases and emotions should be controlled, reduced, or eliminated in scientific inquiry; data should be reduced to its simplest form; and only directly observable phenomena can be regarded as legitimate forms of reality. Unseen or spiritual concepts are de-emphasized, and remain sources of discomfort for recognized helping professionals (McLeod, 2017; Schiele, 2000).

That Was Then, This Is Now …

In this chapter, I have been arguing that the helping professions have their origins in a Christian, colonialist, supposedly scientific worldview that grants them universal authority. This authority allows them to provide guidance and support to individuals from all walks of life, regardless of their cultural or socioeconomic background. The "truths" asserted by modern psychology are, therefore, understood to be true for everyone, everywhere. Like the Black Girl in Shaw's story, I initially took these universal claims seriously. But, like the Black Girl, I wanted to see the evidence for myself.

My search for understanding meant using a magnifying glass to see what I was seeing, and my lived experience highlighted my conclusion that the counseling profession still demonstrably believed in its own universality and authority, despite the passing of time. The more I saw, the more I came to believe that the Western approach to helping was simply a new version of the Christian, colonialist worldview that had been imposed on Africans during an earlier period. The "culture bombs" were still being dropped. This was driven home to me in a particularly vivid way when I went to Zambia on a research trip in the late 1990s, as I will explain in the second part of this chapter.

Universalism and Authority in Action

The first time I went to Africa, at the age of eighteen, I learned a valuable lesson. While visiting a secondary school in Choma, Southern Zambia, I had been called on to direct a school play for a drama competition. Being eighteen and fresh from a standard English education, I naturally assumed that I knew the "right" way to put on a play. I therefore ignored the ideas of my students whenever they differed from my own, which was most of the time. I did my best to create a piece of universal modern theater and to turn my students into African "thespians" on the English model. The result was that my group lost badly. My production was almost universally baffling to the audience, the judges, and my own students. It simply said nothing to them.

The winning play, on the other hand, was, to me, painfully stilted and didactic. It would have made audiences in England squirm with embarrassment, and in my universalistic arrogance I could scarcely believe that this "clumsy" production could beat out my "sophisticated" attempt to transplant the West End to rural Zambia. But the winning play spoke to the local audience and fulfilled their expectations of what a play should do. Although it took me some years to absorb the lesson, this experience made me begin to realize that my English standards were not universally applicable.

Twenty years later, I returned to Zambia, this time with a much greater openness to learning what was really there. I wanted to find out how healing was conceived of and practiced in an African context. I had chosen Zambia because I already had friends there who could provide accommodation and further contacts, and generally make my investigation a smooth one. I also hoped, through my friends, to be able to have a more integrated experience of life in the country than would be the case if I had to stay in hotels, eat in restaurants, and travel by taxi, meeting by and large only "professional" contacts. Day-dreaming of the trip while going about the mundane activities at the social services department where I was then working, I looked forward with eager expectation. I had good memories of my time in Zambia, and I couldn't wait to see my friends again. Unlike many of my African friends born in England, my previous experience of the African continent meant I did not have either romantic or cynical expectations. I did not expect either unspoiled innocence or primitive degradation.

Still, I felt a responsibility to "give something back," and so perhaps a bit paternalistically, I had collected donations of gifts from friends and colleagues to distribute when I got to Zambia. Indeed, this was a conscious aspect of my research method. I wanted to avoid just taking from them, and wanted to ensure I had something to give. I anticipated that the process would be reciprocal, but was conscious that I was likely to get more out of the experience, both personally and professionally, than I would be able to give.

On arriving in Zambia, I found that my friend had prepared an enormous welcome for me. She had invited all her friends, who plied me with invitations in turn. Everyone seemed to go out of their way to take me to places and events they thought I would enjoy and learn from. At first, I was uncomfortable with this. I wanted to get on with my research. It was only later that I realized that I learned as much if not much more from these social encounters than from my "official" research.

After settling in at my host's house in Lusaka, I visited the Kara Counseling and Training Trust the following day. Although my instinct was to telephone first and make appointments with the people I wanted to see, I was told by my Zambian friends that appointments were unnecessary. I was advised that I should just turn up and "take it from there." I accepted this as a sign that the center probably had a culturally relevant orientation.

Encounter One: England Comes to Africa

I had begun my research in England by looking up Zambian counseling agencies on the Internet, and had selected the Kara Counseling and Training Trust as the first one I would visit. Before I left for Zambia, I perused the Kara website for several weeks and came to some tentative conclusions about what the nature and style of the center was likely to be. I already suspected that Kara's goal was to transplant the standard English counseling model to Africa. But I had no idea just how complete that act of transplantation would turn out to be.

The glossy style and familiar jargon on the website suggested an attitude that was universalistic, authoritative, and Eurocentric. For example, the website announced that Kara was the only counseling center in Zambia, and implied that Kara was the authority on counseling in that country. There was no acknowledgment that there even might be other models of counseling going on there. The entire history of Indigenous African counseling, the practice of traditional healers, family members, and elders was ignored. The implication was not that an alternative, African model of counseling was not effective, but that it did not even exist. Counseling was what Kara did, and the way Kara did it was the only way to do it.

Still, I reflected that the main purpose of a non-governmental organization website is to attract and reassure funders. I hoped this accounted for at least some of its authoritarian flavor, and I assumed that the center's practice on the ground would be more African-oriented. After all, it had been operating in Africa, apparently successfully, for nearly 10 years.

I learned from the website that the Kara Counseling and Training Trust was a non-governmental, non-denominational, charitable organization that started as a project in 1989 and became an independent registered trust in 1991. Its mandate was to provide HIV/AIDS counseling and testing services, support, and care for persons living with HIV/AIDS, training of HIV-positive persons in community AIDS awareness, positive living and peer-education skills, training in counseling and home-based care for health practitioners, and care for AIDS orphans and street kids.

Kara trained some 560 counselors and home-based care providers per year, did HIV counseling and testing for about 200 self-referred clients per month, trained about 20 HIV-positive persons per year, visited about 100 organizations per month to do community AIDS education and outreach, was supporting and counseling 30 AIDS orphans and street girls, and also provided general counseling services for an average of 28 clients per month. It was a busy and ambitious organization with about 60 employees.

Kara's particular counseling model was EC (eclectic model). Officially, the Trust was not a religious organization. However, it was run by Irish Catholics (funded from Sweden). Its original brief was only to offer HIV pre- and post-test counseling, but over the years it had developed and broadened into all areas of counseling. Logically, I would have expected it to take a holistic view of the counseling task.

On arrival, the first person I met was one of the center's cleaning staff, and this meeting was the first in a series of disconcerting events. When I was introduced to this mature woman by my Zambian friend, she curtseyed to me. I was taken aback, as no one had ever done that to me before. Even on my previous visit to Zambia, I had not encountered this—presumably because, at 18, I had been seen as a child. The curtsey upset me, but, on the other hand, I could not pretend that I was not flattered by what I saw as the extravagance of her gesture. It took a few more people curtseying to me before I realized that this was simply a cultural nuance, which I was not yet acclimated to.

Later on, my Zambian friend explained that curtseying was simply what Zambian people do when they meet someone they respect. I felt relieved that it was not something that should make me feel important and privileged, which was a feeling I did not like or want, as I felt I had done nothing to deserve it. It was important to me personally, and to my research, that I should be treated like an ordinary person, rather than be deferred to as a privileged outsider or, worse, an "expert." I felt that only in this way would my research be relevant to its objective of conceptualizing an Indigenous African-centered approach on counseling.

The next step was to see the center's receptionist and ask to speak to a counselor and, later, to the director. The receptionist told me I could meet one of the counselors simply by waiting in line with other clients, but that I would have to make an appointment to see the director. This distinction struck me as significant. I could understand why the director might not want to have people dropping by unannounced, but I also knew directors in other centers who did precisely that and functioned no less efficiently. I took the Kara director's policy as a possible indicator of an authoritative, formal approach, and settled for an appointment the next morning. I was then shown through to the client waiting area to wait until one of the counselors was available.

As I entered the waiting area and sat down, a familiar feeling came over me. The room was a virtual replica of a typical waiting area in a British counseling center. There were English-looking chairs arranged in a square around a coffee table covered with miscellaneous popular English-language magazines. On one wall was a bulletin board pinned with various notices and announcements, while the other walls featured an assortment of healthy-living posters, again in English. I looked around for signs of anything Indigenous, anything which reflected local African culture, but literally everything in the room looked like it had been transported straight from England. I was reminded of the waiting rooms in the nationwide counseling agency I had worked for in Birmingham. Every waiting room in the offices I visited around the country looked exactly the same, and that look was very like the look of this room in Zambia. The atmosphere, as a result, was not only very formal and clinical but also incongruous and disturbing for me.

At the same time, I reflected that for the African clients, this was perhaps the scene they expected. I assumed that for them "counseling" was a European thing to be done in a European setting. Certainly, this approach to interior design could only have the effect of reinforcing the idea that counseling was something European, with the prestige and authority that was supposed to go with other imported European products. I also suspected that this was the intended effect. However, I did wonder how the counseling environment, being so familiar to me with my Englishness, could be culturally appropriate and comfortable for Zambian clients.

In any case, the other people waiting with me were generally looking uncomfortable and alienated, if not downright fearful. Many were nervous and fidgety, clearly waiting anxiously for their HIV test results. One couple held hands (discreetly, as Zambian culture discourages this). One man was sitting rigidly, in a tense, traumatized state, perhaps abetted by the cold, intimidating atmosphere of the room. But I reflected that while I was just there to chat, others were waiting for a perceived death sentence to be confirmed and, as such, I could only surmise that how the room was decorated would be the least of their concerns. But I did wonder why no effort had been made to make the waiting area feel more friendly and sympathetic in relation to local culture. On the other hand, I was impressed by the amount of information available, particularly in a colorful brochure on HIV/AIDS displayed on the notice board. Unfortunately, the forbidding atmosphere in the room seemed unlikely to be conducive for absorbing or relating to the information.

I was shocked again when my turn came and I entered the cupboard the counselor was pleased to call her office. This tiny room barely held her small desk and two chairs, plus an enormous pillar smack in the center of the minuscule space. I actually found myself wondering how they had been able to squeeze even this minimal amount of furniture in there. To intensify the cramped atmosphere, the room was dark and airless, the only window a small grille high on the opposite wall. The pillar passed directly down the front of the counselor's small desk, so that we both had to sit off-center at the left edge.

This desk was completely clear of papers, which I found strange and disconcerting. The counselor sat behind her desk, pen in hand, but apart from this initial formality, seemed comfortable seeing me and happy to answer my questions. When I briefly introduced myself and the reason for my visit, she seemed genuinely interested, making eye contact and leaning forward to listen and reply. I had no prearranged questions. We merely chatted, moving from topic to topic as the flow of our conversation directed. To avoid the impression of an interview, I took no notes at the time, jotting some down afterward when I came out of the room.

When I asked her about her training, she told me the agency offered an in-house training consisting of a 2-week course and a 6-week attachment. She had gone through this program and had then been fortunate to get a job at the center. She was happy to be employed (the unemployment rate in Zambia was astronomical) and considered the training program a success from that point of view. However, when I asked her whether she felt her training had adequately prepared her to do the kind of work she was doing, she readily admitted that she felt it had not. She told me there were clear guidelines and policies in place, which she followed but felt little commitment to. She considered she was "just doing her job." She also revealed that only 1 hour in the training course had been given to the issue of culturally appropriate counseling, and that this had consisted merely of a discussion of "cultural issues." She was able to reflect on the inappropriateness of this and acknowledged that the traditional African healer takes an approach which was more in line with local people's expectations. She felt that this was because traditional healers give advice and instruction. She explained that from the traditional perspective, counseling is spiritually guided, with God speaking through the healers or the ancestors. She said this was what most people wanted from counseling—to be "directed" by God, though not in a dogmatic way. They wanted to feel in touch with the spiritual domain and directed by it through a process which caused them to reflect on their situation and understand it from a spiritual perspective. She also pointed out that some traditional healers were not honest anymore, and that when a treatment or advice did not work, they would say that this was because the patient/client "didn't follow instructions," thus reducing the spiritual component to the level of a recipe, which is a distortion of the tradition.

She was aware of and frustrated by the fact that most people came to her with similar expectations. They wanted her to tell them what they should do. However, she was trained precisely to avoid doing this. She also noted that clients expected that she would talk about herself and "bring herself into" the counseling relationship as traditional healers do. Clients expected her not only to tell them who she was but also to justify why they should be coming to her for help in the first place. Their attitude was: why should we come for help to someone whose own life may be messed up? However, this common sense attitude went completely against her training in "professionalism" and "objectivity."

As she made clear, the traditional healer in African culture is expected to be involved with their clients and community, and to display the values of wholeness and healing in their own life—whereas she felt that what she had been trained to do, and was being paid for, was actually the opposite of this. As a result, her work, though welcome for the sake of the financial security it provided, was fairly traumatic and stressful for her. For example, she revealed that it made her feel "divided" in her life. She also noted that there were no follow-up procedures at the center, which she felt was a serious drawback. She pointed out that in the traditional healing system, the healer personally knows and interacts with clients in the community and, therefore, sees how they are doing afterward through normal social interactions, without the need for any formalized follow-up.

Because of these dissatisfactions she presented as being very excited, looking within the culture for appropriate methods of counseling. She clearly saw the method of counseling she had been trained in as a move away from African traditions, and problematic for that reason. At the same time, she revealed that she sometimes did "direct" clients, even though she knew that she was not supposed to—a clear acknowledgment of her practical awareness of the need for a more culturally relevant approach. She was obviously struck by the irony that I was from Britain, yet was talking about African-centered approaches, whereas she, an African working in Africa, was constrained to follow Eurocentric methods which she and her clients did not really believe in or find helpful.

As I left the counselor's cramped office, I gave her some references for material that I felt she could benefit from. I thanked her for her time and for sharing her feelings so willingly with me, and came away from the meeting with the clear impression that, though she saw herself as only doing a job for money, she also had a curiosity about alternative approaches. Unfortunately, there was nowhere she could go to feed that interest.

Encounter Two: Authority Figures

The following day, I went to see the director and found him ready to see me. When I entered his massive office, the contrast to the counselor's room was overwhelming. Fr. Kelly reminded me of a character from the 1960s television series, "Land of the Giants." He seemed swamped by the enormity of the room and sat authoritatively behind a massive L-shaped desk from which he did not move. The desk faced into another area where meetings were apparently held. I sat in this area with a big gap between us.

The atmosphere made me feel as if I was intruding, and I suddenly felt the need to justify my presence in his office. I showed him my university (PhD student) ID card, literally having to get up and walk several steps across the room in order to hold it up for him to see. At the same time, I felt perplexed by this feeling that, in the presence of this white authority figure, I needed to provide concrete evidence of my credentials and prove I had a legitimate reason for being there.

Ironically, Fr. Kelly was not interested in my ID or credentials, or indeed in me or my visit. He immediately asked me what it was I wanted to know. This startled me, as I had not come prepared with the list of questions he apparently expected. Instead, I had been looking forward to my preferred research method, an unstructured conversation with no pre-set agenda, like the one I had had with the counselor the previous day. I believe in a give-and-take approach, where I am part of the process, rather than a subject-interviewer situation where the subject provides information and the researcher, standing outside the frame, "objectively" records and processes it.

However, I quickly improvised a few questions, which had the effect of producing a flow of information from Fr. Kelly. He more or less conducted the interview from that point on, providing data about himself, the organization and its funders, and even giving me with copies of his publications as he went along. In the process, it emerged that there was one ongoing problem that bewildered and frustrated him, and about which he was quite frank. He felt that professional helping training did not seem to provide any self-development for the counselors who were trained. In particular, he was disappointed with the counselors who studied in the United Kingdom, because he found that they returned able to articulate counseling theory, but unable to reflect on themselves and their own behavior. In other words, they had good command of the theory and jargon, but showed little or no evidence of being able to practice what they preached.

The most interesting thing for me was that Fr. Kelly seemed genuinely at a loss to explain this phenomenon, whereas to me it seemed clear that the cause was that the training was not culturally appropriate. I wanted to ask him: what can you expect by sending Africans to be trained in Eurocentric theories that contradict their own culture? However, I said nothing, as it was obvious he was not interested in discussing the issue but merely telling me about it, imparting information rather than sharing experiences. To me, this was in keeping with the whole atmosphere produced by the room and Fr. Kelly's manner. The approach to "communication" was one-way, authoritative, and stifling. Nevertheless, I was intrigued by what I was hearing. At this point I still had no definite idea of the exact focus of my research, but I could see that Fr. Kelly's dilemma, when put together with what the counselor had shared with me the day before, suggested a path to follow. I would have benefited from the opportunity to discuss my emerging ideas with someone in Fr. Kelly's position, but unfortunately this was obviously not the time or the place.

However, Fr. Kelly was pleasant and friendly and appeared to enjoy the opportunity to give me his views on counseling. He was also eager for me to attend a Kara training course that began the following Monday, and I agreed that I would. I realized that I had not said anything about my research or what I was hoping to find, but

I put this down to my feelings of insecurity and intimidation produced by an environment which did not encourage questions. I felt that Fr. Kelly was certainly in control, and that, as director of the center, he assumed that his vision was the one that needed to be followed.

While waiting to pay fees for the course and to be picked up by my friend, I sat in a large, empty hall. It had lots of space and windows, but its emptiness and coldness produced an ominous feeling. After sitting alone for some time, I was greeted by an elderly English nun who introduced herself as one of those who had originally helped set up the project in 1989. When she heard my London accent, she seemed surprised and asked me where I was from. I took great pleasure in telling her about the United Kingdom, but she was not satisfied and asked me where I was really from. She seemed to think that she knew what was British—a category that could not include me—and that was all there was to it. I took offense at this, having become used to such questions as an expression of racism (based on the assumption that anyone who is not white cannot really be British) when I was growing up. I therefore answered, somewhat sharply, that the slave traders had done a remarkably good job in my case, as I had no idea where my family originated on the African continent.

This clearly shook her, and I could sense a growing hostility, so I tried to soften things by explaining that my parents had immigrated to England from Guyana and, since most of the slaves transported there had come from Ghana, we presumed our origins went back to somewhere there. I also told her that over the years I had noted various resemblances (food, clothing, customs, etc.) between Guyanese and Ghanaian culture, which supported this theory. I was trying to be friendly and informative, but sensed that the damage to our relationship had already been done. I could feel her discomfort with what she apparently considered my "uppityness" or "chip on the shoulder." As soon as she could, she changed the subject to the innocuous one of the decorations in the hall. At this point the training director arrived, and the nun introduced him. He gave me the details of the course and said he looked forward to seeing me on Monday. My compatriot then informed me she would not be able to attend, as she had recently retired and was on the point of returning to England. When my friend arrived shortly afterward to pick me up, the first thing I said to her was that I was sure I had offended the nun.

After the less-than-satisfying visit to the counseling center, the weekend came as a revelation. I spent it socializing with my friend and her friends and was struck by how warm and welcoming everyone was toward me. People seemed to take an uninhibited interest in me and my visit. They came to my friend's house to see me and to take me out and treated me in a way that was clearly meant to make me feel at home (and they succeeded in doing so). The atmosphere was one of acceptance and integration, in stark contrast to the coolness and compartmentalization of the counseling center. Here was the opportunity I had looked forward to, and which my research method presupposed; of learning by being involved in the life of a community rather than as an "objective" researcher. For example, at a nightclub, I was introduced to the *rhumba*, which turned out to be very similar to soca/*calypso* dancing, so I picked it up quickly and felt at home as a result; no-one in the crowd could tell I was "different." I felt part of the community.

These integrative feelings disintegrated as soon as I walked into the training room for the first session of the course on Monday morning. After the warmth and authenticity of the weekend, I could scarcely believe what I was seeing at first. It was a re-entry into the world of universalism and authority. I could have been in a training room in London or Leeds. There appeared to be no difference between this environment and a typical British training set-up, even down to how the chairs and partitions were arranged, not to mention the tiles on the floor, the flip charts and papers ready for use, the "talking walls," and the program, with its brainstorming sessions and plenary. The participants, numbering about twenty, were seated in the conventional semi-circle, with the trainer and flip chart positioned in front, lecture-style. As far as I could see, there was not a single visible element of culturally specific material. Everything underscored the universal applicability and authority of the Eurocentric counseling training model.

I retreated to a seat at the back of the room, with the sole intention of hiding and observing, not engaging. However, as the session proceeded, despite the reminders to myself that I was only here to observe, I finally began to share my concerns, realizing that a key part of any Indigenous African-centered approach is to take responsibility, be a scholar-activist, get involved, and give back. One incident in the session stood out. A counselor shared with us how she had seen a man who came in for counseling with his wife and asked the counselor: "Can you tell my wife not to be awkward? I have been making love to her for 15 years standing up, and now she wants us to lie down." The counselor then learned from the wife that she was pregnant and tired, but when the counselor went back to the husband and suggested that he should have some consideration for his wife's situation, he became angry and walked off. The counselor was at a loss to know what she should have done, but the trainer had no idea either, nor did the rest of the group.

I then raised some issues of gender and sexism, and raised some alternatives, such as whether it might have been better for an Elder to counsel the husband. I also posed a question about why more men were not coming forward for counseling. I was dismayed to find my questioning treated as a diversion or distraction, rather than as a way to explore the issues and learn more. I was trying to broach the issue of cultural appropriateness, but the trainer was so wrapped up in notions of professionalism and objectivity that he couldn't see that in such a case it might have been better to have approached the problem outside the "counseling" model altogether. During the tea break in the canteen, I began talking to participants and asking them about their training. Not one of them said that cultural issues or alternative counseling approaches had been part of their training.

At lunch, there was an even greater shock for me. The training director came up to me, handed me my money back and asked me to leave the course. He claimed that as I had not done the first part of the course (we were now doing Psychosocial Counseling Skills II), I was not qualified to continue. I found this excuse dubious, to say the least, as neither Fr. Kelly, when urging me to attend the course, nor the training director, when accepting my fee in the first place, had shown any interest in whether I was qualified. Due to the history of racism in my life and the attitude (and power) I had recognized in the nun the previous Friday, I immediately suspected that she was the one who was behind my "expulsion." I speculated that it had something to do with her resentment at being challenged. Had she used her power to make sure I was sent away? Or had the trainers felt threatened by my questioning attitude? Despite my intention to only watch and listen, like the Black Girl in Shaw's story meeting the Old Testament Gods, had I been naive enough to take Western philosophy at its word and presume that urging the participants to share their concerns and ideas was a genuine request? This is why I had decided to raise issues of alternative counseling models. Had they felt threatened by this, as the Missionary in Shaw's story felt threatened when other missionaries pitched camp nearby? Was sharing and participating only acceptable as long the schedule remained on target or the theoretical model was not questioned? How legitimate could a training model claim to be that feared making room for questions that challenged its fundamental ideas?

Whatever the explanation, I could only say my goodbyes, exchange contacts with some of the participants, call a taxi, and leave the Kara Counseling and Training Trust to its authoritarian ways.

Clarifying Encounters

A few days after my experiences at the Kara Counseling Center, seething with questions that were beginning to propel my thinking in new directions, I had a meeting with Hector Chimbola, the director of the University of Zambia Student Counseling Center. Mr. Chimbola had been thoroughly trained in Eurocentric counseling models, having obtained his Masters in Counseling from Reading University. Nevertheless, he readily agreed with me that mainstream counseling is essentially Western in orientation and that this is a major weakness. Despite his training, his experience trying to apply the Western model in Zambia had convinced him that there was an urgent need for a professional helping model that would be culturally appropriate.

Mr. Chimbola's key point was that professional helping, if it is to be effective, has to be an intrinsic part of a society and its culture. He provided me with a living example of what he was talking about by inviting me to his home. He seemed relaxed, and openly discussed issues of HIV/AIDS and the need to find ways to help the young people he worked with to change their sexual attitudes and behaviors. However, the university's counseling center worked closely with Kara, and in the end, Mr. Chimbola felt that it was necessary to go along with Kara's authoritative, universalistic model of professional helping. In spite of his misgivings, he took the approach that a Eurocentric counseling model is better than no model at all. I felt that he was another example of conflicted acceptance, although in his case the issue did not seem to be job security but rather the feeling that there was no viable alternative available. He was not happy with this situation, and indeed had concluded that it was not very effective but, perhaps because he had received such an excellent training in Eurocentric counseling, he did not seem to be able to see past the assumptions of "scientific" authority and universal applicability that he had internalized.

I then visited the famous Chinamon Mental Health Hospital, the only such institution in Zambia and one of the major legacies of the colonial health system. Here I met Silva Chilimba Hamavhwa, a clinical officer who was the only psychotherapist at the hospital. Like Mr. Chimbola, he was British-trained and was thoroughly familiar with Western psychological and counseling theories. He was also thoroughly dissatisfied with these theories when applied to Africans.

There is no question that Mr. Hamavhwa had an extremely challenging remit. Chinamon's catchment area was the whole of Zambia, and it was expected to deal with every variety of mental illness. In reality, however, Mr. Hamavhwa offered counseling mainly to ex-patriots who resided in Lusaka. This was because Indigenous people were not coming forward; he had great difficulty convincing them that he could help them by "just talking." Nevertheless, he occasionally had the opportunity to counsel Africans, and he allowed me to sit in with him with a woman from a rural village who had suffered a breakdown and whose family had been bringing her for counseling. After the session, we talked at length about the case. For me, it was not just an issue of her not being able to cope with being abandoned by her husband and left to raise three children on her own, without economic or family support, nor community outcry about her husband abandoning his responsibility to the children; these seemed to be obvious contributable facts to her current situation. But then we focused on solutions—which for me could only be found in a holistic package of care, and could not be dealt with on the micro level. I was not surprised to find that he had also reached the conclusion that a holistic, culturally relevant method of treatment might be more effective. He was clearly frustrated by the fact that the psychiatric hospital where he worked was modeled on classic Western lines from the turn of the last century.

My next step was to talk to the head of the psychiatric department at Chinamon, but this was not to be. Having been escorted to his office, I was abruptly asked to leave, with the brusque explanation that he was too busy and had no time to see anyone. I was not offended or hurt by his refusal to see me, but rather by his dismissive, uncaring attitude. Our brief encounter inescapably reminded me of a scene from the movie *Roots*, with the slave master waving his hand and the slaves having to respond.

On the positive side, the reception I got from the head of psychiatry was a powerful reminder of the colonialist roots of mainstream mental health care in postcolonial Africa. I now began to piece together the impressions and ideas which my various Zambian encounters, both the negative and the positive, both the social and the "professional," had given me. As I did so, I began to consider that a way forward had to involve some form of liberation from the essentially colonialist authoritarianism and universalism of the Eurocentric counseling model. As I struggled to conceptualize this challenge, my research was pushed a step further by a chance encounter with an African doctor whose dilemma with mainstream counseling was, like mine, both highly personal and at the same time resonant with the much broader lack of fit between Eurocentric theories and African perspectives.

I met this person, a senior pediatrician who also held a key position in the Zambian national Counseling Evaluation Service, not during one of my official research visits to institutions but at a social event where I never expected to meet anyone who would have such a direct and important bearing on my thinking about counseling. Yet, the social and "non-professional" nature of our relationship was precisely what enabled Dr. Kaunda (not his real name) to reveal his personal dilemma, and to have such a profound effect on my perceptions of the limitations of mainstream counseling.

I was introduced to him simply as a visitor from England. But when, in the course of the conventional getting-acquainted small talk, I revealed that I was in Zambia to do research on counseling, Dr. Kaunda was astounded. Not only was he deeply involved in the committee which had been appointed to examine the effectiveness of counseling programs in Zambia, he was also in the midst of an intense personal crisis which had completely altered his view of the Western counseling model. He told me about his position on the committee, but before revealing anything about his own dilemma, he asked me about my views on counseling. I told him frankly, but with a certain amount of trepidation (since I saw him at that point as the representative of officialdom), that I had come to the conclusion, now strongly reinforced by my experiences thus far in Zambia, that Eurocentric counseling was both ineffective and oppressive. To my surprise he promptly concurred with me, and it turned out that we were both equally relieved to find that the other was a "dissident." This created a bond between us and led, over the next several days before my return to England, to a fascinating and rewarding exchange of ideas and experiences. I talked mainly about the frustration and pain I had felt while struggling to fit in and work effectively within the British counseling establishment. Dr. Kaunda talked mainly about the emotional crisis he was then going through. After being married for 10 years, he had been divorced about a year earlier and had experienced enormous difficulty coming to terms with the situation. Divorce, although not unknown, was still generally frowned upon by the society, and from his traditional culture, he could not help feeling shame and loss of face on this account. At the same time, another part of him saw the situation from a more "modern" (Western) perspective. The fact that the marriage had produced no children made him feel even more conflicted, as this was seen by his family and community as a sign of his personal weakness and failure. To make matters worse, his ex-wife had recently had a child with her new husband.

I concluded that Dr. Kaunda found himself torn between the traditional attitudes of his community and the Western attitudes that he had internalized as a result of his education in England and his lifestyle as an affluent, urbanized professional and leading member of the small Zambian Westernized elite. In an attempt to resolve the conflict, he had done precisely what someone with his education and scientific training could have been expected to do: go for mainstream, Western counseling. However, it had simply not worked, and he confessed that he was feeling increasingly confused and conflicted, not less. On the one hand, he had come to the conclusion that the model of counseling was not only not working for him, but that it was contributing to his distress. On the other hand, he could see no alternative, as he had internalized the Western view of traditional forms of counseling as primitive and "unscientific."

Although we had several conversations about both his personal dilemma and his professional role, with my own ideas still only half-formed, no doubt I seemed to him as confused as he seemed to me. I was astonished, however, by finding such a vivid example of a man who appeared on the outside to be the very model of professionalism, control, and Westernized sophistication, a highly qualified and eminent practitioner of specialized Western medicine and the very picture of the suave, confident physician (I spent a day following him on his rounds and marveling at his skills and self-assurance) but who, beneath the surface, was so desperately conflicted. Some months later I received a letter from a friend who told me that Dr. Kaunda had committed suicide.

Despite the ending of overt colonialism, the legacy of the colonial missionary/native, master/servant relationship appeared to me to be still prevalent in virtually every aspect of relations between Africa and the West. This is nowhere clearer than in the continuing domination of the human and social "sciences" by assumptions of the universal applicability and authority of Eurocentric models of rationality. As counseling developed and became increasingly "scientized" and professionalized, it appears to have absorbed these attitudes of universalism and authority. From its outset, professional helping did not take a culturally appropriate stance. Instead, it adopted a Eurocentric authoritative stance, expecting its professional helpers and helpees to submit to its underlying authority. Those in authority who have had the opportunity to formulate and regulate what they defined as counseling and assumed that their model would be appropriate for all regardless of cultural differences. Most of the practitioners I met in Zambia, both Black and white, agreed that the Western counseling model was inappropriate; but they could see no alternative, and with mental health problems abounding, any model was regarded as better than nothing.

But I feel the question must then be asked: is it actually better than nothing, when the profession itself is in disarray? It is unable to define itself, and its training courses, on the whole, promote a narrow view of professional helping theories. Students who superficially show competence in the accepted theories qualify as professional helpers. The hope that this industry elicits among many may be so devastating when it is betrayed that it may have terrible consequences—as in the case of Dr. Kaunda. It was relevant for me that "clients" were falling back on their traditional, local methods of helping rather than seeking formalized counseling. They appeared to be using the services of counseling centers such as Kara because of the free HIV/AIDS testing service, but with little or no faith in the efficacy of the psychotherapy that accompanied it. This is most probably because the model being promoted as the only legitimate model simply does not take into account the specific needs of the local community.

To me this meant that, as for the Black Girl of Shaw's story, the search for an Indigenous African-centered understanding of counseling was starting its journey from submission and conflicted acceptance toward something else, unquestionably fueled by a desire to find a corrective alternative for a more effective counseling practice.

Fr. Kelly projected both authority and authoritativeness. He clearly assumed the universal applicability of the "objective" Western counseling theories. When something did not work or went wrong, it was not the theory but the counselors who were to blame for not internalizing the principles or exhibiting enough self-discipline in practicing them. The most interesting thing was that Fr. Kelly recognized that there was a problem somewhere in the training cycle, but did not seem able to see outside his paradigm—despite living and working in the midst of an African culture that had its own counseling paradigms. The counselor I met evinced a "questioning acceptance" of Eurocentric counseling theories, but felt she had to operate from a dual perspective for practical reasons (financial security), while the nun, I thought, projected "Englishness" and (probably unconscious) racism. Her authoritative manner was obviously influenced by her religious faith, which convinced her she had access to an authoritative Truth. For her, there seemed to be only one way of doing things: her way. I sensed that she resented my refusal to acknowledge her authority and was, therefore, unsure how to handle me and suspicious about my intentions. My questioning attitude did not correspond to her expectations of how an African should behave in the presence of "those who know best" (i.e., whites like herself). Even though they had a structure and system in place, and could therefore give the impression of being better than nothing, I felt that it led to people living a lie. To accept this authoritarianism, I felt, was detrimental to my living more satisfyingly. I felt I had to move on.

I acknowledge that, having just arrived and with strong, preconceived ideas, I was eager to share my views with others. This could have contributed to my being problematic for the center. Perhaps a more circumspect attitude had been called for. Whatever the case, I came away from the experience convinced that the professional helping model being presented at the center as authoritative, objective, and universal, yet was simultaneously being questioned by the counselors who were trying to use this model in an alien environment, simply did not fit. However, they felt powerless to challenge the situation, mainly because, in a poverty-stricken country ravaged by AIDS, counseling was being able to do "something." Additionally, they were motivated by being employed, and not to help fellow members of the community live more satisfyingly. Yet, unable to divorce themselves completely from their culture, they were nevertheless adapting their methods as they saw fit when they could get away with it.

This Western conceptualization and practice of helping has and continues to have fundamental difficulties regarding its very definition and nature. However, like the Missionary who sought an honorable escape by "settling down in the African forest to teach little African children to love Christ and adore the Cross" (Shaw, 1932, p. 7), it has found a superficial cover of respectability in its popular general appeal. As the Missionary has improvised and created doctrinal replies to questions raised by the Black Girl, so too does helping. However, we are told that the character of the Missionary, from her early childhood, had looked at authority in awe and had limited understanding of her own personal love relationships. Does the profession of counseling acknowledge its roots of authority and universalism in the oppressive practices of colonialism or its theoretical foundations in oppression? Regarding the Black Girl, Shaw tells the reader that she is an unsatisfactory convert, questioning and committed to seeking answers. It is from such a position that I sought to find answers to these questions.

Part II
Making Past Wisdom Modern

Chapter 3
The Lord of Hosts and Nailer: Sacrifices and Sophistry

"I am seeking God" she said "Can you direct me?" "You have found him" he replied. "Kneel down and worship me this very instant, you presumptuous creature, or dread my wrath." (Shaw, 1932, p. 9)

The first "God" the Black Girl encounters in the African forest is the Lord of Hosts, the "vengeful white Old Testament God" (Davis, 1994, p. 127). He professes to be a God of love but immediately disgusts the Black Girl by callously killing the mamba that had befriended her. Having been taught by the Missionary "never to kill anything if she could help it," the Black Girl immediately feels "her heart harden against him" (Shaw, 1932, p. 9). She recognizes his hypocrisy. Next, the argumentative God, Nailer, disappoints the Black Girl by his useless and self-serving interest in argument for argument's sake. He has identified the hypocrisy and contradictions found in the Bible but is not prepared to do anything about them; he simply wants to argue and theorize for the sake of it, and to create an illusion that He really does care. The Black Girl dismisses him because "a god who cannot answer my questions is no use" (Shaw, 1932, p. 13). Though they are very different, both the Lord of Hosts and Nailer contradict what the Black Girl has been told about God by the Missionary. She, therefore, concludes that they are both false gods. For Shaw, they represent the hypocrisy of Christianity's two fundamental conceptions of God. The Lord of Hosts commands people not to kill, yet demands bloody sacrifices from them as He is only interested in obedience and worship. Nailer pretends to be interested in ideas, but only wants to argue and split hairs, not to help people. He is a sophist.

Both of these figures have their parallels in contemporary helping professions. In particular, I see their hypocrisy at work in the form of therapy known as person-centered counseling. Person-centered counseling presents itself as an effective method of enabling people to live more satisfyingly, but may actually oppress through unconscious assumptions about the universality of Western philosophical standards and values—proving itself to be congruent not with positive human qualities, but with the double standards and incongruence of its Judeo-Christian foundations. It demands either sacrifice or sophistry from those giving or receiving counsel.

G. Berry, *Helping?*, https://doi.org/10.1007/978-3-031-88586-0_3

After exploring the shortcomings of person-centered counseling, I turn to a series of encounters that reflect my personal awareness of this issue and of how I and my clients, in attempting to apply the person-centered approach, had sacrifices demanded from us or found ourselves substituting theory for action.

A Mirage of Hope: The Person-Centered Approach

Carl Rogers was one of the most prominent American psychologists of the twentieth century, and his research has had a profound impact on the development of psychotherapy. Like Sigmund Freud, he developed his theoretical approach directly from his work with emotionally troubled people, which led him to conclude that the basic force motivating the human organism is self-actualization, and that individuals have an innate tendency to move in the direction of growth. By recognizing which actions are progressive, the individual, through self-knowledge, chooses to grow rather than to regress. Rogers does not deny that there are other needs (biological ones, for example), but sees them as being subservient to the organism's motivation to enhance itself. His belief in the primacy of self-actualization forms the basis of his non-directive/client-centered counseling method.

The foundation of Rogers' method is the self or self-concept (Rogers, 1951). The self consists of all the ideas, perceptions, and values that characterize the "I," including the awareness of what I am and what I can do. This in turn influences peoples' perception of the world and their behavior. Rogers believed that the individual evaluates every experience in relation to self-concept, and that people want to behave in ways that are consistent with their self-image. Experiences and feelings that are not consistent are threatening, and so may be denied admittance to consciousness. Unlike Freud, however, Rogers believed that such repression is neither necessary nor permanent. The more a person denies experiences because they are inconsistent with self-concept, the wider the gulf between self and reality grows, and the greater the potential for maladjustment. If the incongruities become too great, the person's defenses may break down, resulting in severe anxiety or other forms of emotional distress.

At the same time, Rogers believed that each individual has a concept of the ideal self, a conception of the kind of person they would like to be. The closer the actual self is to this ideal self, the happier and more fulfilled the individual becomes. The well-adjusted person has a self-concept that is consistent with their thoughts, experience, and behavior; the self is not rigid but flexible, and can change as it assimilates new experiences, ideas, and self-knowledge. According to Rogers, any large discrepancy between the ideal self and the real self results in an unhappy, dissatisfied person (Elliott & Farber, 2010). A person's self-concept is also an important determinant of behavior, and the role of the therapist is to facilitate the process of the individual's self-development by bridging the gap between the real and the ideal self, not by asking confrontational questions, but by recognizing that the individual is the only person who can decide on the direction that change should take.

This framework led Rogers to conclude that in order to facilitate maximum expression of feelings, attitudes, and problems by the client, the counseling relationship should be one of warmth, acceptance, and the absence of any coercion. For Rogers, the relationship has to be a well-structured one, with limits of time, of dependence, and of aggressive action (which apply particularly to the client) along with limits of responsibility and affection that the counselor imposes on him or herself. Through this unique experience of complete emotional freedom within a well-defined framework, the client is free to recognize and understand his or her impulses and patterns (positive and negative) as in no other relationship. The counselor's key role, Rogers suggested, is to act as a sounding board who can enable the individual to explore and analyze their problems. The goal of a person-centered counselor is to facilitate this process—not to solve problems, but to assist clients in their growth process. Ideally, this should equip the client to become a fully functioning human being able to cope effectively with current and future problems.

It is hard to overstate the extent to which Carl Rogers revolutionized the field of psychotherapy, and the impact of his ideas can be seen in everything from nursing, medicine, and public health to education, religion, and business (Masson, 1988). There is no doubt that he did away with some of the blatantly oppressive practices within the profession—for example, by substituting the more positive term "client" for the label "patient," opening training to those without professional credentials, avoiding labeling and diagnosis, stressing the counselor's responsibility to provide a growth-producing climate, insisting on the "core" conditions of empathy, genuineness, and acceptance, and focusing on enabling clients to move towards their potential. But Rogers' person-centered therapy only appears to be more genuine than the more austere Freudian one it largely replaced. The clinician may have a warmer demeanor, but they are still playing a role that enshrines their own power. And this power can manifest in subtle but extremely damaging ways.

Rogers based his work on the systematic recording of his own attitudes and behavior during counseling sessions over the course of more than 20 years of research and practice, and in this sense he followed in the Freudian tradition. Freud saw himself primarily as a seeker of philosophical knowledge, and assumed that by reasoning from his own experiences and those of his clients, he could build a universal account of human psychology. But critics of Freud, including Masson (1988), have highlighted the plight of women in Germany in Freud's time to disprove the basis of Freud's work. Masson stresses that the common practice of incest and sexual abuse reported during this period may have been misinterpreted by Freud as female hysteria (a creation of the female mind), instead of being based on factual events. As a result, Freud may have ignored the realities of women's lives and instead presupposed that there must be something psychologically wrong with them (i.e., they weren't actually being abused, but were only imagining these things because of some internal illness or maladjustment in themselves). This didn't just marginalize the women in Freud's clinical care; it also contributed to Freud's understanding of mental illness itself. Rather than seeing the symptoms his female patients were exhibiting as being understandable and even natural responses to the conditions they were living in, he presented them as being the result of mysterious complexes buried deep in his patients' psyches. By following a similar path, Rogers made similar mistakes. His approach was inevitably tainted by his failure to account for his privileged position within society as a white male scholar in racist America of the mid-twentieth century.

Person-centered counseling's core conditions of genuineness, empathy, and unconditional positive regard are often considered as being enough to outweigh the difficulties presented by cultural differences and bias. With the counselee technically defining and leading the process, there is an illusion that "the client runs less risk of being judged by the dominant culture's definition of normality" (Usher, 1989, p. 69). But Rogers' approach is still guided by Western normative values which emphasize individualism and downplay the role social conditions (such as structural racism, poverty, gendered violence, etc.) can play in a client's experience of mental distress. Counselors often end up encouraging their clients to conform themselves to the world as it is.

Person-centered counseling may be a method of "normalizing" people to Western standards, ignoring actual social and economic causes of psychological distress and trying to convince a person that the solution to their pain is through a process of self-actualization. This further oppresses because it is itself an expression, if unconscious, of racism; it assumes the universal relevance and applicability of Western cultural values. It also ignores the fact that the period in which Rogers completed the bulk of his research—the 1950s—was one in which racism was rampant in American society, and when it was nearly impossible for minority scholars to get their work published (Guthrie, 1976). Like Freud before him, Rogers studied a small slice of white, male experience in the United States, and assumed he could extrapolate from it universal rules that governed all of humanity.

Sincere Hypocrisy?

I have no doubt that Rogers' work is a reflection of his sincere beliefs. But these beliefs were conditioned, at least in part, by the culture he was raised in. We know that Rogers loved reading the Bible and was involved in religious groups when he was an undergraduate at the University of Wisconsin (Parrott, 1997); indeed, for a time he felt that he was called to the Christian ministry, and joined the liberal Union Theological Seminary in New York. Two years later, however, he transferred to Columbia University Teachers College, where he earned his PhD in clinical and educational psychology in 1931. Having doubted the wisdom of following any one strict religious creed, Rogers concluded that a truly authentic meeting between equals, in which the client was understood, cared for, and respected as a person capable of positive change and growth, should be the catalyst for living more satisfactorily.

Clearly, Rogers brought aspects of his spiritual beliefs into his counseling practice. The congruence between his professional practice and what he personally believed meant that he considered that the core conditions he advocated for should spring from the counselor's very being. However, although Rogers may have considered that he was being congruent, we need to ask whether his congruence may have been founded on an incongruent foundation. In other words, Rogers' concept of congruence may be based on the contradictory values that dominated the interpretation and practice of Christian beliefs throughout the majority of his life, particularly when he was doing his initial data collection. Such contradictory values may convincingly give an outward appearance of acceptance, genuineness, and empathy (as they do for the Missionary in Shaw's novella), while at the same time making practitioners unaware of or unwilling to accept that their beliefs may be oppressive.

The history of Christianity reveals a clear pattern of hypocrisy in relation to non-Europeans, just as the words of love from the Lord of Hosts in Shaw's story are revealed to be meaningless when he kills the snake merely as a show of his power. Mato Nunpa (2020), who grew up in the Yellow Medicine Community of Minnesota colonized by the Europeans, shares a nearly identical example to that of the Black Girl from his own childhood:

> When I was eight or nine years old (1948 or 1949), several incidents occurred with the missionaries and their Christian teachings. One incident, which I vividly remember, involved my cousin asking one of the young Assemblies of God missionaries the following question: "Some of our grandmothers and grandfathers, who have died, didn't know Jesus as their savior. What happened to them?" The Missionary, a young man from Texas, replied, "If they didn't know Jesus Christ as their personal savior, they are burning in hell right now." I remember this like it was yesterday, even though this happened over seventy years ago. The Missionary's words seared my heart and became indelibly etched in my memory.
>
> Now that I am in my elderly years, and as I look back upon this and similar incidents, I have questions. One is this: Why would this Missionary tell young children such a hurtful thing? Our grandparents were good people, kind and generous people. They cared for others, and they helped people in need. A final question: The Assemblies of God missionaries taught us that God is love, that God is a loving God. Why would this supposedly "loving God" punish or banish people who never heard of Jesus Christ to eternal torment in hell? In my end-time years, I still don't know any good answers to these questions.

Mato Nunpa could not reconcile the hypocrisy that was taught to him by the missionaries about a God that was both loving and so vengeful.

"Manifest destiny," or the "divine ordination and the natural superiority of the white race that they had a right (and indeed an obligation) to seize and occupy all of North America" (Morris, 1992, p. 67) served as the Christian justification for the European invasion, killing, religious suppression, and imperialization of the entire continent of North America. The key role played by the church in the development of the Atlantic slave trade is also well known. In the fifteenth century, Pope Nicholas V issued two papal bulls, *Dum Diversas* and *Romanus Pontifex*, justifying slavery and colonization. Subsequently, slavery was sanctioned by the church as an instance of divine providence which brought salvation to soulless people. As the National Joint Action Committee of Trinidad and Tobago observes, a legal system based on such Christian moral values made the law as well as the church sanction oppressive practices. They note:

> As a Jesuit Priest called Vieira told some slave, "I know of your wounds and scourgings, your hunger and fatigue and reviling; but if you endure these sufferings with patience, following the example of the blessed redeemer, you shall have the merit as well as the torment of martyrdom. Your bondage might become a new calvary; but you must not, merely because your labor is hard, shirk your duty." (NJAC, n.d., p. 7)

Christian missionaries in slave societies in the Americas and the Caribbean were conscious that their role was to create "good slaves." They taught that disobedience of the earthly master was disobedience of the heavenly. Brent (1973) notes in his record of the life of an enslaved girl that, after the alarm caused by Turner's insurrection had subsided, slave owners concluded that religious instruction might dissuade the slaves from murdering their masters again. As Nat Turner himself pointed out, the missionaries were basically saying: "This the way it go: be nice to massa and missus; don't be mean; be obedient, and work hard. That was all the Sunday school lesson they taught us" (p. 69).

As Ani (2000) argues, the irony is that European slavery and imperialism violated every original Christian principle, while, on the other hand, the peoples being enslaved and colonized generally showed, in their simple and peaceful ways of life, far more congruence with these original principles than their oppressors. She therefore asks: "why should a people who were [in fact] non-Christian [i.e. who behaved in contradiction to their professed beliefs in peace, love, justice etc.] and who were slaughtering [true] Christians [i.e. people who actually lived by the values Christianity espoused] encourage them to become Christian themselves and begin to slaughter their brothers and sisters in order to make them so?" (p. 166).

As far as Ani (2000) is concerned, the current helping professions derived not only oppressive beliefs from their foundations in Judeo-Christian religious and spiritual misinterpretations, as discussed in the previous chapter, but may also have absorbed the belief that their practices do not *have* to be congruent with their professed beliefs. This has subsequently resulted in counselors who profess agreement with the positive qualities espoused by Rogers' core conditions, but whose individual and organizational actions nullify their good intentions. Their "authenticity" simply consists in outward appearance, illusion, or rote-learned skill. And since they lack understanding of their own or others' oppressive practices, they end up only helping to perpetuate oppression.

Psychology and "Scientific" Racism

Christianity was not the only ideological framework to shape the helping professions, of course. They are also a product of nineteenth-century European ideas about race and eugenics that emerged following the publication of Charles Darwin's *On the Origin of Species* in 1859. With the rise of evolutionary thinking, the Christian tradition of sincere hypocrisy, founded on a belief that some people were "saved" while others were "damned," was joined by the "scientific" notion that certain groups of humans were inferior or "less evolved" than others. This line of reasoning led many psychologists to turn their research energies to investigations of sensory and intellectual differences between individuals in order to solve the puzzle of human successes and failures.

Galton, a cousin of Darwin, provided one such linkage between scientific naturalism and psychology. Galton's *Hereditary Genius: Its Laws and Consequences* (1869) argued that genius and greatness followed family lines; *English Men of Science* (1874) and *Natural Inheritance* (1899) were written to substantiate this claim. Galton tried to show that great men inherited not only general intellectual ability but specific types of talent (for literature, medicine, music, etc.). His intense concern with the importance of inheritance led him to propose a science of heredity which promoted the idea of racial improvement through selective mating and sterilization of the unfit—he coined the term "eugenics" to describe it. Dalton's claim that good mating "could give more suitable races or strains of blood better chances of prevailing over the less suitable" was quickly followed by the work of Herbert Spencer, who coined the phrase "survival of the fittest" in the belief that since less "suitable" races had the ability to procreate more quickly, only selective breeding of the fittest could bring about a superior race. He did not hide his belief that unfit persons should be exterminated.

In 1887, G. Stanley Hall, founder of the *American Journal of Psychology* and first president of the American Psychological Association, theorized that Africans, Indians, and Chinese people were members of "adolescent races" in a stage of incomplete growth (Gordon, 1998). Thus, they required intervention to save them from their inevitable "negative" fate. While Director of the Kaiser Wilhelm Institute of Anthropology, Human Heredity, and Eugenics in Berlin, psychiatrist Eugen Fischer urged the annihilation of Negro children, theorizing that Black people were devoid of value and useless for employment other than in "manual crafts" (Gordon, 1998). In 1913, when Fischer was Professor of Anatomy and Anthropology at the University of Freiburg, he requested and was granted permission by the governor of German South West Africa (now Namibia) that a preserved Bushman penis be mailed to him. His petition was prompted by the controversy surrounding a claim by an Australian academic Franz Seiner, in a number of publications, that the distinguishing character of "Bushmen" was the penis, which could be used to distinguish between the various tribal groups. It is not known whether the requisition was actually fulfilled (World War I was declared shortly after the request was made), but it is known that the governor felt that the request should be executed in such a way as "not to create an outcry" (Gordon, 1998).

Such an outcry did erupt in 1992 just prior to the opening of Barcelona Olympics, when the display of a stuffed "Bushman" from southern Africa was discovered and forced to be taken down at the Francesco Darder Museum of Natural History in nearby Banyoles, Spain. The remains had been on display since 1916. Parsons (2000) raises the question about the (re-)presentation of dead human bodies in museum displays by highlighting that this is just one of many cases, as also on display in the same room where the African was displayed were "two complete human pelts, stretched out ... a circular hole where the genitals have been removed. Crinkly black hair on the flattened scalps indicates that these two specimens are also African"

(p. 6). Numerous dissections were performed on the bodies of Africans in order to make comparisons between Black people and apes, between criminals and "lower races" and the mentally subnormal. Physicians argued that treating the diseases of the Negro required special expertise. Negro inferiority was obsessively asserted again and again with all the weight of the new scientific measurements and calibrations, and with all the diagnostic powers of psychiatrists and doctors specializing in the pathologies that were said to blight the Negro. Thus, the Negro was "proven" to be intellectually and morally inferior to the white man, and prone to particular pathologies that explained any resistance to oppression as illness. It is clear that the invention of such specific psychological ailments served to naturalize slavery and colonial oppression as the "normal" or inevitable condition of Africans, and to pathologize the behavior of those who resisted and refused to resign themselves to their oppressed status (Mama, 1995).

In 1906, a paper entitled "Some Psychological Considerations on the Race Problem" became one of the earliest American writings specifically to criticize the accuracy of psychological research and the interpretation of accumulated data (Miller, 1906). The author, Herbert Miller, criticized the paucity of psychological training of those who performed the research. He underlined the need to recognize the importance of social conditions and environmental factors when interpreting data pertaining to oppressed minorities, and stressed the "inappropriateness of drawing conclusions from unequal environments" (Guthrie, 1976, p. 42). His evaluation of earlier studies dealing with quickness and accuracy of perception, disconnected memory, rational instinct, suggestibility, and color preference found no significant difference in these respects between Black and white people. However, little recognition of Miller's work came from the psychological establishment, and he appears to have been an isolated voice in the field of "established" psychological research. Miller's colleagues started by assuming the inferiority of Africans, and then devised methods to prove this assumption (Guthrie, 1976). Nevertheless, the 1928 annual meeting of the American Anthropological Association had to concede that "anthropology provides no scientific basis for discrimination against any people on the ground of racial inferiority, religious affiliation or linguistic heritage" (p. 26).

Carl Jung is revered for being the father of "transpersonal psychology" and has unified the human race through his concept of the collective unconscious that connected the human race to the greater cosmos. He is reputed to have been a great equalizer and unifier, and it is said that his philosophy is one of balance and humility. Jung, however, posits that the modern African is equivalent to prehistoric humans (Dalal, 1988). According to Jung, prehistoric humans are not conscious of self as opposed to contemporary humans—namely, white ones. They have no individuality, and their relationship to the world is collective. In the prehistoric psyche, there is no differentiation, with the consequence that thoughts and feelings are tied to sensation. Jung uses the modern African as evidence for his theory on prehistoric humans, stating that the modern African is primitive and prehistoric—this is the a priori postulate on which all else is based. And so the modern Black person is, according to Jung, steeped in emotion and governed by unseen forces. Jung makes it quite clear that he perceives the darker races as some sort of disease, a highly contagious one that infects the white race.

Has Anything Changed?

Many helping professionals will no doubt bristle at the idea that their practices are rooted in Christian hypocrisy or eugenicist ideas about race. But despite the growing diversity of researchers and therapists, many of the core philosophical assumptions Western helping skills training programs today—most notably, universalism and the primacy of the Western scientific method for describing the world—can be traced back to these ideas. This is one of the reasons why, despite the helping profession's attempts to become more accepting of difference, the system consistently continues to fail non-European populations.

We can see this clearly in mental health training programs, which tend to emphasize more passive attending skills as informed by the Rogerian approach. Parham et al. (2016) warn that therapists so trained may be ill-equipped to work with culturally different clients who might find a more active approach relevant to their own needs and values. In a 1979 study conducted by Berman, it was concluded that "Black and White counselors appear to adhere to two distinctive styles of counseling." When shown a videotape of culturally varied clinical vignettes and then asked "what would you say to this person?" at the same point of the session, white counselor trainees recommended more passive attending skills significantly more than Black trainees, who tended to recommend more active expressive skills. Trainees who are not from the dominant culture that Rogers' style and approach was borne from (white, male, etc.) may be trained out of their authentic counseling style in favor of the dominant passive attending skills that continue to be emphasized in counselor training.

Even in 2021, amidst the COVID-19 pandemic and "racial reckoning" that followed the murder of George Floyd, some researchers noted the lack of progress made in helping skills training programs to move beyond the passive, Western counseling training approach (Branco & Jones, 2021). Despite the acknowledgment that "client racism toward BIPOC counselors is a systemic problem and therefore requires a systemic response, to include counselor educator and clinical supervisor efforts, to avoid BIPOC counselors shouldering the weight of racism and microaggressions in isolation" (p. 282), the recommended skills and strategies to "support Black and Indigenous and People of Color Counselors" falls short of supporting and training counselors in being genuine and authentic.

For example, though reportedly consistent with Critical Race Theory (CRT) and *microinterventions* "response strategies" created "in an effort to dismantle the potency of a microaggressive encounter" (Branco & Jones, 2021, p. 284; Sue et al., 2019a, 2019b), the microcounseling interventions developed by the authors adapted the basic counseling skills taught in counseling training programs while remaining aligned with the counseling profession's ethical standards. These interventions are designed to provide guidance for counselors dealing with racism in the workplace, especially from clients, and they provide scripts for how a counselor can respond to microaggressions, such as a client asking whether their therapist is legally allowed to work in the United States. In addition, counseling supervisors are encouraged to help the counselor in such scenarios to reflect on questions surrounding how the microaggression made them feel, what self-care and wellness strategies they have for support, and when they have experienced similar microaggressions before (Branco & Jones, 2021, p. 292).

Purportedly, these counseling skills and intervention recommendations were developed to combat the cultural supremacy inherent in traditional helping skills training. "BIPOC counselors, who enter the training experience and profession with lived racialized experiences, may benefit from clinical skills instruction, rather than replicating the current White hegemonic counselor education framework" (Branco & Jones, 2021, p. 282; Fuentes et al., 2020; Spanierman & Smith, 2017). Yet, it is unclear how the "White hegemonic" counseling training framework is being disrupted at all. Instead, it appears that it is being strengthened by the claim that it can be "adapted" while adhering to the same basic counseling skills and counseling ethical standards. It disregards the humanity of students of color and asks them to do the same in favor of upholding a false sense of a therapeutic relationship for the client. Given the helping professions' public apologies and pledges to anti-racism issued in the same year as the article by Branco and Jones (American Counseling Association, 2020; American Psychiatric Association, 2021; American Psychological Association, 2021; National Association of Social Workers, 2021), the Western helping professions' commitment to hypocrisy is made abundantly clear in its suggested interventions to "support" people of color working in the helping professions.

Thus, the comments continually being highlighted by those counselors who have vocalized their work academically seem to indicate an incongruence with the core conditions considered necessary to facilitate a client's self-development. Consequently, such a position requires those who adhere to varying cultural norms to sacrifice themselves by molding themselves to the dominant helping approach, rather than challenging it.

A Multicultural Alternative?

The ideology of multiculturalism began in the 1970s in the context of the American Civil Rights Movement. It was an attempt to reflect diversity, and to foster awareness and appreciation for the role that non-European civilizations have played in creating American culture. The intent of this movement was to promote an expanded American identity, one that recognized previously excluded groups as an integral component of the whole, and the development of awareness, appreciation, and knowledge of the heritage and social history of racial and ethnic groups. Initially concerned with improving intergroup relations, a critical aspect of multiculturalism in the work of counselors was to show that intergroup relations might represent a problem of communication—a lack of mutual understanding—which in turn could hinder the effectiveness of the counseling process. Counseling attempted to understand, respect, and appreciate the cultural elements and critical social issues of groups defined by ethnicity, race, and socio-economic status. But with competition for power and resources, the multiculturalism movement has become a tool for the benefit of special interest groups. Under the umbrella of multiculturalism, groups based on gender, religion, and other characteristics, including sexual orientation, disability, and age, have staked claims for recognition.

In the helping professions, multiculturalism has led to the development of culturally specific approaches to psychotherapy, with their methods designed to be congruent with the cultural characteristics of a particular ethnic clientele, or for problems believed to be especially prominent in a particular ethnic group. However, the continued persistence of oppressive practices, despite raised public awareness, has meant that within the world of counseling, multiculturalism remains problematic. Oppressive practices will not disappear by themselves, but require active intervention. The search for unity in human diversity (exemplified by cultural pluralism and multiculturalism) requires examining, questioning, debating, and taking action in all spheres of public and private life (including the profession of counseling and psychotherapy), and cannot be done in isolation. An organization may present an image that discourages ethnic minorities from applying, and apparently "neutral" and "objective" requirements may create unequal barriers. A stipulation that candidates for training must have a degree, for example, may disqualify more members of some ethnic minorities because of institutional racism in the education system.

Cultural pluralism, as an ideology of assimilation into society, allows for the possibility of people from diverse ethnic and racial backgrounds to retain their identities within the framework of the larger society. The ideology of cultural pluralism opposes the complete merger of minority groups with the majority group, striving instead to preserve the rights of groups to their cultural and social heritage and to afford equality of opportunity for all groups in economic, political, and educational spheres so that these groups can become proficient in the dominant group culture and can operate on an equal footing.

However, this inevitably raises questions about which cultural values are considered to be dominant, and which are considered particular to a certain group. Antiracist movements usually single out white male dominance or authoritative kinds of influences, such as Western culture, as the root cause of racism and oppression of minorities. Radical multiculturalism, therefore, discredits Western civilization as being oppressive, and sets out to deconstruct the foundational ideals of Western civilization. Cultural relativist approaches to multiculturalism, on the other hand, embody concepts of contextualism and particularism, arguing that cultural beliefs and practices can be judged or understood only within the total context of the group in which these things occur. Experience is simply a continuous process of random flux and change that can only be known and explained by the people themselves within the context of their self-perceived group identities and affiliations. No single scale of values is applicable to all societies. Particularistic interpretations of cultures by ethnographers and other scholars attempt to show fundamental differences from one culture to another, but radical relativists contend that each culture can only be understood on its own terms and with its own unique system of meaning. Mental health, mental disorders, and therapeutic procedures all depend on the cultural norms and beliefs of the particular society or group. Behavior identified as mentally disturbed or harmful could be perceived to be normal behavior in another society or group.

Cross-cultural comparisons and differences have not in general provided helpful principles of human culture or society, nor have they generated psychological principles for individual well-being beyond such obvious axioms as that all humans have language, families, forms of religion, political, and economic systems, and emotions and values. Many therefore question whether cultural relativism has "marginalized" groups of people as stereotypes, allowing the individual uniqueness of clients and the universality of common themes to be neglected.

There are still no clear guidelines about what an antiracist or non-racist alternative is and what it means in terms of practical policies and politics. More importantly, the many frameworks that have been put forward have not, as the outpouring of apologies that followed the "racial reckoning" of 2020 illustrate, made the helping professions more capable of responding to the needs of BIPOC clients. Rather than moving us toward workable, resilient alternatives to the dominance of Western ways of thinking, multicultural discourse has often simply descended into sophistry—a series of complicated arguments about terms and definitions that have not been capable of generating lasting change.

What's the Use of Talking If You Can't Get Me Out of Here?

All of this brings us back to where we started, with Rogers' attempt to create a person-centered approach to psychotherapy. More than 30 years ago, Masson (1988) argued that just as Freud misunderstood the oppression of women (leading him to inaccurate findings), so too did Rogers misunderstand or ignore oppression in general.[1] Despite his numerous academic accreditations, and public validation, the fact that Rogers was unable to address the existence of oppressive practices, invalidates his work:

> Without taking a position on these essential points, and this means a political stance, the therapist cannot even acknowledge [a client's] reality, let alone understand and sympathize with the patient's experience of such abuse. *Nowhere in his writings does Rogers acknowledge the existence of such abuse, let alone ascribe to it any importance*. [Italics in original] (p. 235)

[1] In particular, Masson highlights Rogers' lack of sensitivity to abuse, as when he reported a case history of a patient talking about the pleasure he got from killing rabbits and molesting young girls (p. 246).

Masson is particularly concerned about the fact that one of Rogers' own patients, incarcerated in a mental institution, articulates so succinctly the lack of justice offered by his therapeutic method: "What's the use of talking if you can't get me out of here?" Masson concludes that Rogers had to sacrifice *himself* by "blind[ing] himself to injustice or liv[ing] with the guilt of recognizing it and not doing anything about it" (p. 243), using his theory to argue and justify, for example, that he was impressed with the "sturdy, firm, 'masculine' tone of the therapist rather than addressing the fact that the client had just confessed to child molestation" (p. 1). When in the 1980s Rogers sought to bring "racist whites and angry blacks" together in South Africa in American-style encounter groups, Masson cannot but question the lasting effects (p. 237). From an Africanist perspective the "well-adjusted" person, according to the norms of the dominant society, will be one who accepts an oppressive self-concept consistent with their socialization within an oppressive system, thereby avoiding any large discrepancy between the ideal self and the real self that would result in the creation of an "unhappy, dissatisfied person." The person-centered counselor is therefore trained to enable people to achieve this self-actualized position.

Lived Experience: Sacrifices and Sophistry

In this chapter, I have used the examples of Shaw's Lord of Hosts and Nailer to illustrate the two approaches the Western helping professions use in relating to culturally different counselors. Either they must simply obey the dictates of the dominant society by sacrificing those parts of themselves that do not "fit," or they must engage in endless debates that do nothing to dismantle the existing structures of power. In the following case studies, I explore what this looks like in my own lived experience, and in the lived experiences of others. Neither individuals nor organizations are named in the following case study; in addition to maintaining professional confidentiality, I wanted to be as open and honest as possible about my responses to these encounters, and felt that identifying people would inhibit this. In any case, my own development is the focus, and as such my comments are not intended to be critical of others.

For some years, I worked at a counseling agency that supposedly practiced a person-centered approach. Yet, in reality, this agency applied what seemed to me an assembly line approach to clients. There was a set time for counseling sessions (50 min) that could not be varied without attracting unwanted attention. Since I wished to approach each client as a unique individual, I often found myself wanting to counsel clients for either longer or less than 50 min. However, the manager would knock on the door and ask me to hurry up if I went over time or look at me quizzically, as if doubting my competence, if I had finished with a client earlier.

This agency was an abortion clinic, but even though the presenting problem was the "same," each client understood their own experience uniquely. I sought to address that factor by responding accordingly, as some clients only needed a few minutes of counseling just to provide information, while others needed much more, especially those with problems that related, often in very complex ways, to the issue the agency was designed to handle. The agency's specialization simply didn't hold up in practice, and I felt continually frustrated because I wasn't supposed to stray into other areas that clearly had bearing on many clients' difficulties with abortion. How could I be genuine, accepting, or offer empathy when I was feeling as I did?

Here was a supposedly person-centered organization that denied the realities of their clients' lives and, in my opinion, attempted to squeeze individuals into one mold. Like the Kara Counselling Centre in the previous chapter's case study, the agency relied on a codified, essentially authoritarian approach that put rules and structures before people. After several years with this agency, I finally felt it was time to start my own counseling agency. Motivated by my idealism, the wish to explore alternative counseling methods that effectively put clients' needs before abstract or bureaucratic frameworks, and to engage with people as individuals leading complex lives, I aimed to explore and promote what an Indigenous African-centered theoretical approach would be.

I will be the first to admit that my plan was something of an adventure, and what Western science would call an experiment. This was a conscious part of the enterprise, as I interpreted that from this perspective there could be no step-by-step formulas or a rigid criteria to follow. However, from this early stage I realized that this was itself a contradiction. For in trying *not* to develop and use a step-by-step method myself, but rather a lived paradigm, I was feeding into the destructive concept many people have of a counselor as a guru, which Rogers himself had tried so hard to avoid. My journey started from the realization that I certainly was no guru, and that by presenting myself as one I would be sacrificing *myself*. Like the Lord of Hosts, who talked loftily and authoritatively about love, but then killed, I had been talking about holistic counseling in theory; yet, in practice (both in the agency I had been working in and in my writing) I had been killing that principle. Trying to explore what an Indigenous African-centered perspective on counseling would be was going to involve some work.

For this reason, I spent a large amount of time during the early to mid-1990s traveling around Britain visiting "African-centered" counseling projects. For the purposes of this case study, the 50 or so organizations and projects I visited have been amalgamated into one—in retrospect, they feel as if they were a single, generic organization, and the problems with each were basically the same. Indeed, it eventually became a depressing experience, visiting each new project and finding the same old problems. Ironically, another reason for undertaking my grand tour, as I realized later, was my own lack of confidence and desire to avoid taking responsibility. Although I was not aware of this at the time, my interest in the other projects was partly fueled by the hope that I would discover some model or theory that had done or could do the work of creating an African-centered counseling model, so I could do what I had previously done—be an advocate for a method. The growing realization that a ready-made model did not exist was unsettling, because it meant I would need to think for myself and develop my own resources. This revelation, though painful to accept, was a valuable one, for as my search for understanding evolved, I realized that I gained much in the process of discovery.

It was over the course of this process that I latched onto the two metaphors I've been using in this chapter: sacrifice and sophistry. Like the Lord of Hosts in Shaw's story, the Western model of counseling is a jealous God that demands obedience and sacrifice: Obedience to its Eurocentric paradigm and sacrifice of one's own alternative ideas, experiences, and beliefs when these conflict with the paradigm. Like Nailer in Shaw's story, Eurocentric counseling is able to disguise the demand for sacrifice with debates about theories. I saw that these sacrifices were being masked or compensated for through sophistry, that is, through a sterile focus on attractive-sounding theories and arguments that were not being put into practice, and indeed that *could not* be put into practice as long as so-called culturally sensitive projects depended on Eurocentric structures for resources, ideas, and validation.

For example, a project in London had to have the minutes of its board meetings reviewed and approved by the local authority to ensure it was conforming to their rules. This was the local authority's right: It was funding the project, and had to ensure that its money was being spent and managed according to its contracts with the project. Accountability is one of the key principles in the Eurocentric structure of ensuring the "cooperation" of non-governmental organizations. For the project, however, incorporation into these structures seemed to me to involve sacrificing its own responsibility to address the needs of its community holistically. Like other projects that made the same sacrifice in return for public funds, it was prevented (or rather, was preventing itself) from experimenting with new or different methods, and from breaking free of the mold that Eurocentric structures imposed on it in the name of accountability.

The early 1990s in Britain were a period when culturally appropriate counseling for "culturally different" people was in vogue. Different terms and theoretical perspectives were used (cross-cultural, multicultural, etc.), although, significantly, the term "Afrocentric" was not heard. But all were attempts to respond to the fact that mainstream mental health services were clearly failing Black people. Studies had shown that Black people in Britain suffered more mental health problems and had less success in treatment programs than other sectors of the population. They were overrepresented in mental health institutions, while studies of Black clients' experiences at counseling services revealed high dropout rates and general dissatisfaction, along with a widespread perception of racism.

The conventional mental health model was obviously not working, and as the government had also recognized the failure of conventional models, it made considerable resources available for pilot projects. In some circles, there seemed to be a feeling that the Black community in Britain had finally turned a corner in terms of provision of effective mental health services.

My tour of African-centered projects revealed a less rosy picture. I found that some projects were well-resourced and some were not. Some were under-skilled while others seemed over-skilled. But all were ineffective because they were being designed to fit existing frameworks. Whether this was done for accountability purposes, political purposes, or to address prevalent social policies, they all took the dominant culture as their fixed reference point—as labels such as "cross-cultural" and "multicultural" made clear. They were trying to be different and to offer alternatives, but always in the background lurked the dominant model, which I likened to the God of Hosts in Shaw's story, demanding adherence to its "universal" principles, structures of thought, values, and sacrifice. Projects could *look* different, and would be presented as being culturally sensitive, but they still had to adhere to Eurocentric administrative models, Eurocentric definitions of success and failure (and of illness and health), and indeed to Eurocentric conceptions of culture and cultural difference.

Essentially, these projects provided only an illusion that something was being done to address the health problems of Black people on their own terms. This presumably satisfied the politicians and bureaucrats. It also provided an income for a small number of Black mental health entrepreneurs, some of whom saw the poorly managed public funds as an opportunity for personal enrichment. However, it did little or nothing to help the vast majority of clients deal with their issues or live more satisfying lives. Nor did it make any real progress toward developing a practical and effective model of African-centered counseling and psychotherapy.

As I talked to counselors and clients in these projects, I realized that the underlying cause of failure was that the *starting point* of the multicultural ideal never acknowledged the need for a truly *alternative*, non-European paradigm. All the projects had impressive concept papers, project proposals, mission statements, and so on, which rang the right bells in terms of the rhetoric of cultural sensitivity and cultural appropriateness. They analyzed the failure of mainstream services to address Black people's problems or to provide culturally sensitive services, and rightly noted that the root causes were inequalities and racism within the established mental health system. Most also addressed issues of inequality and racism in British society as a whole and recognized that the origins of mental health problems faced by Black people lay there. When it came to their own alternative services, they talked expertly about "partnership," "process-focused approaches," "holism," "commitment," "community development," and so on. However, in terms of practice, every project left much to be desired. They were failing to make the basic paradigm shift that was the necessary starting point. The excellent theories put forward in project documents simply could not be realized. Essentially, these projects were exercises in sophistry. Instead of using theories to develop and test more effective practices, they were substituting theory for practice. Like Nailer, they preferred to argue, debate, and theorize rather than get their hands dirty by truly becoming involved in the lives and in the communities of the people they were supposed to be helping.

The typical "community-based" mental health service that was the most popular model at that time provides a generic example of the situation I found in all the projects. Such projects typically started when a group of concerned members of the Afro-Caribbean community put together a funding proposal for a culturally specific mental health service to serve their members. The chairpersons of these groups were usually qualified professionals in other areas, such as teaching, but often had no experience of mental health. Councils seemed eager to fund these projects and money was available, but by relying on resources provided by the Eurocentric establishment, they, like similar projects, sealed their fate.

Typically, such projects received grants for a limited-term pilot phase. But what were they then to do? By relying on council funding, they had locked themselves into a specific bureaucratic framework that required a whole apparatus of "monitoring and evaluation"—target indicators, service profiles, monitoring breakdowns, outcomes, review meetings, review structures, external evaluations, etc. Instead of getting involved in the community, they had to begin by erecting the elaborate bureaucratic barriers required for the Eurocentric model of "objectivity." To make matters worse, such projects often recruited very junior and inexperienced staff. In more than one case, I suspected that the chairpersons, who were in charge of hiring, were more concerned about avoiding challenges and disguising their own lack of experience than in ensuring that projects were capable of really addressing the complex issues their funding proposals and other documents had identified.

Looming in the background of all project activities was the council funding deadline, usually just 2 or 3 years down the road. I wondered what anyone imagined could be accomplished in such a short period to redress the entrenched effects of hundreds of years of institutionalized oppression. The incongruity between these projects' multicultural pretensions and their Eurocentric bureaucracies and timetables struck me as another form of sophistry. It did not surprise me when I heard a few years later that many of them had ended up offering clients nothing more than a quiet place to sit and have a cup of tea. Local authorities wanted to *appear* to be caring and to be proactively addressing issues of the Afro-Caribbean community, so I deduced that they funded projects that pressed the right buttons in terms of rhetoric and membership. However, the result was these projects were like lottery winners who had no idea of what to do with their new wealth except squander it on conventional signs of affluence.

The failure of these led me to reflect on Malcolm X's famous metaphor of "crumbs off the table." I realized that even if the projects had been better managed and more successful at translating their culturally sensitive principles into action, they would have been little more than drops in the bucket. For example, one project in a large provincial town with a Black population in the tens of thousands had only a total of twelve beds to offer respite for people suffering from mental health problems. What could the long-term impact of such a project possibly be? I then had to ask myself whether *any* project, no matter how large and well-funded, could be more than a sop. Were these projects so popular with the authorities precisely because they provided the establishment with the face-saving illusion that Black mental health issues were receiving attention? Did the projects, as Malcolm X argued about the Civil Rights Movement in the US, not only fail to address the real issues but actually help to prop up the racist system?

The basic cross-cultural principle is that counselors, by acknowledging their own culture and its prejudices and limitations, are able to relate and reach out to the client's culture. However, wherever there is a dominant, hegemonic culture, there is a tendency to sacrifice to it. That is, it is used as the yardstick by which others are measured and valued. When it condescends to acknowledge that other cultures exist, it requires them to perform on its own terms. I was already skeptical of the value of a Eurocentric training model being applied to a supposedly "culturally sensitive" counseling agency. If Black counselors were trained and qualified by the same Eurocentric system that was oppressing other Black people and producing the Black mental health crisis, how could such counselors hope to deal with the problems of Black clients? The image that kept coming to my mind was of a mouse running on a treadmill. The encounters I had with many individuals working within or subjected to this system illustrated the sacrifice and sophistry required to survive in such a system.

Reflecting on my own experience at a major publicly funded mental health project that was ostensibly based on multicultural principles, I realized that the same issues had affected my work there. I had felt that this project gave its clients a false sense of hope about what could actually be done to alleviate or overcome their problems. Meanwhile, the project was receiving funding for its purported contribution to addressing the mental health crisis. It seemed to me that our clients, and indeed the counselors, were being used sacrificially by the powers that be. We were projecting a positive image on their behalf, but getting no results or, in many cases, destructive results that left clients worse off than before. Like the Lord of Hosts, this system craved obedience and worship. The project, it seemed to me, was essentially in the business of encouraging already oppressed people to participate in their continued oppression.

Encounter One: Playing the Game

At a project funded by the prison service to help Black people get off drugs, I had a lengthy and illuminating conversation with one of the counselors. This young man was clearly working out of genuine concern about the drug abuse that was ravaging his community. He felt that the root causes of the problem lay in oppressive practices, and he had come to work in the project with the faith that a culturally sensitive approach to counseling could help Black people take responsibility for their lives and avoid drug abuse. He was not a qualified counselor, but had been recruited on the basis of his commitment and his willingness to learn—or so he had thought.

What became clear was that he had been recruited because he spoke well at the interview and had a Black face. The project had then enrolled him in typical Eurocentric training programs, but far from equipping him to put his commitment into practice, these programs were actually disabling him as an effective counselor, as well as causing him great distress. At the time we talked, he had already been "kicked off" one training course, and felt he was heading for the same result in the course he had then transferred to. Ironically, the problems he was experiencing were the result of taking the training courses' ideals of "honesty" and of "sharing" too seriously. He came from a very self-sufficient community and was self-confident in his outlook on the world. As a result, when the course leaders encouraged him to be open and honest and to speak up and share his feelings and experiences in training sessions, he shared feelings that they found difficult to deal with. He discovered that being open and honest was acceptable only as long as he confined himself to acceptable areas. When he tried to speak about the racism at the root of his own and other Black people's emotional and psychological problems, he felt the atmosphere change and grow tense and hostile. In both courses, he was the only Black trainee, and he could sense that he was upsetting the others, particularly when he tried to talk about the racism he detected within the courses themselves and at his project. He found himself being regarded as "arrogant" and as having a "chip on his shoulder."

For example, he told me that during the first course he had written some comments in his journal (one of the course assignments) about how he felt his white manager at work was being racist. However, when he shared these comments with his training group, the other members insisted that he must be wrong and implied that it was he who had a problem about race, not the manager. This made him feel he was not acknowledged or appreciated in the group and that this was because he was Black. He felt that by raising issues of racism, he was transgressing their expectation that he should be "obedient." He felt that racism was a taboo, and that the other members of the group resented and distrusted him for bringing up the problem.

He confessed that he was now learning to steer clear of racial issues and to stick to "safe" topics, as he needed the qualification to keep his job. However, this made him feel dishonest and conflicted. He felt he was being forced to modify his ideas and behavior, sacrificing his opinions to placate the fears and prejudices of white trainers. The irony of being trained to work as a "Black" counselor by having to suppress his feelings was very distressing to him. To me, it seemed he was being trained to pay lip service to a theory of multiculturalism while having to deny it in practice.

Encounter Two: Faking It

I had an encounter which brought home to me very forcefully what can happen when a Black woman tries *too* hard to sacrifice herself. I was asked to visit a young Black woman who had been hospitalized after locking herself in her room at home and refusing to eat. She was refusing to talk about what might have caused her breakdown, so for our first meeting, I sat with her on the hospital lawn and chatted aimlessly about the weather, the plants, and so on, deliberately avoiding the real subject in order to see how she would respond.

Suddenly she opened up and spontaneously began talking about the racism that she felt had ruled her life up to that point. She had been born in Zimbabwe and had spent most of her childhood there. Her father had fought for independence, but had disappeared when she was still a baby. Though presumed dead, his body had never been found. When she was about ten her mother moved with her to England and later married a white man.

Unfortunately, her relationship with her stepfather, a retired policeman, was problematic, as he constantly teased and tormented her with racial insults and put-downs as she was growing up. She tried to talk to her mother about this but was rebuffed for reasons she could not understand. At the same time, she suffered the "routine" racism at school, at church, and in the streets that so many Black children growing up in Britain experience. She told me she had always wanted to "join in" but had never felt accepted.

She said she had struggled to be "nice," that is, to accept racism without complaining and to behave as white people wanted her to behave—in other words, to sacrifice herself. As a result, she had grown up feeling humiliated and deeply divided. To make things worse, over the years her mother had stopped speaking their native language and started talking, dressing, cooking, and so on according to her idea of how a middle-class Englishwoman should behave. This greatly distressed her daughter and made her feel she had nowhere to turn. At the age of 18, she went to a university in the north of England and found she was one of only five Black students in her year. Her unhappiness came to a head soon after when she was raped. It was then that she had locked herself in her room, refused to eat, and finally had to be hospitalized.

In the hospital, she was very angry at first. She said she felt as if she had been sent to prison for a crime she had not committed. She shouted at the doctors and nurses, refused to eat the "mushy" hospital food (which seemed to be intended for old people, as most of the other inmates were elderly), and deliberately made a nuisance of herself. However, when I met her, she had realized that this was not the way to be "cured" and released. She wanted to get out of this place, where she felt more oppressed than ever, and saw that the only way to do so was to conform to the institution's expectations. In other words, she prepared to sacrifice herself again. She calmed down, pretended to be content, ate the terrible food, and shared with the doctors and nurses only those feelings she knew would be "acceptable." Needless to say, she took special care to avoid talking about racism. Soon after our meeting, she was released.

Her situation reminded me of that of Mr. P, another client I encountered, who also learned to "fake it" in order to cheat the system, but in an even more tragic way. I met Mr. P in prison where he was awaiting trial for the sadistic murder of his girlfriend (and the mother of his four children). He was a man who seemed to lack any sense of responsibility or concern for others. For years, he had been sexually involved with four different women, whom he had systematically abused and exploited. Basically, he had lived off their welfare/dole payments while engaging in petty crime on the side. Predictably, he also had a history of drug and alcohol abuse. He had learned to play a certain kind of vicious game with the system.

The murdered woman had met him when she was a 16-year-old runaway and had stayed with him despite constant physical, emotional, and sexual abuse, mainly, it seemed, because she felt she had nowhere else to go. She had run away from him several times, but had always come back. They had four children together, all under 8 years of age at the time. One day he had come home for one of his "chats" with her (their euphemism for a beating), and as reported by him to me had hurt her so badly she had said: "Why don't you just kill me and be done with it?" For some reason he could not or would not explain, this is exactly what he then did—stabbing her forty-four times, according to the post-mortem report.

At the start of our first meeting, he surprised me by asking, "So what do you think of me?" and I surprised *myself* by replying, without pausing to think or to remember my Eurocentric training in "objectivity": "I think you should be killed." He then confessed that he had to agree with me, though he had no intention, as it turned out, of even paying the penalty of imprisonment. However, my "unprofessional" outburst seemed to establish a strange trust between us. I felt my comment enabled him to open up and tell me about the mental health trick he was planning to play on the system. He could not endure the idea of spending years, possibly the rest of his life, in prison, so he had decided to feign mental illness. He had been in and out of therapy often enough to know how to do this convincingly, and his cynical manipulation of the system and its theories worked perfectly. He spent only 3 years in an institution and was released—supposedly, no longer a danger to society, but as I heard from his mother, he had remained essentially unchanged.

This case struck me as a horrifying example of manipulation of the system and conformity to its expectations in order to survive. Indeed, it could almost be read as a reverse sacrifice. It is not often that Black people "benefit" from the Eurocentric mental-health system. When they do, as in this case, it is often for the most negative reasons. As his case showed, Black people sacrifice themselves not just by conforming hypocritically or self-delusively to the rules of the game, but sometimes by actually pretending to be something they are not in order to cheat the system and get what they want.

Both the Black woman, who faked a cure to get out of the mental health system, and Mr. P, who faked mental illness to get out of prison, falsified themselves and took advantage of the system in order to escape from the responsibility of facing up to their problems. As I thought about them in the context of my struggle with my own practice, I realized that I, too, was faking it. True, my disillusionment with the sacrifices and sophistry demanded by person-centered counseling was genuine, and so too was my determination to find a more congruent alternative, and my faith that this could be done by actualizing an Indigenous African-centered perspective. However, I now realize that I was still only playing a role. I was acting out an image of a counselor and had somehow stopped living. My own practice and life were not congruent; I felt that just as others perceived me as a guru, I somehow appeared to collude with that image. I admitted to myself that I did not want or relish the attention. I wanted what I perceived my grandfather had had, with no degrees or other professional qualifications, nor any counseling theories or ideological labels. He had no need to present himself in terms of others' image of what a counselor should be. People came to see him because of who he was, not because of his credentials, office, or standing in the community. I surmise that it was of his character, his genuineness, his acceptance, his empathy, and primarily his congruent behavior—not with a psychological theoretical perspective, but with his life.

These encounters—and others there is no room to recount here—occurred either during my visits to counseling projects and while reflecting on my search for understanding. Together with my disillusionment, they forced me to act. They made me realize that I had more to offer than I first thought or wanted to accept. As I visited projects and discussed their operations with counselors and clients, I found others listening to me and asking for my advice. I discovered that many others were as frustrated as I was with the Eurocentric counseling model, even (or especially) when it was dressed up in Afrocentric rhetoric. I realized that people *were* refusing to sacrifice or argue, but without really understanding what an Indigenous African-centered model would be or how it would operate.

I recognized my responsibility to walk the walk of Indigenous African-centered counseling instead of just looking for others to provide a model. I had come to several conclusions about what Indigenous African-centered counseling should be like, and I began to put these conclusions into practice. First, it was clear to me that state funding was of primary importance. Public resources brought with them official requirements to conform to Eurocentric administrative, training, monitoring, and evaluation standards that locked one into a time-constrained, "objective" pseudo-scientific, and non-holistic model, no matter how Afrocentric one's counseling *theories* were. I found that people came to my practice with the expectation that I was state-funded and had all the "normal" resources and set-ups—and the normal aloofness and objectivity. I found that many people were impressed to encounter something quite different, while others (I felt, being truthful) had trouble dealing with something different. Many Black people are so used to being treated superficially and stereotypically that they have great difficulty relating to a service that aimed to treat them otherwise.

Second, I saw that a genuinely Indigenous African-centered approach could not "compartmentalize" itself. It could not be cut off from the full life of the community and become a special, professionalized event that happened only in a special place at certain hours between a client and a counselor certified by the Eurocentric system. I thought of my grandfather, who was a carpenter who also happened to "counsel" people. His counseling was not a profession that put him on a pedestal towering above the community; it was a vocation, a calling, woven into the community and into his own and others' day-to-day lives.

For the same reason, I felt that the agency could not just sit and wait for people to come to it. Getting involved with the community was paramount. I spent a great deal of time visiting schools, attending "underground" (unofficial, word-of-mouth) conferences and holding training and motivational sessions for any interested members of the community. My goal was to be truly holistic, similar to a traditional healer who involves themselves in the community.

Paradoxically, I found that in an environment still controlled by the Eurocentric system and hedged in by racism and oppression, this practice tended to dissolve my "normal" status rather than reinforcing it as I wanted. Because what I was doing was different, people unfortunately came to see me as "The Afrocentric Counselor." This was flattering, but also got in the way of pursuing my underlying conviction that the essential point of Indigenous African-centered counseling is that it is about being simply and fully human. I surmised that I would need to continue my search.

As much as I did not want to admit it, I concluded that a truly Indigenous African-centered perspective should enable one to just live as oneself, as the Black Girl does at the end of Shaw's story. The Black Girl's ultimate revelation is that her life is not about being this thing or that, what one or another god or church says she is, but simply about being herself, free of the oppressive categories of gender and race, without needing to fight either for or against such categories because, from a truly liberated perspective, they are no longer relevant. Many readers feel dissatisfied with the ending of Shaw's story because, from a category-bound perspective, the Black Girl seems to be accepting a gendered, oppressive role. In fact, Shaw's point is that she has succeeded in escaping from these categories altogether. I realized that it was time for me to explore this potential in an Indigenous African-centered perspective on counseling, and to do so I now left my experimental practice behind and embarked on the remainder of the journey that has resulted in this book, and which is described and reflected on in the following chapters.

Chapter 4
Koheleth the Greek Scholar: Turning Points

"Take the world as it comes; for beyond it there is nothing. All roads end at the grave, which is the gate of nothingness; and in the shadow of nothingness everything is vanity. Take my advice and seek no further than the end of your nose. You will always know that there is something beyond that; and in that knowledge you will be hopeful and happy."

"My mind ranges further," said the Black Girl. "It is not right to shut one's eyes. I desire knowledge of God more than happiness or hope. God is my happiness and my hope." (Shaw, 1932, p. 14).

When the Black Girl meets the "good looking clean shaven white young man in a Greek tunic," she had been questioning her previously held belief that "white beards and old age and nightshirts" were divine credentials (Shaw, 1932, p. 36). Although both "interested and repelled" by the scholar's appearance, the Black Girl asks him for directions to find God. His materialistic reply puzzles her but, in the spirit of the discipline of philosophy, their discussion proves to be a turning point in her thinking, enabling her to reason that "to know God is to be God" (Shaw, 1932, p. 16). Her encounter with Koheleth proves to be a turning point in her reasoning, prompting her to look inwardly. As a result, she validates her own perspectives and is able to adopt a position of agency.

In this chapter, I explore how an alternative philosophy of life, a worldview contextualized from an Indigenous African perspective, could alter the current dominant concept of professional helping, as well as provide a way out of the problems described previously. However, in attempting to apply such a perspective, some fundamental assumptions need to be made when defining what is "African" and what constitutes an "African" worldview. Like the Black Girl in Shaw's story, my own turning point in discovering such a worldview involved an encounter with scholars. But in my case, they were scholars of philosophy who, in search of an African philosophy, turned to within the Africa continent for answers.

G. Berry, *Helping?*, https://doi.org/10.1007/978-3-031-88586-0_4

Discovering the Rabbit Hole

As I mentioned at the beginning of this book, my disappointment with my academic program set in very soon after I began the program, as I wrote about in a journal article at the time (Ramsey, 1992). I wanted to find that mystical "Black perspective" I heard talked about so much. But where was I to find it? My professors encouraged the Black students to discuss it during lectures, but never shared any research, theorists, or studies. I believed they genuinely wanted to know, but when I responded to the essay question "write about being a social worker from your cultural perspective," and I wrote about the supportive and restorative impact of the work of Black churches, Black politics, and self-directed nation-building policies, my professors deemed it unacceptable and failed my paper. I rewrote the same paper from a white feminist perspective and my paper "somehow" received a passing grade.

I felt this was unfair because—as the mainstream theorists I was studying recommended—I wanted "to be authentic" and "be myself." I concluded that I would need to look outside of the university to see if I could find answers. This was the late 1990s, and unsure of where to start, I decided to check out the pop-up International Book Fair of Radical Black and Third World Books, and made my way to Camden Town Hall in London as if I was on a secret mission. I was not sure what I would find, but I hoped it would be true to the pop-up's stated goal, which was to give a platform to Black and Third World writers. Mainstream bookstores, at that time, did not see such work as being financially viable enough for them to promote.

There was a buzz in the big hall, and it was clear I was not the only one seeking to learn something new. I walked around the musty, crowded space and awkwardly placed makeshift stalls, which were all doing their best to make use of every square inch of their allocated space. I quickly maneuvered up and down, as my initial thought was that I would not find what I was hoping for—even though I had no idea what I was looking for! As I walked toward the exit, I saw a title that jumped out at me: *The Chains and Images of Psychological Slavery* (later republished with revisions as *Breaking the Chains of Psychological Slavery* in 1996) by Dr. Na'im Akbar, an African-American clinical psychologist. What did he mean "psychological chains?" It was a small self-published pamphlet that seemed to get straight to the point. I purchased it along with works by other Black women authors writing about their experiences.

Just one sentence into Akbar's book, and I felt like Alice falling willingly down the rabbit hole. Why had I not heard about this before? Where could I get more information? Akbar's references were specialized and very few places at that time in London carried the kinds of books he cited, so with family in New York, I flew across the Atlantic so I could walk up and down 125 Street in Harlem, where street vendors sold provocatively-titled, predominantly self-published Black authors and political t-shirts with a message to share. I followed the references I found in these books, and their references' references, until I found myself arriving at a new understanding of how we think about things in the first place. In short, I discovered a new philosophy.

Reasoning from the External

As the parent of all academic disciplines, philosophy posits that through philosophical reflections, the nature of the world can be revealed. By the process of questioning, reflecting, and abstracting, human behavior is distinguished from the instinctual or animalistic, providing codes of conduct or sets of principles by which people can live and giving life meaning and purpose. Although classical Greek philosophers initially concerned themselves with the existence of God and the human soul in an attempt to provide a purpose for human life (Leahey, 1996), the work of scholars such as Thales, Heraclitus, Anaxagoras, and Pythagoras laid a foundation which asserted that the world is within human understanding, being made up of ordinary matter. Such reasoning from objectivity came to dominate the Western academic tradition, despite some leading Western scholars who have, over the centuries, argued that understanding the meaning of life can also be determined from a position of subjectivity (e.g., Epicurus, Socrates, Descartes, Spinoza, Nietzsche, and Wittgenstein).

With the publication of Darwin's *On the Origin of Species* (1859), which proclaimed the human species to be just an animal among animals, the foundation was laid for the discipline of psychology to lose its literal definition as the study of the soul (from the Greek *psyche*). When it split from philosophy at the beginning of the nineteenth century, Gustav Fechner's work in 1860 established the less religiously loaded term of "psychology" as the study of the "mind," seeing humanity not "outside of science but brought into the laboratory and accurately measured" (Hall, 1954, p. 13). From this foundation, Freud attempted to build a "philosophy of life," a worldview "based on science rather than on metaphysics or religion" to unravel the riddles of the mind (Hall, 1954, p. 20). In turn, Carl Rogers (1957), as previously described, tried to make the professional helper's experiences scientific and, supposedly, to enable an authentic meeting between equals in which the client was understood, cared for, and respected as a person capable of positive change and growth. Although continuing to address the "vexing questions" about the meaning of life (Leahey, 1996, p. 4), the strong influence of these men has, with few exceptions, resulted in the general acceptance of spiritual and religious experience being interpreted as neurotic and self-deceptive, with talk of God in the therapeutic relationship likened to the need for a security blanket or supernatural teddy bear (Lartey et al., 1994). But, as will be argued in this chapter, from a position of subjectivity, an alternative *weltanschauung* is necessitated, one in which the nature of the therapeutic relationships is drastically altered, with spirituality becoming a central feature.

The Cultured and the Barbarian as Equals

The major thinkers of Greek antiquity articulated social and human geographical differences on the basis of the opposition between the "cultured" and the "barbaric":

> Aristotle defined the human being as a rational animal and supposed that the cultured people (such as the male aristocratic Greeks) were capable of living in a reasonable way and organized their society accordingly (democratically). While the barbarians, the non-Greeks, incapable of culture and lacking the superior rational capacity for the Athenian-style democratic social organization, lived brutishly and under despotism. (Eze, 1997, p. 4)

Even at the dawn of what we now call "Western" civilization, philosophers based their reasoning on an assumed hierarchy between different peoples. It follows that many notable Western philosophical scholars have likewise assumed that distinctions need to be made between those who are capable of reason, and those who are supposedly incapable of it.

The German philosopher Immanuel Kant, who coined the term "Enlightenment," wrote and lectured extensively on Africans (despite basing everything he knew on hearsay), and argued that "the Negroes of African have by nature no feeling that arises above the trifling" (Kant, quoted in Judy, 1991, p. 3), conflating "Blackness" with "stupidity" (Judy, 1991). Similarly, Taiwo (1998) reports that Hegel saw Africans as being arrested in immediacy, exhibiting "the natural man in his completely wild and untamed state" (p. 3). Likewise, Hume, who never visited Africa, surmised "the Negroes … to be naturally inferior to the white," never having created anything that can be considered civilized (Browder, 1992, p. 17). Eze (1997) concludes that the "numerous writings on race by Hume, Kant and Hegel played a strong role in articulating European cultural and racial superiority and establishing a belief that humanity was headed by white Europeans, based on their supposed rational and moral evolutionary capacity" (p. 5).

Works such as *Primitive Mentality* (1923) by Levy-Bruhl confirmed a belief that African culture and thought systems were pre-scientific and pre-logical. Although Levy-Bruhl later renounced this position in his posthumous *Notebook on Primitive Mentality* (1975), the renunciation is not as well known. Even the landmark text by Temples (1959) on "Bantu" philosophy, which supposedly challenged the "primitiveness" of Africa, had the objective of providing its European colonial and missionary readers with information to aid the "mission to civilize." Nevertheless, Temples' work represents one of the earliest and most influential explicit acknowledgments of African intellectual efforts and achievements as constituting "philosophy." It, therefore, marks the initiation of contemporary discussions of African philosophy (Eze, 1997) in the West.

Up until that point in history, Taiwo (1998) notes that an African philosophy had been peculiarly absent from philosophical taxonomy compared with other geographical philosophies (e.g., Asian). This omission, Taiwo suggests, was driven by the West's own grandiose ideas, having "puffed itself up and invited the rest of humanity, or the educated segment of it, to be complicit in this historical swindle":

> It is only insofar as Western Philosophy has passed itself off as Universal philosophy that we may talk of the peculiar absence. It is only insofar as we confront, or have to deal with, or inhabit a world constructed by Western philosophy that we are forced to think of an absence and how to make sense of it. (p. 2)

Incontestably, the myopia and violence of the Western philosophical tradition, coupled with the political domination of Africa, has not only influenced how the rest of the world and its people view Africans, but also how Africa and her people see and understand themselves.

It is, therefore, understandable that African philosophical discourse is predominately based on European concepts of philosophy, forcing African philosophy to be on the defensive, having to justify itself and its existence in relation to Western philosophical standards. The danger of such a reactive stance is the continual reinforcement of its inferiority to the Western-assumed authority or, as Aimé Cesaire (2017) suggests, the process of losing oneself through either fragmentation in the particular or dilution in the universal. In response, many African philosophers have attempted to develop their own frameworks for understanding African philosophy on its own terms. Some have argued that African philosophy didn't need to develop along the same lines as Western philosophy (Omoregbe, 1998), while others have taken the original use of the classical Greek term *philosophy* to mean that wherever there is reflection, there is philosophy (whatever form this reflection may take). Omoregbe (1998) reasoned that just because the philosophical reflections of African thinkers in the past were not preserved or transmitted by written accounts does not mean that they did not exist. Wise sayings, proverbs, stories, and religious ceremonies can also be means of philosophizing, preserved not in writing but in the oral and sociopolitical traditions of a people. Such a position suggests that despite the diversity of the pre-colonial histories and the complexity of colonial experiences, there is someone or something that is distinctly "African."

This view, however, has its critics. Some scholars have argued that the term "African" is readily used to refer to a wide array of social groups and concepts the descriptions of which over the centuries have changed drastically depending on the contexts. The idea of a collective, immutable, and definitive "African philosophy" is therefore ludicrous and absurd (Hountondji, 1983, p. 47). For such critics, "Africa" is above all a continent—an empirical, geographical concept rather than a metaphysical one. There is therefore no sufficient basis for an "African" human identity or solidarity, as there exists no single method for identifying members of ethnic groups.

The question of African philosophy is further complicated by the fact that, prior to political independence on the continent of Africa and the development of civil rights legislation throughout the Diaspora, a written African philosophy had been built up mainly for a European public (Hountondji, 1983 p. 45). Ethno-philosophers made themselves the spokespersons for all Africans facing all-European academia. Those African intellectuals who adopt the European academic perspective thereby expound it over the head of the majority of the Africa populace. As a result, European conquerors, missionaries, and adventurers have written the majority of African historical treaties and studies on her people.

This forces contemporary African philosophers to tackle the question (as Zora Neale Hurston did when asked "how does it feel to be coloured?") by dismissing the possibility of a direct answer and placing it in the context of her reality—"compared to what as of where? Who is asking? In what context (where), with what interests and presuppositions and for what purpose (why)?" (As cited in Van Niekerk, 1998). The who, the where, the why, the when, and the what of African thinking have been the domain of professional philosophers writing for a professional audience, communicating with other philosophers on the nature, problems, and methods of African philosophers. African philosophers forced into such a position argue that philosophy is culturally determined (Coetzee & Roux, 1998, p. xii). Philosophy in Africa is considered in a culture-specific way, which means that philosophy is related to the specific cultural context within which it is practiced. It is therefore possible to understand the idea of "African culture" as a broad, inclusive term within the context of the struggle for liberation from colonial oppression if one takes the imposition of Western cultural values and colonial politics as providing a context for daily life in large parts of Africa, even though this culture is in no way homogeneous. The idea of African culture may provide meaning and purpose, pride, enjoyment, or emotion in the daily lives of African people under colonial rule or threatened with Western (cultural) imperialism.

The responsibilities of African philosophers presuppose the existence of freedom of expression and extend far beyond the confines of their disciplines. African philosophers cannot afford the luxury of self-satisfied apoliticism or quiescent complacency about the established order. To do so would be to deny themselves both as philosophers and as people. As Hountondji (1983) says, "the theoretical liberation of philosophical discourse presupposes political liberation" (p. 46). An "African" identity is not, then, something that is genetic or inherited, or a given and homogenizing way of understanding the world. Thus, according to Asante (1997), an African identity is gained as we read the novels of African writers and recognize in them the challenges we ourselves face. Such a position then gives shape to what is "African," allowing white Africans such as Gideon Strauss, who has immersed himself in the continent and considers that he has become "African inside-out," to define themselves as "African" and tell the stories of Africa as their story "no less than Africans of any skin color or race" (p. 7). What is then defined as "African" is the ability to transform and recreate rather than to assimilate. But for this process to occur requires that one escape the boundaries predominately imposed by Western academia and its norms of analysis that compartmentalize knowledge. The task is to recover a sense of Africa as a place that has produced and continues to produce its own distinct ways of knowing and understanding that have the same legitimacy as other global civilizations.

The Nile Valley Civilization

As I began to read more deeply in African philosophy in an attempt to be able to start reasoning from the internal, I discovered a dazzling world of bold ideas. Scholars like Akbar, Asante, and Diop gave me resources for placing the African experience on an equitable footing with other scholarly examinations of the human experience, a conceptual framework for how the world is seen and understood. This framework centers itself not on the pervading assumptions of the continent today, but rather on those of an Indigenous one, which has been referred to as the Nile Valley Civilization, which some believe to have existed around approximately 8000 B.C.E (Akbar, 1979; Asante, 1988; Browder, 1992; Diop, 1978; Karenga, 1997). Such a position establishes Africans as representative of a distinct cultural group, independent of Euro-North American culture.

As conceptualized by the late Senegalese scholar Chiekh Anta Diop in his seminal work *The African Origin of Civilisation* (1974), the Nile Valley Civilization is considered to be the geographical and historical source of the cultural commonalities shared among the continent's approximately 6000 tribes and countless descendants scattered throughout the Diaspora. Diop understood it to be the source for an African-centered worldview, serving modern Africa in a similar way as classical Greek civilization serves as a reference point for modern Europe. The idea that the Nile Valley Civilization should serve as the classical reference point for the study of what constitutes "African-ness" has come to be known as the "Diopian" school of thought.

Diop's aim was to give the sense of African identity a proper historical depth, rather than a metaphysical dimension. The primary objective of his first book was to demonstrate the Black origins of ancient Egyptian civilization, and thus to refute the contention that the Black race produced no great world civilization. Diop further argues that historians have fully accepted the decisive influence of Egypt upon the early formation of Western civilization in classical Greece, concluding that Europe itself owes an immense cultural debt to Africa. Tellingly, it was not until Martin Bernal, a white professor, published *Black Athena: The Afroasiatic Roots of Classical Civilization* (a study that supported Diop's position) that the white academic establishment took notice of what was emerging as Afrocentrism.

Diop deduced that cultural themes prevalent in the Nile Valley were disseminated throughout Africa when groups began to migrate out of the Nile Valley. He did this by identifying common interests, habits, or characteristics such as oneness, harmony, complementarity, sameness, and spirituality. Diop assumed that these cultural ideas survived the migration of people throughout the continent, the intrusion of European and Arab influences, and the passage of time. While scholars following in Diop's footsteps acknowledge that modifications and diverse practices have occurred, due to the tenacity and resilience of these cultural themes (supported by extended kinship systems, lack of physical contact of many Africans with colonizers, barter economy systems, and the basic desire to maintain customary practices) the essential features of the Nile Valley worldview have been maintained (Schiele,

2000). Contending that such noticeable commonalities exist presupposes the existence of an ontological and cosmological framework for a collective and spiritual worldview that stretches across the various ethnic groups on the African continent and throughout the Diaspora.

Factual Myths or Imagined Identities?

The question of whether the classical Nile Valley Civilization existed or not has been the subject of intense and emotionally charged debate, involving legal writs, accusations of racism, and slanderous statements. Critics accused adherents of the Diopian school of holding onto long-debunked academic arguments of essentialism, taking a too-simplistic view, or making generalized historical conclusions. Diop's African-centered perspective is considered by many to be a pseudoscience fueled by a political agenda which aims to uncover a conspiracy that has been suppressed by racism, atheism, or ethnocentrism (Howe, 1998). Others have viewed it as a romanticized and unrealistic concept of African customs and traditions, which Africans on the continent know is not their experience (Richburg, 1997), or implied that any ideas of "African-ness" are founded on a racial essentialism or spurious cultural unanimism which does little more than mirror Eurocentric racism (Appiah, 1992; Hountondji, 1983; Mudimbe, 1988).

But it is important to understand that Afrocentric thinkers are not theorizing from nowhere. Their ideas have developed as a response to oppression, and it is understandable that Africans have embraced different versions of "African-centeredness" in search of a cultural anchor to establish intellectual, political, and cultural independence from Europe and white domination. In the nineteenth century, Black Nationalist thinkers such as Blyden, Delaney, and Crummel promoted Africa as their motherland to counter the degradation they experienced at the hands of Europeans. Arguing that ancient Egypt was a Black nation and the source of world civilization, they promoted the notion of "Ethiopianism," which held that God had a special destiny for Black people and that this would lead to their redemption in Africa. Ethiopianism, along with Black Nationalism—the idea that Blacks worldwide form a Diaspora, share cultural traits, and have a common political mission—asserted on varying levels the worth and legitimacy of a kind of broad-based African civilization. The supporters of Egyptocentrism link ancient Egyptian ancestry and the heritage of that great civilization and its pharaohs to African Americans. Despite language that is often interchangeable, there are separate and sometimes conflicting movements in what constitutes an African perspective.

Léopold Senghor fashioned a discourse of Pan-African cultural identity, *Négritude*, which was intended as a non-violent revolt against colonialism and, in particular, as a statement against the French policy of cultural assimilation. Négritude used poetry and literature to restore the validity of African culture and to establish a positive image of Black consciousness. Senghor stressed the Indigenous wisdom of African peoples and argued that, beneath the superficial cultural idiosyncrasies that distinguish one society from another, Africans were united by a profound commonality which is expressed in their democratic social structures, their religions, their work practices, their art, and in the rhythm of African life itself. While stressing that African cultures were united, Senghor also argued that Africa was distinct from Europe and that nation-building as a form of anti-colonialism could only emerge if the African personality was rescued from the suffocating pressures of European colonial culture.

Franz Fanon's views of the African situation were shaped by the revolutionary idea of the total transformation of society. For Fanon, the struggle against colonialism had meaning not simply as a means to an objective purpose, signified by the attainment of political independence, but as a process through which colonized man would remake the humanity that had been diminished and distorted by the experience of domination. Fanon (1967) attached a psychological and moral value to violence which is inseparable from his vision of man creating his own destiny in the effervescence of a progressive movement in history.

Afrocentrists, therefore, argue that Africans must see themselves through African eyes, as agents of history rather than as simply subjects of investigation. According to Asante (2007), Afrocentrists do not want to replace Greece with Egypt, but do want a proper recognition of African civilization:

> There is much we know. There is still much more that we do not know because our focus has only recently turned to the study of Africa for its own sake. In the past we studied Africa as it related to Europe, not as African cultures related to each other, and certainly not as Africa related to Asia (p. 46).

As such, Afrocentrism is not, nor can it be, based on biological determinism. Rather, it seeks to promote a dynamic, multidimensional, and real concept of African culture that emphasizes the diverse character of that culture. The historical and cultural connection between ancient Egypt and Black Africa that Diop postulated lead him to affirm the existence of a distinctive African philosophy that originated in ancient Egypt and is perpetuated in the cosmologies of various African societies today. This position implies not merely the attribution of a distinctive historical personality to Africa, but also points to an original heritage of philosophical thought.

Having grown up in a society that taught me nothing beyond European history and European thought, the discovery of this rich world of Afrocentric scholarship had a profound effect on my life. My discovery of Na'im Akbar at that radical book fair was the beginning of a journey into a new way of thinking, one that took for granted the agency of Black people and the legitimacy of our traditions of thought.

Propositions, Assumptions, and Conjectures of African Philosophy

"I am, therefore we are." This famous statement by the Kenyan philosopher John Mbiti actualizes the concept of philosophizing for change. African philosophy accepts the basic premise that the act of philosophizing should be about enabling. Mbiti starts from the idea that since belief in God is primary to all African religions, a common philosophical system is suggested, and defines African philosophy as the understanding, attitude of mind, logic, and perception behind the manner in which African people think, act, or speak in different situations of life. What is central to this thought and behavior is the "spiritual disposition" or "collective consciousness," in a word, the ethos that establishes the context of African philosophy (Mbiti, 1969).

Mbiti's argument has been criticized for approaching the philosophy from religious, sociological, and anthropological perspectives, thereby departing from the methodology of the European academic philosophical tradition. However, as Mbiti (1969) argues, "religion and philosophy are the same phenomena" (p. 5). To understand a people's religion, proverbs, oral traditions, ethics, and morality is to understand their philosophy. Religion is the more observable phenomenon, as it has permeated every aspect of African life. Indeed, in many African communities, religion was such an integral part of the community's existence that there was no specific word for religion. There were also no sacred texts or scriptures. The community's religion was handed down from generation to generation via oral and performative traditions. In addition, traditional African religions were not proselytizing. The people *were* their religion and thus could not preach to others; nor could there be any distinction between the spiritual and the physical.

Cosmologically, the African-centered worldview understands the structure of reality from the perspective of interdependency. This perspective holds that all elements of the universe, such as people, animals, and inanimate objects are interconnected. Consequently, there is no separation between the spiritual and the material (Asante & Asante, 1990). Reality is viewed as both spiritual and material at once. This emphasis is captured succinctly in the African notion that to destroy one component of the web of cosmic elements is to destroy the entire universe, even the creator (Mbiti, 1969; Nobles, 1980).

Ontologically, the Indigenous African-centered model assumes that all elements of the universe, including people, are spiritual, and that they are created from a similar universal substance (Akbar, 1984; Mbiti, 1969; Nobles, 1980). Spirituality, here, is taken to imply the non-material or invisible substance that connects all elements of the universe. The focus on spirituality within the Afrocentric perspective supports and encourages the cosmological view of interdependency. Epistemologically, the Afrocentric perspective places considerable emphasis on an effective way of obtaining knowledge (Akbar, 1984). That is, from an Afrocentric standpoint, understanding events and reality through emotions or feelings is considered valid and critical. Axiologically, this underscores the value of interpersonal relationships. Indeed, the maintenance and enhancement of harmonious interpersonal relationships is considered the most important cultural value in Afrocentricity. This position fosters a human-centered perspective toward life rather than an object-centered or materialist perspective. For Afrocentrism, the value of maintaining and strengthening interpersonal bonds overrides concerns about acquiring material objects and accumulating wealth.

An optimal worldview, according to Afrocentrism, assumes that there is a spiritual reality underlying all material phenomena, and that there is a unity of spirit (thoughts/feelings) and matter (sense of perception). This unity is positive by nature, and common to all persons (Myers, 1993) and therefore unites individuals with one another and with everything else in the universe (Akbar, 1979). Such a view structures human consciousness toward the creation of the greatest good as conceived by a sense of self-inclusion with venerated ancestors, the unborn, the community, and nature as a whole. Recognizing one's unity with this spiritual reality diminishes the perceived importance of outward differences between persons, and places focus on qualities of character (e.g., honesty, integrity, or compassion). The sense of security engendered by this recognition is felt to lessen defensiveness and fear toward those of other races, ages, sexes, and social classes.

This African perspective has created a feeling of respect for personhood, including persons after death. Although such beliefs may be scientifically unsound, they are philosophically and morally relevant to the development of sane societies. They have the merit of avoiding the problems created by science and technology in modern societies, where the concepts of a person and respect for personhood and human value have lost much of their meaning. This seems to show that a philosophy based solely on empiricism or materialism is inadequate for understanding the meaning and purpose of life or for improving the general condition of people, as opposed to the material measure of all things. The strictly scientific view of life puts human beings under the control of science and technology, and this in turn reduces them to inhuman and inhumane machines. Consequently, in spite of its so-called lack of scientific value, African philosophy has something to contribute to decoding the excesses and abuses of science. When individuals see themselves as separate from the spiritual-material unity, they are more likely to judge others as different from themselves and, therefore, are more prone to engage in discriminatory behavior.

The anthropocentric ontology was a complete unity that nothing could break up or destroy. Everything was functionally connected; to destroy one category completely would cause the destruction of the whole existence, including the creator. God was viewed as the originator and sustainer of humanity, with the spirits explaining man's destiny. Humanity was the center of the ontology, and the animals, plants, and natural phenomena constituted the environment in which man lived. God was the source and ultimate controller of energy, but the spirits also had access to it. A few human beings, such as the shaman, priests, and rain-makers, possessed, to a degree, the knowledge and ability to tap, manipulate, and use this energy. From this perspective, time exists but is elastic. It, therefore, brings together things which have passed, things taking place, and things that will occur (Mbiti, 1969). A person was not considered a full human being until they had gone through the whole rhythmic process of physical birth, naming ceremony, puberty, initiation rites, marriage, and procreation. Then, and only then, were individuals considered to be complete human beings. After physical death, as long as the person was remembered and recognized, they continued to exist in some sense.

Unlike Western philosophical traditions, African traditions do not place heavy emphasis on the individual. It is recognized that each individual becomes conscious of their own being only in terms of other people (Mbiti, 1969). Only through relationship does one learn one's duties and responsibilities toward both self and others. Thus, most African initiation rites are designed to instill a sense of corporate responsibility and collective destiny, so that when a member of the tribe suffered the entire tribe suffered, and when one member of the tribe rejoiced all of the person's kin, living, dead, and still unborn, rejoiced along with them. Whatever happened to the individual also happened to the corporate body, the tribe, and whatever happened to the tribe also happened to each of its members.

To summarize, an Indigenous African-centered perspective is assumed to be rooted in a geographical givenness and directed by a historically shared complex of challenges: the daily life of the individual and the collective (past, present, and future), the experience of racism, slavery, colonial oppression, and exploitation, and now the failure of postcolonial liberation and increasing marginalization in a world marked by material excess. The Nile Valley Civilization may or may not have actually existed in the form or with the values that Afrocentric historians and philosophers claim. It may indeed be a "fantasy." However, this is largely immaterial. What matters is the power of the idea to enable action in the here and now. This is what Afrocentrism has given me, and what it has given millions of others: the ability to claim a tradition that empowers people to imagine a world different from the one European colonial powers imagined, and to work toward making it a reality.

Case Study: Turning Points

The encounters I will relate in this second half of this chapter occurred in 1990, before the research in Africa I discussed in the first chapter, and before I even had it in mind to conduct such research. They are included not simply because they were a relevant part of my life experience, but because, in retrospect, I recognize them as being a turning point in my journey. These encounters provided a key for my understanding of the Indigenous African-centered perspective being delineated here. Like the Black Girl's conversation with Koheleth in Shaw's story, my encounter with the Social Therapy approach to professional helping triggered the realization that it was okay to look inward and use my own resources, and that I had the right to come up with my own approaches and answers. I also began to feel that the path I should take was to explore my grandfather's unschooled and untheorized practice as a helper. Attending a Social Therapy conference made me realize that what I sought could probably be found closer to home.

In retrospect, I have come to see that my encounter with Social Therapy was what began to persuade me that no search for an Indigenous African-centered approach to professional helping's goal of supporting others to live more satisfyingly that had to validate itself using the standards of Eurocentric philosophy could work. Like the Black Girl—and like contemporary philosophers of Afrocentrism—I realized I had to look inward, both to my personal strengths and intuitions and to my cultural and spiritual roots—not just in my immediate environment in England, but that of my parents, from Guyana, South America, and beyond that in Africa.

Encounter One: Meeting of Minds?

I had been interested for several years in the possibilities of more socially conscious, socially oriented approaches to professional helping, after attending a conference at which a New York-based Social Therapist spoke on action-oriented methods. At the time, Social Therapy was still relatively little known in Britain, and I instantly became interested in exploring its ideas and practices. According to its practitioners, Social Therapy is a practical, non-diagnostic, and non-interpretive, short-term method for helping people to re-initiate their emotional development through performance. The Social Therapeutic approach thereby challenges the assumptions of knowledge-based, problem-oriented, anti-developmental psychology, including most forms of psychotherapy. Contrary to conventional psychological wisdom, according to this approach, there are no natural limits to human development. It is the belief of Social Therapy that this development is the "cure" for emotional pain and psychopathology.

From my own frustrations with the lack of a social agenda in mainstream professional helping, I felt that, in theory at least, Social Therapy appeared to offer a way to incorporate a more outward-looking, activist perspective into professional helping. I learned that a major Social Therapy conference would be taking place in New York, and as I had aunts I could visit in Washington, DC, I decided to attend and learn about this alternative to the standard approach with which I had come to be dissatisfied.

I began my journey with a visit to Howard University, as I wanted to do some research in their archives and had a few weeks to spare before the New York conference started. I stayed with my aunts, who seemed to perceive me as still being the 10-year-old child they used to know. Among other things, this meant they adopted a paternalistic attitude toward me, treating me as if I could not make decisions for myself. For example, one day they drove me to a MacDonald's fast-food outlet and, without a word, ordered me a Big Mac, even though they knew I was a vegetarian at the time. When I did not eat the meal, they were upset. I mention this otherwise trivial incident because, by chance, their paternalistic attitude had a major bearing on my experience of the New York conference and what happened afterward.

When my aunts took me to the station to catch the train to New York, their paternal attitude was once more in evidence. Worried that I might miss the train (although there was ample time), they would not let me buy a ticket before boarding and assured me I could buy my ticket on board. What they failed to tell me was that this would cost me twice as much money, in fact almost all the cash I had on me. However, I did not panic, as I had my credit card and had asked a friend in England to credit the account while I was away so that I could access cash in an emergency.

To my enormous distress, when I arrived at New York's Central Station and tried to transfer to my connecting train, the card was refused by the cashier. Distraught, I called the credit card service, but whoever answered my call only confirmed that I had no funds and then hung up. My friend had apparently forgotten to deposit money in the account. I had barely enough money to take a train to the conference center. After that, I would be totally broke in one of the most expensive cities in the world. To make matters worse, there was nowhere in the station to sit and think—the enclosed area was for ticket holders only, and the toilets were filled with bag ladies—so I wandered around the station trying to decide what to do. Finally I realized that, having come so far to attend the conference, it would be a shame if I did not take the risk and attend, and I bought the ticket with my last remaining cash. This act, which was quite foolhardy from a rational perspective, I now believe, greatly impacted my experience of the conference. Finding myself without material resources forced me to fall back on my inner emotional and spiritual resources. My attitude was that my destiny had led me into this situation for a reason, and that all I could do was rely on the same destiny to lead me where it intended me to go.

Another surprise greeted me at the conference. Though well organized, with people waiting to welcome attendees and help them to find their way around, the conference had no preset structure. It was entirely up to us, the group of approximately a thousand people, to make things happen. Collectively, therefore, we were *all* thrown back on our own emotional and spiritual resources. Nevertheless, I found it difficult at first to let go and jump in. I felt preoccupied with my own perilous situation, worrying about how I was going to get back to Washington with no money or friends. I couldn't help but reflect that I was at a conference that was supposed to be about practicing an alternative, socially conscious form of professional helping, yet no one I met seemed at all concerned about my plight or interested in helping out a colleague. The paradox was troubling and gave me my first uneasy feelings about Social Therapy.

Luckily, I was introduced at dinner to a Washington, DC, delegate who, on hearing about my problem, offered me a lift back to the capital—for a price. I was more than a little surprised that she expected payment, but said nothing. Perhaps this was an exotic American custom. She was, however, prepared to wait till we got back to be paid, and her trust immediately took the pressure off and enabled me to focus on the conference.

What I saw there both encouraged and troubled me. On the one hand, the participants were enthusiastic, dynamic, and very welcoming (despite, paradoxically, showing no interest in helping at a practical level). There was plenty of talk and activity in the sessions and intense networking outside them. People were very ready to share experiences and ideas, and I learned a great deal. On the other hand, many of the participants were simply getting up and glorifying Fred Newman, the founder of Social Therapy, and/or testifying about their lives and the wonderful difference that Social Therapy had made. Being used to British reservation and understatement, I felt somewhat overwhelmed. I had difficulty adjusting to what was going on, having no framework with which to understand the proceedings. The closest I could come to relating to the conference was the then-emerging trend for Oprah Winfrey-style confessional and self-help shows.

Although I had arrived with very high hopes for the transformational potential of Social Therapy, what I found revealed a gap between the therapy's promises and its results. I began to wonder if people were being exploited. I shared a therapy space with a colleague who had been seeing her client for 27 years. Another person I met seemed to be looking for a quasi-religious experience and was clearly highly vulnerable to manipulation. Along with many others, he seemed to have elevated Fred Newman to the position of a god. Fred himself walked around with an air of knowing all, similar to that of Koheleth in Shaw's story. People swarmed around him like devotees.

For the first 2 days, I thought of myself only as an observer. Being used to a much more structured approach, I felt disconcerted by the open-ended format and unable to participate in the "official" sessions, despite doing a lot of talking and questioning on a one-to-one basis outside the conference arena. Suddenly, however, on the afternoon of the last day, and much to my surprise, I found myself jumping to my feet in the hall, and intervening in the discussion. I can't remember what prompted me to stand up, or even what the topic was, only that some inner impulse was frustrated with the direction of the discussion and prompting me irresistibly to intervene. I also remember that, to my amazement, my intervention changed the course of the proceedings. From a passive observer, I had suddenly become not simply a participant but a decisive one.

Reflecting later, I realized that something, a new awareness of some kind, had compelled me to get involved. I made the connection that I could not sit on the sidelines, claiming to be interested in Social Therapy only as a theory to be applied to others. I acknowledged that I too was a subject and that, as such, I had to become involved. I realized that change came from within and that it would be difficult from then on to operate as an aloof, "objective" practitioner. I saw that the professional helper had to bring their *own* life into the professional helping work. I was delighted, therefore, when the therapist who gave me a lift back to Washington suddenly invited me to join her therapy group for the rest of my stay (6 weeks)—though again for a fee.

Encounter Two: Therapy and (In)congruence

On the drive back to Washington, I was struck by the fact that, despite all the talk of sharing and concern for others at the conference we had just attended, we only made small talk. Something seemed to be in the way of real communication, as if the principles discussed at the conference had nothing to do with life outside. A similar compartmentalization was evident in the therapy group. Despite the participants' eagerness to talk and share in the therapy sessions, no one seemed interested in carrying this openness into their daily lives. I found it impossible to get close to anyone outside the sessions. They only seemed to care during therapy, as if their lives in the group and outside the group took place in separate worlds. This paradox led me to conclude that the participants enjoyed the group as a sort of haven from reality, a place where they could talk but without needing to act or move, without having to put into practice what was being preached by this therapy. To my mind, this gave a falseness or emptiness to the group. I was participating because I wanted to *change*, and had hoped that in Social Therapy I had finally found a professional helping method committed to bridging the gap between social and emotional transformation. However, I began to suspect that Social Therapy's claim to be different from mainstream therapy was hollow.

The group had a gender mix which, initially, excited me. I had once believed in the need for women-only groups, but later had begun to feel that it would be better to incorporate men after all. However, this group of two white men and four white women turned out to be dominated by the men. Discussions somehow always came back to *their* problems, and they were never challenged on this oppressiveness. Indeed, the women in the group appeared to collude in this male domination. I also came to feel that racism was a problem. I was the only Black person. Had I been invited in for that reason? The suspicion troubled me. However, I kept quiet about race because I didn't want to upset things. I realized from the beginning that the members of the group wanted to talk about "safe" issues: "my mother," "my father," and so on, and I could see that an "uncomfortable" political topic like race would not go down well.

Encounter Three: Therapy and Race

I had briefly discussed race with one of the leaders of the movement at the conference, and after my time in Washington I attended, at his invitation, a special 2-week program put together specifically for me. This program included an all-Black therapy session, a visit to the movement's Castillo theater, and one-on-one sessions with two counselors. The first counselor could not address my questions and passed me on to another, more experienced counselor who also had difficulties. However, they were eager to talk about my concerns and, in fact, I was still talking to the second counselor minutes before my flight home, so anxious was she that I should not leave unsatisfied.

The all-Black therapy session, held in the heart of Harlem, was the most memorable and significant event of the program. To my amazement, I arrived to find that the group was led by a white therapist. I was shocked to find a white person facilitating such a group, due to the supposedly progressive and culturally sensitive view of the Social Therapy movement. However, looking back this makes sense, as one would need to be well-resourced in order to obtain the training to become a facilitator in this particular organization. This type of expense was beyond the reach of most people at that time. My most vivid memory of this session was gazing out of the window and seeing the Nation of Islam headquarters across the street. I had visited it while waiting for the session to start, and had been made, through the warm welcome, to feel spiritually invigorated. From the Social Therapy session, I looked out across the street consumed by nostalgia and longing, and pondered the contrast between the atmosphere I had encountered there and the atmosphere in this room, where the lack of spirituality and recognition was striking, despite my being a technical stranger to both groups.

I had met the white male therapist earlier at his house to discuss the movement with him and others. He had acknowledged that my questions were valid, but I nevertheless had sensed failure to recognize me as *other than* Black. I felt he saw me only as a Black person, as a stereotype. Thus, when I saw him at the therapy session in "control" of this group of 30 or so Black people, I felt there was something he was not seeing in us (or rather, that he was only seeing *one thing* in us). He seemed genuine and well-intentioned, but unable to see past our "race," and unable to recognize our need to have the space to do the work ourselves.

My experiences in New York and Washington clearly indicated a gap between theory and practice, and, more importantly, a lack of a program within the Social Therapy movement to recognize and address this gap. The need for professional helping to be *lived* in order for real development to take place did not appear to be a priority. There was a hollowness and irrelevance at the core of the theory. More crucially, for me as a Black person attempting to overcome racism and oppression at both a personal and a community level, Social Therapy fails to provide for an African-centered perspective.

I cannot fault Social Therapy philosophically; I can only report my undeniable feeling, thrown into stark relief by my brief glimpse of the alternative offered by the Nation of Islam, that I at least was not going to find the congruence I was seeking in it. Despite the movement's admirable principles of activism, social consciousness, and cultural sensitivity, I sensed, at a gut level, the persistence of the status quo and a familiar resistance to accepting new approaches that are not "packaged" in conventional ways. Though Social Therapy is a major advance over mainstream professional helping approaches, it still has difficulties thinking outside the box when it comes to race. The idea that a specifically Black philosophy or worldview is either possible or desirable does not seem to fit into Social Therapy's paradigm, progressive and well-intentioned as it is in other respects. However, this realization pointed the way forward for me. I now saw that the next stage in my journey needed to be precisely an exploration of a specifically Black approach to helping.

Conclusion

Just as the Black Girl is left "thinking harder" about her journey, but feeling she has benefited from the encounter with the Greek scholar, Koheleth, so too has African philosophy benefited from its engagement with the Western philosophical tradition. Its encounters with Western philosophical views has meant that, from its initial reactive position, it has moved to one of being proactive, and concluded that it can derive its own assumptions from which to view and understand the world. Thus, as the Black Girl of Shaw's story concludes, African philosophy assumes that "knowledge of self is knowledge of God" (Nobles, 1976). For my part, my encounters with Social Therapy had made me realize that I too needed to look inward, initially by turning to a specifically Indigenous African-centered perspective.

Chapter 5
The Myop: Seeing Things Differently

> *"I am not interested in wisdom" he replied: "in fact I do not know what it means and have no reason to believe that it exists. My business is to learn something that was not known before. I impart that knowledge to the world, and thereby add to the body of ascertained scientific truth."*
>
> *"How much better will the world be when it is all knowledge and no mercy?" said the Black Girl. "Haven't you brains enough to invent some decent way of finding out what you want to know?" (Shaw, 1932, p. 23)*

In the figure of the Myop, Shaw represents a modern, scientific God. The Myop takes a fundamentalist approach to the scientific understanding of human behavior by insisting that all knowledge is empirically derived. He has made this discovery as a result of "25 years of devoted research" and takes great pride in the adulation offered by the scientific world as a result. The Black Girl is loath to accept his doctrine because, in the quest for the acquisition of knowledge, he has cruelly tested his hypotheses at the expense of animal suffering. The Black Girl finds a less cruel way to demonstrate his hypothesis that the universe is a system of conditioned reflexes by telling him that he is seated upon a crocodile and frightening him into climbing a tree. Then, just as effectively, she proves that he can descend from the tree by claiming a vicious snake is hovering at his shoulder. However, the Myop's belief in science, and his conviction that knowledge has nothing to do with either faith or the soul, eventually drive her away.

For Shaw, the Myop illustrates the short-sighted, paradigm-bound nature of Western science. For me, he typifies the same flaws in Eurocentric helping strategies, with their pretensions to being "objective" and "scientific" and their denial of spirituality. In contrast, an Indigenous African-centered perspective adopts a position of agency, and accepts spirituality as a key component for understanding human behavior and thinking. Within this framework, psychological work aims not just to add to the "body of ascertained knowledge" (Shaw, 1932, p. 23), but also to realign people to the spiritual laws of the universe.

G. Berry, *Helping?*, https://doi.org/10.1007/978-3-031-88586-0_5

Rejecting the "Norm"

At a meeting held by the King's Fund in London, on 29 January 1997, which had been convened to examine the question "Are mental health services bad for Black (African-Caribbean) people?" Professor Sashidharan observed that Black people's experience of the mental health system had, for decades, mirrored their wider experiences of marginalization and containment in white supremacist societies. It was vital, he argued, to think more radically and to develop new forms of mental health intervention that are more appropriate. However, the vested interests of psychiatrists, who continue to dominate planning, could easily hold this back:

> Black people are better off avoiding psychiatry, particularly in deprived areas where the problems are at their worst. Mental health services fail to assess the problems correctly so dragging more people into institutions is unnecessary. What is needed are innovations away from hospitals and a challenge to their role as the bastion of power in mental health services. (Sashidharan, 1997, p. 2)

Paul Boateng, who was the British junior health minister at the time, was acutely aware of the raw deal being given to Black people under the mental health system (Amokeodo, 1998). "I get sick and tired of the approach to research and development which sees Black people like laboratory mice which have to be seen under a microscope largely by white laboratory technicians," he told MIND's annual conference in 1998. "But the mice are biting back and there is a big mouse in charge." He saw an increased emphasis on talking therapies as a possible option.

Two and a half decades later, these problems persist. During the COVID-19 pandemic and associated global "racial reckoning" sparked by the highly publicized murders of George Floyd, Breonna Taylor, and Ahmaud Arbery in the United States, major mental health associations issued public recognitions and apologies for those shortcomings highlighted by Sashidharan and Boateng (and many, many others). For example, the American Psychological Association (October 2021) stated:

> The American Psychological Association failed in its role leading the discipline of psychology, was complicit in contributing to systemic inequities, and hurt many through racism, racial discrimination, and denigration of people of color, thereby falling short on its mission to benefit society and improve lives. APA is profoundly sorry, accepts responsibility for, and owns the actions and inactions of APA itself, the discipline of psychology, and individual psychologists who stood as leaders for the organization and field.

The APA had previously said it was "committed to identifying, understanding, and rectifying our past injustices, as well as developing anti-racist policies that promote equity in mental health for all," and issued an apology to its "members, patients, their families, and the public for enabling discriminatory and prejudicial actions within the APA and racist practices in psychiatric treatment for Black, Indigenous and People of Color (BIPOC)" (January 2021).

The National Association of Social Workers (NASW) acknowledged that social work "had not always lived up to our mission of pursuing social justice for all," and apologized for "supporting policies and activities that have harmed people of color"

(2021). While the American Counseling Association (ACA) did not issue such an apology or acknowledge its participation in perpetuating racism in mental health, it did denounce

> the historical legacy and destruction caused by institutionalized racism and violence against Black people, perpetuated at the hands of law enforcement, the hatred bred of White supremacy, the deafening silence of dehumanizing and complicit inaction to address these systemic ills within our society. (2020)

It also acknowledged that the ACA has "a moral and professional obligation to deconstruct institutions which have historically been designed to benefit White America."

Despite these public apologies and pledges to anti-racism, it is unclear what the proposed steps forward are—but it is clear that there is no proposed plan to relinquish the foundation of Western philosophy, or to meaningfully adopt an Indigenous perspective.

From an Indigenous African-centered perspective, restoration and healing would have to involve acknowledgment of human interconnectedness and our shared connection to the spiritual realm. The solutions to systemic racism and inequalities in mental health care have been in existence since pre-colonization, but implementing them would involve an actual paradigm shift to welcome the ancient wisdom of Indigenous philosophies. Given that Western helping professions exist within economic systems that rely on mental illness, addiction, poverty, disempowerment, and family dysfunction, it is difficult to trust that this paradigm shift will take place, as there is no economic advantage to the helping professions if global wellness and empowerment were to be actualized.

As the Association of Black Psychologists (2021) articulated in its response to the American Psychological Association's (2021) apology:

> The American Psychological Association (APA) cannot simply dismiss the full history of Euro-American psychology that is rooted in a legacy of the pathology of Whiteness with a simple apology and questionable claims to now combat racism, oppression, and white hegemony. The APA, in fact, has played a large hand in the oppression of the Black community in education, health, housing, the media, the work sector, criminal justice, and practically all domains of life necessary to thriving and optimal well-being. Borrowing again from this transformative concept of Sankofa, we also know that "the white man will try to satisfy us with symbolic victories rather than economic equity and real justice," underscoring that while the apology and resolutions may appear genuine, it is far too late for it to mean anything to Black America and sorely lacks several opportunities for real and meaningful apology and atonement, which are inextricably linked to restitution and restoration.

Like the Missionary of Shaw's story who went to Africa with the good intentions to "save" the souls of African children, these Western professional associations may genuinely believe that they are helping. However, as we saw with the Missionary, her own faith was not a lived one and it was not incorporated into her day to day. She was unequipped to deliver helping to those she aimed to serve in Africa because she wasn't even able to address her own psychological problems.

These formal apologies of the professional healing organizations put me in mind of something Malcolm X said in a 1964 speech: "I will never say that progress is being made. If you stick a knife in my back nine inches and pull it out six inches, there's no progress. If you pull it all the way out, that's not progress. The progress is healing the wound that the blow made" (MalcolmShabazz, 2018). What Malcolm X was calling for was not anti-racism or decolonization, but restoration.

Terms such as "decolonization" and "anti-racism" have gained popularity in recent years, and they are meant to signal that things are actually going to be different moving forward. But a rational step-by-step analysis of the evidence from the history of Western mental health so far points to the fact that racism, injustice, and oppression have played major roles in the development of the helping professions' infrastructures. Awareness of this fact is a necessary first step—but what evidence is there to suggest that these helping professions are now capable of constructing the next steps? There will be platitudes of imagery and diversity hires to give the illusion that alternative voices are being heard. Yet without system change to fundamentally respect and collaborate with alternative perspectives, this will result in hiring individuals who cannot exercise the agency to offer their alternative perspective or are not equipped for the job of "decolonization" due to their prior indoctrination in the Western training system.

This is a fundamental difference between the Western helping process and the Indigenous African-centered perspective on helping. In going where the evidence has taken me throughout my journey of understanding, I have recognized the role that spirituality plays in the restorative helping/healing process. When this element is absent in the helper, the helping institutions, and their policies and procedures, true healing and *restoration* cannot take place—regardless of their supportive words or intentions to "decolonize."

From this perspective, what constitutes helping is that which facilitates self-knowledge, emotional acceptance, and growth to promote the optimal development of personal resources. The process aims to provide an opportunity to work toward *living more satisfyingly* and resourcefully. Therefore, a professional helper operating from such a perspective acknowledges the need for cultural construction and reconstruction. In this instance, seeking answers from Indigenous philosophy means having the goal of transforming or re-aligning people to the natural order.

A Missing Ingredient?

As we saw in the previous chapter, spirituality is central to Indigenous African-centered philosophy, and so we must question the current perception of spirituality in the therapeutic setting and taking into account specific cultural expression of spiritual beliefs. The academic study of spirituality is rarely an aspect of therapists' training (Jafari, 2016). Indeed, the overall attitudinal matrix of a psychology-oriented education tends to foster a negative attitude toward religion. With few exceptions, traditional psychotherapists have been subservient to Freud's assessment of religious life as neurotic and self-deceptive (Genia, 1995).

Strongly influenced by Freud's thinking about religion, psychoanalytically oriented counselors and therapists tend to perceive all religious or spiritual conviction as illusive and neurotic, and interpret reliance on a "god-figure" as an outmoded continuation of childhood dependency (Pargament & Lomax, 2013). They contend that infants and young children perceive their parents as omnipotent god-like figures, and that they are especially prone to idealize their fathers on whom they rely for protection and support. Although healthy adults relinquish their childhood illusions, Freud contended that most continue to long for someone to protect and comfort them. He concluded that this universal need for a surrogate father is the psychological force that draws people toward religion. Thus, from a psychoanalytic perspective, religious practice is a neurotic repetition of early childhood anxieties. Since the world is frightening and unpredictable from the moment of birth, Freud theorized that the human race created an exalted Father in order to feel protected and secure. According to Freud, the pinnacle of human enlightenment will be achieved when this illusion is vanquished by science.

Aversion to religion and spirituality in order to be accepted as "scientific" has also been rampant in Cognitive Behavioral Therapy, a subgroup of the behaviorist school that emphasizes the importance of cognition in determining human behavior (Carlson & Gonzalez-Prendes, 2016). In contrast to psychoanalytically oriented therapists, who link psychological dysfunction with childhood trauma, cognitive-behaviorists relate emotional problems to distorted thinking patterns. They propose that negative emotions and interpersonal problems stem from irrational beliefs that people have about themselves and the world. From this theoretical perspective, such irrational beliefs are assimilated through social and cultural norms and the influence of the mass media. Following the anti-religious bias of Albert Ellis, founder of Rational Emotive Therapy, many cognitively oriented psychotherapists presume that all religious beliefs are irrational and immature. For Ellis and his followers, atheism is the only road to optimal emotional health and well-being. In a 2013 survey of members of the Association for Behavioral and Cognitive Therapies, 36% of respondents reported some discomfort in addressing spirituality and religion issues with clients, 19% reported never/rarely inquiring about spirituality and religion, and 71% reported little-to-no previous clinical training in this area (Rosmarin et al., 2013).

In contrast, the emphasis placed on values, love, and faith by the Humanist school of thought appears to indicate that it recognizes the place of spirituality in the counseling relationship. Allport, Maslow, and Rogers all share a closeness with religious values, and see individuals as being propelled by an inner thrust toward growth and maturity. Thus, on the surface, the Humanist (or Existential) psychological orientation seems more compatible with religious or spiritual values than either the psychoanalytic or the behavioral perspective, especially as issues at its center, such as mortality, freedom and responsibility, isolation and intimacy, and ontological meaninglessness parallel the concerns of all major religions. Nevertheless, humanists tend to regard the transcendent as nothing more than a higher level of consciousness. Consequently, humanistic and existential practitioners may be as unsympathetic toward traditionally religious clients as other practitioners.

However, psychotherapists are generally less religious and spiritual than the populations they serve (Delaney et al., 2013; Plante & Thoresen, 2012), and thus a paradoxical situation is created, as their use of theological language and imagery, together with a set of convictions and moral stance, can be equated to religious faith. Such an incongruent position ensures, from the Indigenous African-centered perspective, the perpetual ineffectiveness of such therapeutic models, while at the same time providing an explanation for the "counseling makes no difference" theses (Eysenck, 1952; Truax & Carkhuff, 1967) and research findings that conclude it is the therapeutic alliance, and particularly the therapist's personal contribution to the alliance, which has most to do with effectiveness of treatment (Baldwin et al., 2007; Wampold, 2010).

The Indigenous, Africanist identification of spirituality as a key component in the counseling relationship is certainly not a new phenomenon. Brown and Pedder (1992) quote the work of Ellenberger (1970) who identified the foundations of psychiatry in exorcism, magnetism, and hypnosis. Ellenberger makes a direct link with both the psychotic and somatic illness of "possession by evil spirit" and goes on to state that "[traditionally] healing was … naturally in the hands of religious leaders or traditional healers, such as shaman, witchdoctors or priests" (Brown & Pedder, 1992, p. 8). Jung also recognized the importance of the spirit (soul) and its place in the counseling relationship.

And yet despite developments like the "logotherapy" (logo meaning spirit) of Victor Frankl, the Existentialist who most notably recognizes the role of the spirit in the therapeutic relationship, Freud's influence remains overwhelming. As a result, spirituality and its place in the counseling relationship have largely been rejected (Katz, 2017; Lartey et al., 1994).

Creating a Solution

From an Indigenous African-centered perspective, developing appropriate psychological approaches that incorporate spirituality is crucial (Katz, 2017). With the concept of time being interpreted as holistic, the current generation is always seen as charged with the responsibility of preparing a path for future generations. It is recognized that the current oppressive status quo will remain unless a change is made in the present. Thus, because of the inherent interconnectedness of individuals and collectives, the entire society should be working to redress problems. The application of an Indigenous African-centered perspective to the therapeutic/counseling process sees the counselor/therapist charged with providing the community with leadership in terms of guidance on overcoming personal as well as societal oppression, and realigning people to the natural order of the universe/God's laws (Akbar, 1995; Grayshield, 2010; Katz, 2017; Mkhize, 2021).

It needs to be noted that not all Black psychologists agree with the above definitions of an African perspective on psychology. However, I am arguing in this chapter that adopting a position of *agency* enables the proponents of an Indigenous African-centered perspective to speculatively create their own frame of reference that, by inference, may alter the current concept of professional helping. Agency is then defined not in terms of dependence or independence, but as interdependence (Nyamnjoh, 2001):

> Agency in this sense is open to individuals and groups alike, and discussions of it should not be limited to the empowerment of the individual alone, but extended to include how the quest for individual fulfillment negotiates conviviality with collective interests which may include but are not limited to their cultural dimensions. We should provide for agency that guarantees not only individual rights and freedoms, but also the interests of the communal and cultural solidarities (which interests are more than just the composite of many individual interests). In Africa in particular, where individuals and groups are hybrid in more than the conventional sense and where marginality limits action and creativity for both individuals and groups, discussions of agency should be informed by the reality of the creative quest for survival on the ground. (p. 1)

Afrocentricity in particular seeks to relocate the African person as an *agent* in an effort to eliminate the illusion of being on the fringes in human history (Waldron, 2010).

It is, therefore, necessary to philosophize from the standpoint of Africans as human agents, rather than as objects as in a European framework. Afrocentricity is a philosophical source and theoretical perspective, arguing for pluralism in philosophical views with all cultural centers being respected (Mkhize, 2021). From this position, an Indigenous African-centered theorist takes into account the shared responsibility of all members of society as being interconnected and interdependent in the effort to transform the status quo, being mindful of contributions made from the past and those yet to be made (Charema & Shizha, 2008).

In support of this position, Flick (1981), in his analysis of why Malcolm X used "myths to destroy myths," argued that he considered that the status quo of oppression was supported and "given life by a series of symbolic themes," which is why he used the same method to dismantle them (p. 167). This approach challenges the perception that "to have the ability to define the world and the entities located within allowed man to have control of that world" (p. 169). Consequently, Malcolm X considered it necessary to work outside the confines of white scholarship and to reject the imposition of white doctrines in terms of both language and method of operation. As has been shown, psychology and other social sciences and related professions have been developed to support and maintain the interests of European culture. This is why an Africanist perspective has long understood the role of psychologists as explaining and providing clarity for Black people in the context of "Black" reality, and therefore considers it necessary to develop new and alternative methods that work on behalf of the oppressed rather than the oppressor (Semaj, 1981).

As the work of Franz Fanon (1967) emphasized, these requirements should center on the creation of a positive self-image and self-esteem, and a pride in one's appearance and in Black cultural creativity in order to redress the negative image of

"African/Black" established in the colonial era. By using the Nile Valley Civilization as a frame of reference, it is assumed that a message of human growth and inspiration can be revealed that will uplift people to a higher spiritual reality—one that enables them to develop themselves. This approach also represents a movement away from the original focus of "Black/African" psychology (namely, to understand the behavior and thinking of "Black/African" people) toward a theory for understanding humanity in general. Viewed from this perspective, Western society, with its emphasis on materialism, has arrested human development, revealing a "low-level moral expectation" of humanity that only stimulates lower human appetites (i.e., behavior that is motivated purely by sex, violence, and/or self-destruction) (Akbar, 1979).

Indigenous African-centered psychology, accepting a cosmological framework, requires a system of knowledge (philosophy, definitions, concepts, models, procedures, and practices) concerning the nature of the social universe. Thus, it becomes fundamentally different in origin, content, and direction from that recognized and practiced by Euro-American professional helpers (Clark et al., 1975; Mkhize, 2021). An understanding of African cosmology, as identified, for example, in the Nile Valley Civilization, is essential to an understanding of African psychology. The ontological principle of this cosmology is harmony with nature. Thus, all aspects of nature, including consciousness, are interrelated and interdependent, forming one phenomenal reality—a communal phenomenology. In its stress on "groupness" (survival of the group), commonality, corporateness, cooperation, collective responsibility, and interdependence, the Indigenous African-centered perspective thus centers on, derives from, reflects, and reinforces the basic principles supposedly established in African antiquity, interpreting psychology as articulation, institutionalization and perpetuation of a fully human/natural psychology, as opposed to an adaptation of Western psychology with a "Black" face. Thus, African psychology differs greatly from mainstream psychology, seeking to take literally the definition of "psychology" as the study of the *soul*. This is mirrored by Indigenous psychologies across the world.

A Shared Global Philosophy

While my search for understanding was guided by one particular Indigenous philosophy from my own cultural context (an African-centered lens), there is a universal aspect of Indigenous philosophy. This universal concept is the idea of oneness, interconnectedness, and alignment, though each culture has its own unique interpretation or way of expressing this philosophy.

We can see this in the proverbs, sayings, adages, and maxims that reflect this foundational Indigenous philosophy of interconnectedness from their respective cultural contexts across the globe. For example, an African-centered lens is captured by the concept of *ubuntu*, the philosophy which underpins cultural values and beliefs of indigenous groups in Southern Africa (Hlongwane et al., 2018). While *ubuntu* has no literal translation in English, it is generally understood as meaning "I am because we are." Aboriginal and Torres Strait Islander people of Australia recommend that helping and wellness approaches must recognize the importance of one's interconnection to "land, culture, spirituality, ancestry, family and community, and how these affect the individual" (Gee et al., 2014, p. 55). A Maori proverb, "He waka eke noa" translates in English to "A canoe we are all in with no exceptions" (or, "we are all in this together"). Sa'di of Shiraz, the thirteenth-century Persian poet, expresses something similar in his poem "Bani Adam": "The members of the human race are limbs one to another, for at creation they were of one essence/ When one limb is pained by fate, the others cannot rest./You who are unsympathetic to the troubles of others, it is not fitting to call you human" (Sa'di., 2008, p. 22). Even the Italian saying *Quando finisce la partita il re ed il pedone finiscono nella stessa scatola* translates to "When the game ends, the king and pawn end up in the same box." The Dalai Lama offers the following statement from a Tibetan perspective: "I don't think of myself just as a Tibetan or a Buddhist, but as a human being. We have to think of the whole of humanity. Being human is the common ground in our efforts to create a better world. Remember, we all survive in dependence on others" (Gyatso, n.d.). The Mexican Proverb *Arrieros somos y en el camino andamos* translates to "we are all mule drivers in the fields" reminding us of our one-ness, while the Japanese phrase *Okage Sama De* translates to "I am what I am because of you." The Bahá'i Persian-American author Marzieh Gail similarly states:

> Oneness, of course, should not be confused with sameness, which is a tedious, artificial thing, entirely alien to a world where no two grains of wheat have ever been alike. The peculiar curse of the times is an effort at standardization; gum is chewed on the Himalayas, and everyone is trying desperately to be like everyone else, or more so. (Gail, 1976, 119)

The universalism illustrated by these proverbs and maxims is, therefore, very different from the universalism described in Chap. 1, because it does not rest on a single paradigm or doctrine: it acknowledges that interconnectedness and oneness do not require uniformity across cultures.

Theories for Change

Because they have designed their theories to penetrate well-established myths about Africans' lack of human potential, because they emphasize spirituality and community, and because they see humanity as more than the "Darwinian assumption that man is a glorified ape" (Akbar, 1979), Africanist theorists have often been misunderstood. Their willingness to transgress the Western scholarly norms in their research and presentation, together with internalized racism and negative attitudes toward anything African/Black, has led to its public image being narrowly defined as encouraging only Black nationalism and ethnic pride. The Africanist use of emotive, non-jargonistic, readable language, designed to transform themselves and others to enable the entire human species to live more satisfyingly, is somehow lost amid the outcry of reverse racism.

However, for the Indigenous African-centered theorist, the more important question is how these insights can be used to create alternative theories of helping that are better equipped to serve the needs of Black people. The Myop of Shaw's story is so focused on a narrow, materialistic conception of the truth that he is unable to see what is actually happening around him. Like the Myop, Western professional helping—like Western academic thought more generally—is so committed to seeing the world in a single way, it refuses to see the harm a reductive, materialistic paradigm is causing.

Thus, Azibo's (2015) model of psychological functioning, which argues that healthy psychological functioning for people of African descent must be based on principles that affirm an African reality, can easily be dismissed as essentialist, emotive, and unscientific. However, Azibo's model depends on the assertion that persons of African descent must be in harmony with their creator, and that mental disorders for persons of African descent must be conceptualized within a culturally relevant framework. Consequently, with these assumptions as a basis, he developed a classification system of disorders that he believed are peculiar to the African personality, and which are not present in the Diagnostic and Statistical Manual of Mental Disorders (DSM-5).

For her part, Linda James-Myers developed an Indigenous African-centered model of psychological functioning called Belief Systems Analysis (BSA) (Montgomery et al., 1990). BSA seeks to introduce the client to a worldview that is more conducive to spiritual growth by comparing and contrasting the consequences of differing belief systems, which she calls "optimal" and "sub-optimal." Myers posits that adopting a worldview based on optimal conceptual systems leads to peace and happiness. This optimal system is based on integrating the spiritual and the material, and thus on harmony, communalism, intrinsic self-worth, self-knowledge, diunital logic (union of opposites), extended self-identity, and a holistic worldview. In contrast, the sub-optimal conceptual systems are based on materialism, competition, extrinsic self-worth, dichotomous thinking, individualism, and a segmented worldview. BSA therapy seeks to facilitate increased self-knowledge by monitoring thoughts, feelings, and behaviors using a variety of techniques. Myers believes that therapy is working when (a) client's self-esteem increases, based on intrinsic self-worth, (b) they are empowered to define reality for themselves, and (c) they develop a spiritual base manifested by faith, a positive belief system and patience. Again, however, her framework for creating an optimal state for a human being can easily be dismissed as idealistic.

Another Indigenous, Africanist therapy is NTU, which is spiritually based, and predicated on an integration of ancient African philosophy and humanistic psychology. NTU is a Bantu concept that means "unifying force" (Phillips, 1990, 1994). The core principles of NTU therapy are harmony, balance, and interconnectedness. The NTU therapist uses talk therapy along with culturally specific techniques, such as teaching the principles of the Nguzo Saba,[1] libations, Afro-drama, and prayer. According to Philips, these techniques are carried out within a highly spiritualized relationship with the client. The therapist believes that healing is natural, and that it occurs *through* the therapist, not *because* of the therapist. However, NTU's fusion of Western therapeutic techniques, critics claim, clings to the use of Western methodology—but Phillips argues that the goals of NTU therapy are to increase self-knowledge, to promote authenticity in interactions with others, and to arm the client with tools to manage difficulties in life.

Akbar's (1991) primary focus is to help Black people understand themselves by reversing the accepted European concepts of mental health disorders. He wants to promote the restoration of good mental health (defined in terms of behaviors that foster mental growth and awareness as opposed to those that hinder awareness and growth). Akbar regards an Indigenous African-centered model of psychotherapy as spiritual, which is central to healthy human development. This model posits that inner peace and harmony are acquired by co-operation between what Akbar calls the components of the community of self: motors, senses, emotional ego, memory, reason, conscience, and will.

Akbar defines motors as instinctual behaviors that move an individual toward pleasure or away from pain. The senses are used to communicate with the external world, while the emotional ego protects the individual from harm by responding to people and events on an affective level. Memory retains experiences in order to enable the individual to learn and to grow, while reason organizes and assesses the information coming from the senses. Finally, conscience controls all the other components of the self for the good of the community. It represents the will of God operating within each person. Thus, Akbar (1991) insists that, in a healthy person, conscience rules over the other components and maintains them in a correct balance. Consequently, mental illness is essentially the result of a lack of balance among the different components of the self. To maintain or regain balance, an individual must acquire self-knowledge by listening to the "inner voice" of conscience that connects them to the creator. Akbar asserts that increased self-knowledge results in self-acceptance, self-help, self-discovery, and self-preservation.

Akbar suggests that living in a Eurocentric society based on unnatural principles has made Black people live disordered lives. An alien self-disorder causes them to reject natural dispositions and to see only materialistic goals, and thus they acquire an individualistic European perspective on the self as opposed to a collective one. This anti-self-disorder then produces racial self-hatred. They become willing workers against the survival of their own people, craving approval from the oppressor. Eventually, the individual also has to destroy his or her own self. Thus, instead of recognizing and fighting the root causes of the oppression, psycho-physiological malfunctions are embraced which, Akbar upholds, explains why so many Black people live "disordered" lives. He gives a list of alleged psychic disabilities among

[1]The Nguza Saba are African-centered principles of Umoja (Unity), Kujichagulia (Self Determination), Ujima (collective work and responsibility), Ujamaa (cooperative economics), Nia (purpose), Kuumba (creativity), Imani (faith).

African Americans (laziness, obsession with status and showy consumption, disrespect for leadership, clownish behavior, inferiority complexes, divided communities, weak families, internally divisive color complexes) which is remarkably similar to that drawn up against Blacks by classic expressions of white American racism.

At the level of the individual, Akbar (1995) proposes a "natural psychology" based on the assumption that human beings are fundamentally spiritual entities whose physical forms merely reflect or materially express their true spiritual nature. Thus, the individual's physical existence is not by any means his or her whole existence. For the same reason, intuitions, hunches, and "vibes," according to Akbar, need to be seen as spiritual phenomena. Natural psychology is proactive as well as reactive. It is also political; through self-definition and self-determination, it seeks to reaffirm the human essence of Africanity and in so doing affirm its centrality in the natural order. Akbar describes three stages of personal development. In stage one, the self/soul hungers for something beyond the satisfaction of physical needs but is unable to move beyond material needs. He argues that the Western psyche is trapped at this stage. In stage two, a critique of the self emerges. The self/soul becomes self-accusing and is no longer driven by material desires. Stage three, representing the completed self, is achieved when one's self-critique produces submission to God.

How relevant is such a psychology to counseling promoting the well-being and agency of African people? Taking into account that, to a large extent, conditions that have been formulated and controlled from outside the African social experience, an Indigenous African-centered approach to helping first of all accepts that the system which dominates the world is oppressive. It then recognizes that, having emerged from within this system, mainstream professional helping methods are also oppressive and so need to be replaced. Consequently, application of an Indigenous African-centered perspective to professional helping means that helpers must no longer perceive through the tunnel vision of the school of therapy in which they were trained. Rather, their perceptions must take into account the natural and spiritual order of the universe within a communal context. From this perspective, then, it can be seen that professional helping does not necessarily have to be confined to a certain time or place or to certain procedures, but can and should be incorporated into the community life process itself. Helping should be part of everyday life, and not a compartmentalized, "professionalized" activity.

Additionally, an Indigenous African-centered approach would challenge Western psychology's universalistic ideology that "man can heal himself" by replacing it with the idea that the wisdom of God or the spirit is required for any healing process. Healing comes from self-understanding, but knowledge of self is knowledge of God or the spirit. For understanding of self to occur, self-examination, self-analysis, and self-correction are necessary to allow the self-accusing spirit to be heard. It is only when they are awakened morally that people can face the self-accusing spirit that will lead to their transformation (Akbar, 1995). Therefore, the chief task of someone who aims to empower others is their own mental liberation. Through the process of life being regulated by a person's submission to the assumed spiritual rules of life, and by maintaining a healthy internal rhythm by observing basic notions of self-respect and respect for others, recognition of the universal life force can reinforce one's interconnectedness with the community as a whole. Therefore, as Myers (Montgomery et al., 1990) argues, incorporating spirituality into the understanding of human behavior establishes an optimal state of being.

Some theorists consider the major problem with this idea to be the fact that there does not seem to be a compelling alternative to change the old or "dislogical" way of living and thinking. But when we bear in mind the fact that society's unwritten oppressive curriculum is continually being transmitted, whatever new paradigm that is constructed must redress negative internalized concepts of the self and build new, positive concepts in the light of current knowledge.

Case Study: Constructing a New Reality

My first direct experience of the Nation of Islam was while attending the Social Therapy conference in New York (see the previous chapter). I visited the movement's Tape Connection and, like most people, I knew little about the movement except what I had read or heard in the media concerning the organization's leader Louis Farrakhan and his alleged "bigotry" and "extremism." While browsing through the tapes, I naively asked the salesperson why the movement was anti-Jewish and anti-white. To my surprise, she did not become defensive but simply invited me, sensibly enough, to listen to a number of tapes of Farrakhan's speeches before making a judgment. I purchased some tapes and, as I listened to them, interpreted the message to be "know (and heal) yourself." I felt that Farrakhan used a strategy similar to Shaw's. He was deliberately controversial and provocative to shock his listeners out of their conditioned responses, and to perhaps force congruence of adherent's behavior.

From my frustrations with mainstream professional helping, I had already become convinced that my clients' problems (and my own, for that matter) could not be solved in isolation, and that oppressive philosophies and attitudes that had been perpetuated for centuries had to be redressed. I recognized that effective helping must tackle and address such oppressions. I had come to New York because I hoped that Social Therapy could provide a model for a socially conscious, activist, form of professional helping. However, as I began to recognize its limitations, I simultaneously began to feel that the Nation of Islam went a step further by integrating "counseling" into a way of living, a way of being, and that this pointed to a way forward. I glimpsed, from a helping perspective, an environment that seemed much healthier than being "in therapy," and was intrigued. And so I made a point of visiting the Nation's headquarters in Chicago. I was exhilarated and inspired by the welcome and sense of fellowship I experienced there. The experience was particularly striking as it was in such contrast to the sterile and alienating atmosphere of the Social Therapy session I had previously attended, with its bewildered Black participants and well-meaning but controlling white professional helper.

When I began my research several years later, I was determined to delve more deeply into the philosophy and work of the Nation of Islam. In particular, I wanted to uncover why the movement's approach had given it a reputation for being so much more effective than other forms of therapy in transforming people's lives. I felt that an answer to the question of how an Indigenous African-centered perspective on helping might actually operate could perhaps be found here. And so I returned to the United States with the specific goal of studying the Nation of Islam.

I started by visiting the organization's head office in Chicago and then moved on to the New York and Los Angeles facilities. These visits awakened me to the reality of a truly alternative form of therapy, one that is integrated into people's lives and enables people to care about themselves and each other and to take responsibility for transforming themselves and their communities. This awakening occurred continuously over the course of several weeks. However, in order to present it coherently, I need to focus on the following series of specific incidents that highlight the key insights I experienced.

Encounter One: Chicago

When I attended an education conference in Chicago sponsored by the Nation of Islam, a woman there said:

> I became interested in the Nation of Islam when I was driving my daughter to school one day, and a man was selling the *Final Call* newspaper on the corner. I stopped for a red light, and he approached me and asked me if I wanted to buy a paper. When I told him I had no money, he just smiled and gave me the paper, saying I could pay him next time. It may seem like a small thing, but I was so moved; I realized I'd forgotten the feeling of being trusted.

Although the actions of the paper seller could easily have been a technique of manipulation, this simple story moved me (as it did the woman who told it) at a level that was deeper than the mere "concept" of trust. I had similarly been trusted at the Social Therapy organization, but this somehow felt different. Though almost trivial on the surface, at a deeper level it suggested a potentially far-reaching integration of theory and action, that is to say, praxis. In effect, she (and I by listening and responding to her) had experienced a counseling transformation, yet the "counseling" was not a compartmentalized, professionalized experience but an actual interaction growing out of everyday life.

Encounter Two: Los Angeles

At the Chicago conference I met Aiesha, a Nation "sister," who invited me to Los Angeles to stay at her home. When I got there, she fed and cared for me, and showed me around for 2 weeks—yet before the conference, we had never set eyes on one another. Although such an act of kindness is duplicated throughout the various religious and non-religious groups, to me this meant: Here was somebody who really was acting on and living out the principles she professed.

The particular incident that struck me most during this visit was another apparently trivial event. I arrived at Sister Aiesha's home after my flight from Chicago and, after settling in, was asked what I would like for dinner. Aiesha gave me five different options from which to choose, based on what she had in the house at the time, and assured me, in a way that I could sense was not simply a matter of being polite, that it would be no trouble for her to prepare any of them.

Another simple incident struck me because it reminded me of a time when I was doing my MA and was invited to dinner by a very well-intentioned white liberal who was going out of her way to be my friend as I was one of the few Black people she knew. I had an African friend staying with me at the time, so I asked if I could bring her along, and we went together. In contrast to Aiesha's hospitality, the meal in this case was already settled. We were to have what our host wanted to eat and that was that. She was proud of her progressive tastes, not just in politics but also in food, and so she had prepared a fashionable organic meal. Unfortunately, this meant that there was no salt in the food, nor in the whole house. My African friend ate the food out of politeness but found it completely unpalatable. By doing her best to give us a healthy, holistic meal, she had imposed her own ideas on us without bothering to ask us about our own tastes. As an "enlightened" person, she assumed she "knew best" but, ironically, she was acting out of the familiar superior, controlling attitude of Eurocentrism. By contrast, even though the Nation of Islam maintains a strict food regimen, Aiesha made no assumption that what *they* believe is best should be imposed on others. Perhaps a somewhat sweeping generalization on my part as a result of two isolated examples, but it is from these experiences I concluded that congruence with one's beliefs through one's actions is necessary.

Encounter Three: New York

I attended a Nation of Islam's meeting at its New York headquarters and was quietly observing from the back of the room when a gust of wind blew the door open behind me and a cold draught invaded the room. Before I could even begin to wonder who was going to attend to the problem, all but two of the twenty men and women at the meeting sprang to their feet to close the door. Once again, a small incident forced me to connect theory and practice. The event was an illustration, simple yet all the more vivid for being so simple, of the Nation's principle of collective responsibility. The attendants were exercising the principle of *acting* on their beliefs, and doing so without having to think about it. I recalled the organization's policy of asking new members to state one problem about themselves that they wanted to change and then giving them a 6-month deadline to match their actions to their principles by actually ending the problem. Thus, in the movement, if you see that something is wrong, even if it is only a piece of rubbish on the floor or an open door, *you need to do something about it*.

Conclusion

The Myop in Shaw's story is too short-sighted to realize he is oppressing others. This is like Eurocentric psychology, with its assumptions that this is the way it is for everyone, thereby creating, usually with the best of intentions, an oppressive system for those who are *not* like "everyone." By contrast, an Indigenous African-centered perspective like that of the Nation of Islam recognizes that solutions depend on where the problems are coming from and where oneself and one's community are coming from.

The fundamental goal of the Nation of Islam is to allow the wisdom of God to come through in people's lives. Wisdom is understood as being in possession of knowledge and experience *and* having the will and the power to apply one's knowledge and experience to solve real problems and transform one's own and others' lives. I was particularly impressed by this as I recognized it as an attempt to modernize and actualize something I had already seen existing in traditional African practices (e.g., in the work of Zambian healers). The movement, I felt, is attempting to make these principles accessible and operational by the use of culturally specific language and imagery. Their strategy is often confrontational and directive, but these qualities are also shared with traditional African healing practices. However, what the example of the Nation of Islam offers appears to be a culturally relevant method of actualizing principles of African antiquity.

In regard to professional helping, I decided that the lesson is that one cannot isolate helping in some separate domain of experience, as something that can only take place in a special setting (a counseling center, say) between 8 a.m. and 5 p.m. on weekdays, between a specially trained, "objective" helper and a "client/patient." Instead, helping works best when it is incorporated into a way of living. This is because, from an Indigenous African-centered perspective, a holistic environment designed to promote healthy living is necessary to produce healing. Healing cannot take place unless it addresses the whole context of the individual and community and accepts the reality of spirituality and its place at the center of human life.

Social therapy recognizes this and makes an attempt to put this insight to work, but my experiences made me feel that it does not go far enough. It fails to put its principles into action. However, the Nation of Islam takes the next step by actually trying to construct a community and environment where people can work through their problems as a way of life and live more satisfyingly as a result. Instead of using counseling just to obtain relief from problems that remain outside the professional helper's office, the movement sets out to construct an alternative, transformative social reality. I could understand why they feel they need to build a separate community, but at the same time I felt that, for me, to live more satisfyingly means being able to feel comfortable and at home in *any* environment. This realization brought me back to my memories of traditional healers in Zambia, and gave me the idea that the next step is to realize that the wheel does not have to be re-invented. I now began to feel that an Indigenous African-centered perspective on professional helping need not promote any formalized system and theory of helping at all. In traditional healing practices based on *ubuntu*—the topic of the next chapter's encounter—I discovered that an integrated, spiritual form of helping is already in existence as a living practice.

Part III
Tools of Reconstruction

Chapter 6
The Cathedral Carriers

> *"Do not believe the fisherman. Do not listen to those other fellows. Mine is the true Church." At last she had to turn aside into the forest to avoid them, for they began throwing stones at one another; and as their aim was almost as bad as if they were blind, the stones came flying all over the road. So she concluded that she would not find God to her taste among them. (Shaw, 1932, p. 30)*

When the Black Girl encounters Peter, an ancient fisherman carrying an enormous cathedral on his shoulders, her first reaction is to offer help, thinking that the cathedral is made of stone. The fisherman's disclosure that his burden is only made of paper, together with his pleasant grin and dance that made "all the bells of the cathedral tinkle merrily" (Shaw, 1932, p. 30), is seen by the Black Girl as a lack of congruence between his image and reality. When other people emerge, similarly adorned, calling her to join their "true" churches but then proceeding to fight each other, she quickly concludes that "she would not find God to her taste among them" (Shaw, 1932, p. 31). This chapter examines issues of congruence within liberational Indigenous theories, with particular application from African-centered theory, arguing that congruence is the key to achieving genuine transformation, and also to achieving counseling's objective of living more satisfyingly. A case study using further encounters in Zambia is presented to illustrate such congruence.

The Reality of Psychological Well-being?

In 1969, the anthropologist Marjorie Shostak traveled to the Kalahari Desert and spent three years living among the !Kung San people, one of the last remaining traditional hunter-gatherer societies in Africa. Her landmark study (1983) became renowned for the gendered lens she used to look at the community. By prioritizing the life of Nisa, fusing traditional ethnography with a biographical, narrative style, Shostak, highlighted shared human values between the reader and the !Kung

G. Berry, *Helping?*, https://doi.org/10.1007/978-3-031-88586-0_6

people. And despite being criticized for romanticizing the !Kung, and her unprecedented reliance on a single informant, her work remains influential because it gives us access to the voices of the Indigenous peoples themselves. Whether intentionally or not, her work highlights the relationship between the !Kung's people's closeness to nature and spirituality, and their lack of psychological difficulties.

Shostak notes that the realm of the spiritual infuses all aspects of the !Kung's physical and social life, and is seen as a fundamental determinant in the delicate balance between life and death, sickness and health, rain and drought, abundance and scarcity. Can we then also deduce from this groundbreaking study that the !Kung's psychological well-being was supported by their integration of spirituality into their society? Nisa's interpretation of her community's spirituality is comparable to that illustrated by the Indigenous African-centered perspective, which sees spirituality as a person's life and activity in relationship to God and self, fellow people, and all other things. The essential element in this spiritual life is the pure desire to see things clearly and to "live rightly." In secular terms, this might be interpreted as a constant search for honesty: For whatever is true, honorable, just, pure, lovely, gracious, excellent, and worthy of praise.

A lot has changed for the !Kung San people since Shostak's 1983 publication. Researchers seem to have shifted their focus to seeking to understand the impact of globalization, climate change, or how the !Kung San people's traditions are adapting to modernity or are being eroded. The !Kung people themselves, once reliant on hunting and gathering, have transitioned to residing in villages and participating in wage labor and cash-based economies. Living on the land they once called their own now requires politicians, government officials, and lawyers to help them navigate land rights policies to challenge illegal settlers, cattle hearers, and others who have encroached on their territory. Unsurprisingly, practices that have kept them psychologically well for millennia have diminished, and are being replaced by depression, alcoholism, and a plethora of mental health issues. A McCall and Resick (2003) study on PTSD, which required the translation of the DSM manual into the language of the !Kung people, found "how technically challenging such an investigation can be," but "even in an extreme non-Western society, assessment (for PTSD) is feasible, given culturally appropriate modifications." The appearance of helping in this context, with all the cultural considerations that need to be taken into account, reminds me of the Cathedral Carriers in Shaw's novella. Would it lead to a restoration of the psychological well-being of the !Kung community?

The Failures of Liberation Theology

A lived spirituality is demonstrably different from the approach to religion brought into Africa by Christian missionaries as part of European colonization. Religion as "the formalization of ritual, dogma, and belief, leading to a systematic statement of syntactically suprarational tenets that may lose or may not issue from a spiritual conception of the universe" was "integrally related to the development of ideology in the West" (Ani, 2000), and the relationship between European religion and other aspects of culture has been symptomatic of a persistent de-spiritualization and desacralization of experience which can be shown to be characteristic of "Western-ness" since its archaic stages (Ani, 2000). This contradicts the concept of religion from an Indigenous African-centered perspective, which defines spirituality as resting upon the "conception of a sacred cosmos that transcends physical reality in terms of significance and meaning" (Ani, 2000). In this African concept of religion, as in many other primary religious formulations, it is the spiritual-emotional needs of the people within the culture that are served; the values of the culture are sanctioned and the mechanisms for its continuance are sacralized (Ani, 2000).

From an Indigenous African-centered perspective, spirituality is considered to be infused into every aspect of the human life cycle as a way of being. While established religious doctrines may embody spiritual truths metaphorically, when taken as literal truth they may also embody particularistic elements that fuel human oppression and thereby omit the necessity for congruence with professed belief and practice. Thus, as Semmes (1997) says, Africanists have had to search for "an appropriate way to embody an uninterrupted African-based spirituality in a formal religious structure that is empowering, status enhancing and liberating" (p. 162). American, continental, and other Diasporic Africans have undertaken this search in a number of different ways.

Some have attempted to "Blacken" or Africanize Eurocentric Christianity by emphasizing its African roots. This involves things like using Black images and/or African rituals, dress, and music in Christian religious services. Others have gone further, and claimed that the Christian scriptures refer specifically to African people and that Jesus is the Black messiah. Still others have tried to reform Western Christianity and link it to the Black struggle by emphasizing a theology of liberation.

However, Azibo (1994) argues, such liberation theology, despite its motives of redemption, "failed even as it was born and nurtured by a legion of dedicated Black liberation theologians" (p. 336). As with the glaring hypocrisy of Peter in Shaw's short story, and Carl Rogers' "sincere hypocrisy" (which we saw in Chap. 2), the failure of liberation theology is grounded in the incongruence between what it tries to do and its roots within the dominant culture. As Azibo (1994) argues that:

> We should expect such faltering even more so when the authors of a religion are initially driven by reaction to the hegemony of a religion based in an alien conceptual universe in a societal context of oppression. (p. 341)

Azibo concludes that "Black liberational theology is spent and thereby incapable of liberating Africans" (p. 345). Despite its efforts to "Africanize" Christianity, "there is no victory in having the Catholic (or any alien conceptual based) church reflect social change [such as using African garb and music] while remaining essentially unchanged itself" (p. 343). Those who seek liberation (defined in this book as the search to live more satisfyingly) cannot do so as long as there remains an "unconscious" adoption of the Western dominant cultural concept of religious/spiritual practice, which lacks spiritual congruence. Christianity's conception of the world is fundamentally at odds with an Indigenous African-centered understanding of spirituality.

Sincere Incongruence

The same is true of Black theology. In July 1966, at a national conference of Black churchmen in the US, this incongruence was highlighted when a group of Black churchmen issued a statement asking for power and freedom from political leaders of America—while at the same time asking for power and love from their white counterparts in the church (National Conference of Black Churchmen, 1999). The incongruence of their requests, however, is totally understandable: In the light of the dynamics of political oppression, together with the Christian church's role in supporting this position, Semmes (1997) concludes that it has been difficult to separate doctrines and forms of religion from deeper spirituality. As Semmes argues, oppression forces the oppressed to "maintain contradictory ideas simultaneously without any apparent recognition of the need to resolve these contradictions" (p. 158). He believes this has created a distorted consciousness in which new knowledge does not necessarily alter behavior or belief, especially when the new knowledge conflicts with beliefs that have been deeply ingrained through oppression.

As a result, Semmes observes that many people have difficulty separating spiritual truths from the institutional forms of religious life acquired through enslavement (p. 158). Semmes calls such self-enslaving behavior "conditioned dislogic," which he defines as the continuation of beliefs and behaviors that are culturally negating, oppressive, and logically untenable. These beliefs and behaviors cannot be confronted by those who hold or engage in them because the result would be too traumatic. The trauma, of course, arises from the possibility of having to reject a familiar social reality, one that is supported by tradition and linked to a complexity of reinforcing institutional forms.

Unfortunately, as we have already seen, enslavement, colonialism, imperialism, apartheid, and other oppressive practices have resulted in the distortion of an Indigenous African-centered perspective and, more importantly, the imposition of a way of being which is oppositional. Western religious imperialism, with its normative white supremacy, obscured the process of cultural effacement through universalistic claims and has consistently avoided confronting its inherent and underlying intolerance. As a consequence, religious imperialism has helped to spawn among Africans the perennial problems of religious fragmentation and cultural disunity, intragroup religious intolerance, self-alienation, psychological dependency on white approval, and weakened institutional development.

Despite much-welcomed political changes that have taken place on the continent and across the Diaspora, particularly during the last fifty years, a strong residue of such abhorrent practices remains. For liberation to occur, we must devise an epistemology that can research, rescue, and restore African perspectives, and challenge the paradigm violently imposed by European colonialists and their Christian missionary partners. African psychology, with its foundation in a worldview rooted in a culturally relevant perspective, "is better framed for the development and promulgation of a holistically healthy African psyche that is in alignment with the natural order and inner self" (Phillips, 1994, p. 358). This means returning authentic spirituality—not the obfuscating doctrines of European religion—to its rightful place at the heart of human life.

Natural Congruence

As a result of her discussion with the old philosopher, the Black Girl of Shaw's story creates her own reality. It is a reality that is far from her original intention, but is "coerced" by her from what is available. She decides that she needs to reach a space where she can be happy and settled, and then goes about creating that space using the knowledge she has gained in the forest. Similarly, the challenge for an Indigenous African-centered perspective on helping is to adopt an approach that will enable individuals to use their spiritual resources to devise their own ways of living more satisfyingly—in harmony with the community, but free from artificial theories and models that constrain their choices or impose false standards. The project of adapting and/or modernizing the techniques that are said to have been founded in ancient Africa aims to be long-lasting and to achieve the goal of satisfying the soul. To this end, a combination of three key ingredients is essential: inner strength, external strength, and praxis (the congruence between them).

What might this look like? Black liberation psychology originated as a reaction to Western models of psychology. It was felt that the Western models produced unnatural human beings based upon unnatural assumptions about human functioning and development. At the root of this, as we saw in the previous chapter, was the materialistic assumption that human beings are simply another kind of animal. By converting the living inner being into a material being, man's potential to capture and master his animal form was lost. In fact, *psyche* became a servant to the animal disposition identified by Western psychologists as the core of the human creature. Originally, an African psychology rooted in African culture and philosophical premises (and not expressed in terms of Western understanding) must have existed before Western impositions. Once we accept that Black people are not being effectively treated by the bickering Cathedral Carriers of white psychotherapy, we can, like the Black Girl, begin to explore approaches to healing that genuinely reflect an Indigenous African-centered understanding of the cosmos.

All the requisites to achieve reactive rebirth (transformation out of oppression-induced psychological states) and proactive natural development (participation in an African survival thrust) are integral to African psychology. Hence, the term "Black liberation psychology" is to be understood as no more than an appellation connoting these particular characteristics of African psychology. To speak of liberation psychology is to speak of African psychology in the sense of underlying disciplinarity. Its focus may be on religion either as a practice or as a framework of ideas and beliefs, but the two elements are interdependent. Faith and worship are unintelligible without some idea of what they are directed toward, while religion's characteristic conceptions are such that certain practices and responses are seen as appropriate and even mandatory.

Rediscovering the Link

Spirituality from this Indigenous African-centered perspective can, therefore, be defined as "a recognition that a person is connected to the creator (God) from the cradle to the grave." This concept is made more explicit by Paris (1995) when he argues that contrary to the opinions of most of their predecessors, contemporary scholars of African religion generally agree that all peoples throughout the continent believe in a self-existent supreme deity, and that this deity constitutes the primary cohesive power in every African cosmology: The power that unites the realms of nature, history, and spirit.

Traditional African societies embraced and actualized this concept of spirituality by developing a civilization that regulated the life of the community, where people were progressively introduced to the mysteries of life by a guru-like master. Through a long process of preparation and training, these men and women were made capable of discerning good and evil. An art of living and respect for moral values was at the heart of this initiation. Mbuya-Beya (Abraham & Mbuya-Beya, 1994) suggests that the lack of points of reference between traditional African spirituality and Christianity could account for the destabilization which African and Black people now feel. At the same time, however, she argues that African spirituality contains the possibility of incorporating Christian spirituality. Therefore, an authentic Christian experience for Africans, she suggests, must be based on both the gospel and African tradition.

In traditional African societies, spiritual guides would teach and translate the knowledge of God so that individuals could receive guidance on how to tackle and resolve their own problems. The traditional healer, as Afua (1992) states, is someone who has, through their personal experiences, learned to utilize life's obstacles for growth and development. When an obstacle, problem, or illness is overcome and a new experience of benefit is born out of an old problem, true healing has taken place. An individual is then in a position to extend their healing experience to others to guide them through their experiences. Thus, a healer is created and the process is continual.

Spiritual guides and healers recognize that change occurs only by God's grace. They also recognize that no human being should step into God's shoes by imparting information, acting, or behaving as if he or she is God. Thus, they see their role as assisting a person to become balanced in alignment with the natural order. Although their tools differ slightly (herbs, prayer, fasting, etc.), the result is the same. The person seeking guidance, healing, or doctoring is restored to a state of peace, a balance of mind, body, and spirit. The guide, healer, or physician is proactive, taking on board the personal responsibility to stay in balance and harmony with the natural order. This is required in order to be in a position to heal others. The process is used to realign the client with the natural order, with the counselor taking on the role of "vessel" to enable such realignment to occur.

Throughout Africa, a member of the extended family, often an uncle or aunt, was dedicated as "counselor." This was the person to whom a member of the family would turn, depending on the sex, in the event of a problem. The uncle or aunt was consulted during marriage preparations, marital problems, funerals, divorces, and remarriages. If disputes could not be settled, they were referred outside—to the headman or chief. Such guidance and counseling were daily occurrences and activities. Elders informally educated children around the fire in the evening, and counseling was offered through tales, stories, allegories, proverbs, and legends.

In this environment, the counselor was fully involved in the life of his or her community—rather than a professional looking on from an "objective" distance. As a result, his or her own life was continuously relevant to his or her practice. Thus, as Messing (1972) reports in his field study investigating traditional healing and new health centers in Ethiopia:

> People usually treated the community nurse as another type of midwife, and if she herself had not had a baby, her instructions were merely listened to politely but regarded as theoretical and not followed. (60)

Messing goes on to describe traditional healers as eager to employ the best practices to care for the people who had confidence in them. Holistic healers are rooted in a life that is interrelated and forms one whole, and so the counselor is a member of the community who is spiritually congruent, and who shares their knowledge of living more satisfyingly so that others might achieve the same end.

Case Study: Sincere Incongruence Versus Natural Congruence

After my disappointing experience at the Kara Counselling Centre, I carried on my formal "academic" program (library and archival research, visits to Chinamon Mental Hospital and the University of Zambia Counselling Centre, interviewing the chairperson of the National Counselling Review Committee). These activities were useful in building a fuller picture of mainstream, formalized counseling in Zambia at that time. However, although I found many worthwhile programs being carried out and met many hard-working counselors, the impression I carried away of a dependence on an authoritative, objective, and fundamentally alienating Eurocentric approach was largely confirmed.

More useful in developing my ideas about an Indigenous African-centered perspective on counseling was my parallel experience of fitting into the life of a typical Zambian family and community. Besides the day-to-day family interactions and visits to and from the larger community, I attended a wedding and a funeral, and also traveled upcountry for Christmas with the extended family in my host's "home" village. As a result of these varied experiences, I was able to contrast two worlds (Eurocentric and Afrocentric) and gain valuable insights into both the social context and actual practice of Indigenous African counseling methods. These insights came into focus in a series of specific incidents involving traditional advisers or healers.

Encounter One: An Elder

My host, whom I'd known for twenty years, was the junior wife in a polygamous marriage. In principle, she had no problem with such an arrangement, and it was an accepted part of her culture. However, her husband had lately been spending more time with his first wife, and my friend felt neglected. She, therefore, decided to confront him at the first wife's house, which was in another town, and demand that he come and spend time with her.

The visit resulted in a scene that greatly upset both herself and her husband. All three then agreed they had to resolve the problem, and the husband went to seek the advice of an elderly man in the same town. He had never met this man, but knew he had a reputation for being able to decide cases. Without any notice the Elder agreed to come out of his house (at 9:30 in the evening) and hear the case. He talked in turn to the husband, the first wife, and my friend, and then brought the three together for "judgment." He pronounced that my friend was in the wrong for coming uninvited to the first wife's house and confronting her at her own door. He also told my friend to pay compensation to the first wife. He then declared that the husband was also in the wrong for neglecting his junior wife, stating that if a man decides to have more than one wife, then he must take responsibility for their well-being and share his time equitably with them. Consequently, he also pronounced that the husband should pay my friend compensation (which took the form of a new dress).

To me, this incident was a revelation. What I took from it was the following: The problem was addressed there and then, it was addressed by a stranger (and an "amateur") who nevertheless showed concern by getting involved, and the Elder assumed responsibility for helping to solve the intimate problems of other members of the community. This reminded me of what my grandfather was known for doing in Guyana, and connected with the idea that had been forming in my mind ever since my experiences with Social Therapy and the Nation of Islam. Indigenous African-centered counseling needed to be something *lived*, and could be re-established in the Diaspora (as I saw being done in the Nation of Islam). Finally, I was impressed by the fact that the Elder took responsibility for directing his "clients" regarding what they must do. He made no pretense at "objectivity," but simply delivered his judgment in line with the norms of the culture.

Encounter Two: The Cousin

My friend went back home, but the neglect continued. She then requested a male cousin, who was considered to be the head of her extended family, to talk to the husband. The cousin immediately visited the husband and told him:

> This is the only time I'm going to talk about this with you, as you are not a child. The only reason my cousin is unhappy is that you are not spending enough time with her. You've already been told by the Elder that you are in the wrong and that you need to share your time fairly with your wives. Therefore, if I hear that you do not remedy the situation, I will take responsibility, as head of the family, and put an end to the relationship by telling her to leave with her children.

When I heard about this, I was again astounded. What I took from the incident was the following: The "counseling" had been short, sharp, and to the point. The cousin used highly directive language; he did not try to spare the husband's feelings or to draw out the discussion with theory or abstractions. His approach would probably be seen from a mainstream perspective as authoritarian and even oppressive, but in fact it was a response to oppression. In reality, the husband was oppressing his second wife, and the cousin was taking responsibility for setting things right. Eurocentric counseling methods would ironically have sustained the oppression in the name of not being oppressive (i.e., directive).

Encounter Three: Traditional Healer, Lusaka

With my friend as translator, I visited a traditional healer in Lusaka who specialized in "male problems," and interviewed him about his methods and how he understood his role as a healer. I first asked him why he became a healer. He answered that his father had also been a healer and that the instruction to follow in his father's footsteps had come from God in a dream when he was a child. He then trained under his father and eventually became knowledgeable enough to operate on his own.

Next, I asked him to describe how he operated. He told me that the key was listening and that, though he used herbs, he essentially cured his patients by listening to what they told him about their problems. In a very real sense, then, he was as much a counselor as an herbalist. Equally interestingly, he shared that he saw his role as being in the center of the community. He explained that what he meant by this was that he had to know the community and be involved in it and, just as important, be known by it. For example, the community had to know how he treated his wife and children, as he literally could not function unless his own life was "clean" and known to be. So above all, he needed a reputation for being healthy and happy himself. This reminded me of something the counselor at the Kara Centre had told me: That people did not want to be counseled by someone whose own life might be messed up. Finally, this traditional healer made it clear that he saw himself as doing what God wants. He considered himself a servant and instrument of God. As he explained, it is really God, not the healer, who heals. Thus, it is vital that the healer be a fit instrument, which is why he had to carefully watch what he did, what he ate, what he said, and so on.

This meeting summarized for me what a traditional healer really is and clarified the approach counselors need to take if they want to adopt an Indigenous African-centered perspective. Therapy has to be seen as an integral part of one's own and the community's ongoing life, not some separate, "special" activity divorced from daily life and compartmentalized by jargon and "scientific" theories. Moreover, the Indigenous African-centered counselor, like the traditional healer, has a responsibility to be healthy himself or herself. One cannot heal others without healing oneself. Although similar in essence to that required of practitioners by Western models of counseling, its "community check," or requirement that there be evidence of congruence, establishes its difference.

Encounter Four: A Secret Healer

Two weeks later, I interviewed another traditional healer in town. In contrast to the first healer, who followed his vocation openly, this healer lived in a community dominated by the church, and did not want the general public to know what he did. Consequently, he did not make his work public but trusted that the ancestors would send him people who needed him. Despite the authoritarian presence of the church, he did not lack clients, but they too had to keep quiet, so the healer's practice operated as an underground network within an apparently staunchly "modern," Westernized, Christian community. Indeed, he revealed that many of his clients came from the sections of the community that were ostensibly the most Westernized, such as doctors, lawyers, and other professionals. He appreciated this irony, and enjoyed the fact that he did not fit the stereotype of the "primitive" traditional healer.

Whereas the first healer received his guidance directly from God, this healer worked through his ancestors, whom he saw as intermediaries between himself and God. I asked him how he operated, and he told me it was through dreams. The things he needed for healing (stones, bones, plants) were visualized to him in dreams, so his principal tool as a healer was himself, specifically his own mind. Like the first healer, he had to carefully watch how he lived in order to maintain himself as a suitable vessel through which the wisdom of God and the ancestors could be expressed.

He then told me a fascinating story of how he had once traveled to the Netherlands, thinking of going there to live. However, as soon as he arrived, he developed a severe earache, which no doctor there could diagnose. He sensed, however, what was wrong: He was not meant to be in the Netherlands. His mission was at home with his community. He immediately returned to Zambia, and as soon as he got back the earache went away.

Encounter Five: A Traditional Sex Therapist

This encounter occurred, ironically, in the midst of the first encounter. At the hotel where my friend and I were staying when she went to confront her husband at the co-wife's house, we met a woman who was introduced to us as a traditional sex therapist. Never having heard of this profession before, I asked her what it was she did. Her response could not have been simpler or more direct. She said: "I teach women how to make love." Intrigued, I asked her how she did this, and she replied that she simply taught, taking nothing for granted (i.e., not making assumptions about what her clients already knew or should know), avoiding abstract language, and, above all, accepting sexuality as normal and healthy.

Struck by her practical and matter-of-fact approach, which totally avoided either the shame and false modesty or the scientized technicalities of talking about sex in modern Britain, I recalled my own experiences as a counselor, and blushed to remember how hard we worked to avoid the issue of sexual "performance" as much as possible, and, when not possible, couched our discussions in either abstractions or innuendos. By contrast, this traditional counselor used no formalized, objectified structure, nor did she beat around the bush. For her and her clients, sex was simply an important element in life, which it made sense to know how to do well and to enjoy.

From all these encounters, what kept coming across was that counseling need not be something sterile, cold, and artificial, but could be—and succeeded best when it was—incorporated into everyday life. I thought of the conclusion of Shaw's story, when the Black Girl marries the Irishman. Most readers find this, as I did, surprising and, initially at least, disappointing. The Irishman hardly seems the most appropriate mate for the Black Girl, but she goes ahead and makes the best of the situation. In effect, she creates her own reality. Similarly, I reflected, we often find ourselves in situations we did not plan or expect, and the outcomes of even our best efforts are rarely ideal. However, through our attitudes and practices, we have the power to make the situations we find ourselves in healthier and more positive.

In this increasingly technological world, perhaps we have forgotten how to be satisfied with what we have and to value things that are positive but not ideal. At the same time, we have fragmented and compartmentalized our needs: Work is in one compartment, family in another, hobbies in a third, and so on. Counseling, too, has been compartmentalized, converted into a special activity that takes place in a "center" during office hours, is facilitated by a "professional" and, as a result, is divorced from the rest of life. What the study of traditional healers showed me was that from an Indigenous African-centered perspective, there is no counseling as such; only various practices integrated into the life of the family and of the community that express the value one has for other human beings and enable people to take responsibility for ensuring that their actions actualize this value. For me, therefore, counseling is not about sitting with a counselor, but about doing—that is, about living.

Conclusion

From an Indigenous African-centered perspective, spirituality is central to the therapeutic relationship and is a relevant factor when offering counseling. The issue, however, cannot be fully examined without taking into account the historical, sociological, psychological, and theological factors that have affected African/Black people so uniquely. The key to the Indigenous African-centered perspective is spirituality, but questions regarding the validity of this perspective must still be raised. When applied to counseling, for example, how can spirituality be evaluated and measured? Does counseling from a spiritual perspective differ from pastoral counseling and, if so, how?

These questions have been debated predominantly by African-American psychologists, researchers, and scholars, and have only recently entered the wider academic field. This work has resulted in the creation of departments and programs devoted entirely to the study of African-centered perspectives (Black Studies programs). The Association of Black Psychologists in the United States, for example, has focused its work on the development of theoretical and practical models of counseling and psychotherapy. The premise behind this work is that Eurocentric therapeutic methods are influenced by racism and its oppressive assumptions and approaches, thereby making them inappropriate when applied to the unique experiences of those who accept a theocentric or God-centered philosophy.

Chapter 7
The Knobkerry and the Bible

> *For when the Black Girl, receiving her teacher's reply very literally took up her knobkerry and strode off into the African forest in search of God, she took the bible with her as her guidebook. (Shaw, 1932, p. 8)*

In Shaw's story, the Black Girl takes the two things she feels are most important to her when she sets out on her journey in search of God: her knobkerry and her Bible. The Black Girl uses the knobkerry to defend herself against the ignorance of those she encounters, and I take it as representing her external strength. Her Bible, on the other hand, is a more complex symbol. It was given to her as a birthday gift by the Missionary, but "whether the ants had got at it, or, being a very old book, it had perished by natural decay, all the early pages had crumbled to dust which blew away when she opened it" (Shaw, 1932, p. 11). From the beginning it is a problematic image, the significance of which is obscure. Moreover, as the Black Girl continues on her quest, her Bible continues to disintegrate until nothing remains of it. In line with this, I interpret the disintegration of the Bible as representing the Black Girl's internalization of spiritual principles. She at first thinks that she needs the Bible for support and reference, as a theoretical guidebook in the search for life's meaning. However, as she pursues her quest, she learns not to depend on the doctrines of her Missionary teachers, and finds she does not require their Bible as a constant source of reference. Instead, she learns to depend on its basic spiritual principles, which she has internalized (as opposed to the trivial points of doctrine argued by Nailer or fought over by the Cathedral Carriers) and which are in tune with her own culturally derived spiritual principles and first-hand experiences.

These core principles are shared by those who believe in a natural order of the universe and who rely on spirituality. The key issue is congruence between one's beliefs and one's actions. By learning to be congruent with spiritual principles (as espoused in the Bible but rarely followed in practice by those who claim to follow its teachings), the Black Girl learns to be guided from *within*. Like the Black Girl taking the advice of the philosopher, I sought to cultivate my own "garden" in my career as a professional helper. Finding myself in a world so far removed from an Indigenous African-centered philosophy meant cultivating an understanding of

G. Berry, *Helping?*, https://doi.org/10.1007/978-3-031-88586-0_7

cultural differences, being in alignment with my internalized spiritual principles, and valuing and appreciating interconnections—even though I do not always see and understand them initially. "Marrying the Irishman," for want of a better term, to me means making the most of a difficult situation, or making the most of your life. You, as a human being, have the right to do what resonates for you.

To me, the connection between Shaw's final chapter and being a professional helper is that if you have chosen to do this work, this should be something you are passionate about—that you feel you have been put on this earth to do it. You have come to this earth with a purpose, and your goal here is to find that, as scary as that is. But know that there will be challenges along the way. These challenges are not meant to deter you, but instead to help you find different ways of strategizing so that when difficult situations arise, you have the resources to navigate those challenges.

Cultivating the Garden

As a clinical practitioner with the professional desire to *effectively* help, my journey of understanding has allowed me to reach a point where I see helping as looking at the complete picture as far as possible, and taking that into account in any intervention. From an Indigenous African-centered perspective on helping, restorative empowerment is of paramount importance.

In this final chapter, I will introduce the framework of "synergy" (Katz, 2017) to provide a succinct context for understanding what Indigenous African-centered helping looks like in practice. Using the ten strands of synergy (Cornish & Berry, 2025), alongside examples from my own professional development, I will revisit the previous chapters to show how the principles of an Indigenous African-centered philosophy can be applied to helping. Synergy can be considered both the process and the outcome of a system that operates from an Indigenous philosophy (Katz & Murphy-Shigematsu, 2012). Cornish and I have identified ten strands of synergy (though we are aware there may be more), which are:

1. ***Agency,*** or the belief that all human beings have capacity and power;
2. ***Truth and reconciliation,*** to rebuild harmony within and between communities to redress historical harms;
3. ***Empathy,*** or understanding and ability to display respect for diversity of perspectives amongst humans and the impact of injustices on communities;
4. ***Growth-orientation,*** or believing that all human beings have capacity for learning and evolution through challenge and support;
5. ***Flexibility,*** or the commitment to adaptability and open-mindedness;
6. ***Interconnectedness,*** or the belief that all human beings are connected and dependent upon one another for survival and thriving;
7. ***Awareness,*** the ability to reflect on our impacts on one another;
8. ***Contextualization,*** recognizing the unique contexts of individuals life experiences, communities, and sociopolitical society;

9. ***Creativity,*** or encouraging imaginative thinking and practices;
10. ***Diplomatic disruption,*** to encourage disruption to current dominating systems of care while recognizing the sensitivity of growing pains involved in disruption.

I then turn my attention to you, the reader, to summarize the takeaways I hope you will receive from each part of the text. I also offer some questions for you to reflect on for your journey of professional helper development.

The Missionary: Acknowledging the Starting Point

Just as the Black Girl at first accepts the Missionary's concept of what God should be but then sees through its hypocrisy, I initially accepted the mainstream person-centered theory of helping, but soon found that it could not enable me to achieve congruence. Like the Black Girl with God, I started with a Eurocentric and oppressive perception of what helping should and should not be. But by being open to evidence from my professional experiences, I was forced to accept that this concept could not enable me to live more satisfyingly. Glaring contradictions became apparent within the theory. My first case study, in Chap. 2, highlighted the continued existence of a universalistic and authoritarian stance adopted by the helping professions, which perpetuates itself due to social, political, economic, and educational factors. Eurocentric professional helping expects its concepts and methods of practice to be adopted unquestioningly, "with sweet docility," despite the fact that the profession's public image as a "science" is increasingly being questioned. With such basic issues remaining problematic, it can be concluded that the profession has inappropriately claimed universality and authority for itself.

Case Example: Indigenous Philosophy in Case Management

One memorable case that displayed my growing sense that I needed to rely on my own critical thinking rather than uncritically accepting my training was when I was a social worker in London with an immigrant man from Ghana. This man woke up one day to find himself to be permanently blind (he later learned it was due to untreated syphilis). The shame and embarrassment, coupled with the belief that his sight would miraculously return, meant he had not sought treatment and lived each day in isolation. Upon learning what the cause was, his wife took his kids and returned to Ghana, so the man did not have a support network and had to rely on the social services care network. Naturally, after losing so much at once, he stayed in his house depressed.

The home help contacted social services and they sent me, an intern, out to talk to him. The home help said that he would stay in his pajamas each day until 3:00 p.m., and she was really worried about him because he was apparently very depressed. She was concerned about his safety. He had not let any of the previous social workers sent to his home inside. When I arrived, I knocked on the door and he opened it a crack. When I popped my head in and introduced myself, he said "No, go away." When he finally let me inside, I did what I had been told to do, which was take him to the Center for the Blind.

When I came back in the afternoon to pick him up from the Center, I asked him how it had gone. He said it was *horrible*. People didn't talk to him, he just sat there making baskets all day (which he didn't think was useful). Needless to say, he didn't want to go back. So, just as I would have appreciated being asked what I would like to eat instead of being expected to eat what my hosts made for me as discussed in Chap. 5, I said, "OK, what do you like?" He said he liked to play the organ, and that he missed his food from back home in Ghana.

According to my training, I should have labeled him "resistant" for not wanting to engage with the prescribed intervention. Instead, I decided to get his permission to talk to the Ghanaian embassy to see what events, activities, and resources they offered in the community. I learned that they had an expat lunch twice a week. I also got his permission to call up the church he previously belonged to, and the minister arranged for a bus to come pick him up from his home so he could play the organ at the service. I also took him to the post office so we could arrange for him to be issued a white walking stick and a statement from the disability officer (which he was uninterested in, until he realized it could help him get free taxi service to attend other activities he enjoyed). From then on, he got into the cab and took himself to the Ghanaian lunches twice a week. The last time I spoke to him he said he just really appreciated being able to speak his language and eat his food. When I followed up with the home help later on, they told me they never saw him at home anymore—he was always out and about doing his own thing.

From the perspective of ***individual responsibility,*** I had learned that I could not wait to be *told* what to do in my work with him, I had to use my own critical thinking, discernment, ***flexibility, empathy,*** and ***creativity***. While others may have opted to petition for the Center for the Blind to change to be more accommodating and diverse, what I needed to remember was that I was tasked with figuring out what would be most effective for *him*. He was not interested in the Center, so finding ways to convince him to continue to go there would have been about me following the directions given, rather than being helpful to him. From the perspective of ***interpersonal responsibility***, as a helper who is rooted in nature, I must always seek to empower. Just like a bird, I have to be able to help you fly. Otherwise, it's just about my ego as a helper, as it was for the Missionary, and can create a dependence that harms rather than helps. From the lens of ***collective responsibility,*** I knew that I alone could not provide the resources that he needed—but in recognizing my role amongst the collective, each individual was able to work as a collective, including the client.

To the Reader: It is important to be honest with yourself when entering this field. While it is initially unsettling to recognize the limitations of our training as mental health professionals, this acknowledgment opens us up to be able to take responsibility for our decisions and actions within the context of our very nuanced work. Oftentimes, the "right" path forward may not be right for a particular client or context. Other times, there will be no guidance at all. This means that you must be able to see value in the work you do! And this is why it is crucial to deeply understand your purpose and intentions in what you do in order to effectively help them. We must be very honest with ourselves about our reasons for entering this field and our motivations for helping others.

- What are you most proud of in the work that you do?
- What would you say figuratively "pats you on the back" or gets you excited about the work?
- How do you foster the agency of the individuals you work with when in a system that predominantly fosters dependence?
- What are the strategies that you have used to escape the mainstream structure of Western mental health care and to intentionally practice and think outside of the box?
- What mentorship or support have you sought to help you to do so? Who in your personal and professional life will be honest with you?
- Have you asked questions? Do you feel satisfied with the answers?
- How can you more deeply listen to the individuals you work with to better understand their unique contexts, strengths, and paths to wellness?
- How can you deepen your "why" behind your actions so you can be more creative and flexible?

I hope that, as I have, you find the challenge of going beyond your training while staying rooted in Indigenous principles to be an exciting and rewarding professional journey. When we release our hope to be told exactly what to do, we open our own sense of agency and with it a world of possibilities in fostering the same with our clients.

The Lord of Hosts and Nailer: Awareness of the Starting Point

The Black Girl's encounter with the Lord of Hosts and Nailer provides the framework for the argument in Chap. 3. From a genuine desire to understand their authority and universality, she questions them and finds the Lord of Hosts to be hypocritical and the Nailer to present the illusion of caring while only arguing for argument's sake. This parallels my experience of the person-centered counseling model, whose failure to acknowledge the reality of oppression makes it unable to facilitate a *genuine* process of self-actualization. My early desire to work in the helping profession led me to engage in sacrifice and sophistry, which shows that I myself was not immune to a similar incongruence. In particular, those experiences highlighted the importance that I too had a right to live more satisfyingly.

Case Example: Indigenous Philosophy Across Power and Privilege

It became clear through my journey of understanding that micromanagement in leadership is inconsistent with an Indigenous African-centered philosophy. When I have had the opportunity to lead other professional helpers from an Indigenous African-centered philosophy, I want to be surrounded by people who feel empowered to ask me why I am doing what I am doing. If as a leader you are surrounded by people who are too fearful to have or express an independent thought, it perpetuates the status quo of oppressive systems. And realistically, in counseling centers that serve hundreds of clients each week, micromanagement is impossible. In my most recent full-time role in leadership at a counseling center, I took deliberate time to cultivate human relationships with my direct report Assistant Directors as a space where we could all be honest, vulnerable, and accountable so that we could translate these values to the team and therefore the community we worked with. This required vulnerability, honesty, and trust.

One example of this stands out amongst the others. During a particularly difficult time for the center, when administration changes in the institution were threatening the model that we had been cultivating, I walked out of my office to find a banana directly in front of my door. Because of everything that was going on politically, and experiences of similar racial trauma throughout my own life, it was easy for me to assume that someone that had been targeting me left the banana in front of my door with racist motivation as a scare tactic. Based on my experience with a particular boss, I reached the conclusion immediately that leaving a banana outside my door was something he would do to intimidate me—he had been on a mission to get me to resign for months. In the past, I would not have felt safe enough in the environments I worked in to even believe that others could understand the kind of stress I felt when I opened my door. I would have deliberated alone about what I should do next, and the stress might have consumed me.

However, instead, while very emotional, I went directly to one of my Assistant Director's offices. She was able to understand my being upset yet had the wherewithal to challenge me, even as her "boss." "Okay," she said, "let's slow down and figure this out. Let's ask questions." She felt empowered and trusting enough in our team to send an email to the entire team asking if anyone knew where the banana came from. Within minutes, a staff member on our team responded that the banana must have fallen out of her bag on her way out of the office and that it was hers.

Instead of festering over what might have happened, because I had a team I trusted, I was able to release. In traditional top-down settings, leaders are rarely questioned, and with current Diversity, Equity, and Inclusion (DEI) initiatives, it's likely my Assistant Director, a white woman, may have been afraid to be perceived as someone who was willing to ask questions in such a sensitive scenario, lest she be labeled as dismissive of racism. But to truly ***diplomatically disrupt*** our current mental health systems, all things should be open for question, from leadership to operating theory. I want to be able to have those kinds of difficult conversations with a team who both ***empathizes*** with the oppressive ***contexts*** in which we live and work, where a racist attack such as this is an unfortunate reality, and yet are willing and able to have ***agency*** and discernment to help even their leader slow down.

If I couldn't have that type of difficult dialogue with my team, then why would they be able to have those conversations with their clients? When well-being is the final goal, we cannot lead with fear. I needed to trust the reflection and sensible feedback from those I was surrounded by, and even in the most challenging of circumstances, I could. My willingness to be open with my Assistant Director is directly related to the ***collective responsibility*** cultivated at the center to both sensitivity, and to working together to construct solutions to protect the well-being of the center through our ***interpersonal responsibility*** to both hold space, challenge, and support one another, and our ***individual responsibility*** to be authentic even in the most difficult of situations.

To the Reader: Rather than rely on an authoritative stance or our training in "objective truth," it is important that we are humble enough to be willing to think deeply about the unique person seeking our help. Like the Black Girl, it's important to reject the hypocrisy of helping approaches that, like the Lord of Hosts, require feigned genuineness as opposed to a human-to-human interaction. Instead of becoming a human healer, you can end up being more like a conveyor belt providing the same techniques and interventions over and over again no matter the relevance to the life of the human being in front of you.

As seen in my case example, it is also important to surround yourself with people who challenge you to slow down, listen, and assess the facts in front of you, even at times when that may be challenging or feel threatening to do. In this work, it is important that we believe in and recognize the substance behind what we argue and work toward, rather than be like the Nailer who seemed to enjoy the drama of arguing for argument's sake.

- Are you really thinking about the individual sitting in front of you receiving your help? Are you thinking about who they are, how they live their life, the relevant factors in their life, and how they want to live their life in the future?
- What and who helps to ground you to maintain a stance of openness?
- How do you live your own life in a way that avoids hypocrisy so that you are able to be genuinely *yourself* as a professional helper?
- How do you distinguish between "drama" (or arguing for argument's sake) and arguments that are worth your genuine investment? What is your bottom line?
- How can you maintain the bravery to seek the truth, rather than avoid it for fear of being perceived negatively, or as not "woke" enough?
- Do you surround yourself with people who are afraid to challenge you? How can you change that?

Maintaining a sense of openness is challenging in a field still seeking the prestige of scientific certainty, or an environment where regurgitating social justice terms is reinforced above seeking to understand and apply them authentically. Your willingness to truly listen and analyze each unique situation for what it is, rather than being guided entirely by the trauma from the past or others' perceptions of you, will translate to helping the individuals who seek your support to be brave enough to do the same.

Koheleth and the Greek Scholar: Turning Points

In Chap. 4, I describe how I became disillusioned with person-centered theory and sought answers from the Social Therapy conference in New York. There I reluctantly had to face the fact that I could, and should, look within for answers. Like the Black Girl, I began by trying to reason from a Western philosophical worldview, but found that I had to abandon this worldview and look to an Indigenous African-centered perspective in order to reach a position of agency. This is also the conclusion reached by the developing field of African philosophy. From initially using a Western philosophical framework, it has accepted a position of agency and as such has been able to reason from an Indigenous African-centered perspective.

Case Example: Indigenous Philosophy in Professional Supervision

Recently, one of my former Assistant Directors reminded me that in her first supervision session with me, being new to our counseling center and hired into a leadership role, she had shared that she wanted to make sure our staff saw her as a "boss." She wanted to hold her authority, given that she had not had the advantage of having worked with the staff previously. She recalls me simply responding; "Why do that? Could that be your ego leading or talking? That's just your ego." Taken aback, she followed with: "But how am I going to get people to do things if they don't see me as a boss?" What she remembers most vividly is my saying, "Why did you think that you need that in order to lead?" This made it clear to her that trying to be seen as having authority could be a waste of her personal energy. She said she knew then that her experience at our counseling center was going to be different.

This experience helped the Assistant Director shift her own style of leadership and supervision with her supervisees. She began to genuinely ask them similarly simple questions such as "How are you? Are you having fun? What's working? Why are you thinking about that?" through the application of radical ***empathy*** and an authentic relationship-building perspective of support rather than an authoritative one—just like we wanted our staff to be doing with their students, and the students with their peers. She shared that while at first this shift was intimidating, it "removed all of the pressure of feeling like I needed to assert myself and that, in turn, took the pressure off of how people needed to be around me." In the past, she had learned to check things off of lists as a manager and supervisor, but she now looks back fondly and says "I never had the opportunity to fail at that," once she was guided to see another way. The system that has been built does not lead to empowerment, instead it leads to further oppression. Once you have that knowledge, it can't be taken away from you.

My first job as an Elder is to have the ***awareness*** to be true to myself as a human being every single day. My second job is to encourage everyone else to do the same, in order to create a collective environment of authenticity from which an abundance of well-being can blossom. For example, in my role in leadership at the counseling center, colleagues would often note that I would take an exorbitant amount of time getting from one end of the corridor to the other when I arrived to the office in the morning because I would walk into every office door that was open to greet everyone and ask how they were doing on a human-to-human level. Yes, I had plenty of emails to respond to and plenty of fires to put out awaiting me in my inbox and voicemail. However, from an Indigenous perspective, focusing on the process rather than running to the outcome is always going to result in better long-term effects when it comes to well-being everywhere (Katz & Murphy-Shigematsu, 2012).

Note that this approach does not mean simply being *nice*. In fact, authenticity means learning how to communicate difficult things with respect that people typically do not want to hear. In meeting people where they were and helping them to recognize and exercise their unique strengths, I was modeling the philosophy and way of helping so that staff could translate this parallel process into their authentic and human interactions with students. I made sure our Assistant Directors felt valued and respected as role models in the center. When writing this chapter, I was reminded by one of my former Assistant Directors of the "no drama" policy we worked hard to infuse into the life of the center. She remembered having a minor disagreement with another assistant director early on in our implementation process that could have become a long-standing disagreement. She recalled that once I learned about the conflict between them, I told them we needed to deal with it immediately and had them face one another to work it out rather than speaking with each of them individually. She shared that through the intentional dialogue they were able to "see windows into each other's consciousness," and by setting such a tone for how we were going to handle disagreements with honesty and without drama early on, they developed a collaboration and even a strong friendship that has lasted to this day.

When you are committed to your ***individual responsibility*** to be in alignment over the course of so many years, it becomes easy to see when things are out of alignment (a.k.a., drama). We had to take on the ***interpersonal responsibility*** to be proactive and honest with helping one another recognize and intervene when misalignment arose and to empower our staff to do the same with each other. From an Indigenous philosophy, focusing only on oneself doesn't actually create satisfaction and well-being; there is a ***collective sense of responsibility*** to building and sustaining a culture of synergy. We have to help one another find our own unique dance as we learn to dance together in a collective whole. This fosters a synergistic energy that allows everyone to grow as they bounce ideas off of one another to reproduce well-being in abundance.

To the Reader: As we are all interconnected, being a human means being able to be *moved* in some way by others. However, because this requires vulnerability, we instead find plenty of ways to avoid being perceived as a learner. But just as our Assistant Director was quickly able to realize, maintaining the perception of knowing or being unmoved/unchanged by others or new ideas is one way of giving up your sense of agency. Getting comfortable with the discomfort of not knowing, but being willing to learn, take in new information, analyze, and evaluate from within is what gives us a sense of agency. In the adventures of the little Black Girl, the point of the Greek scholar is to remind the Black Girl of *her* ability to have the agency think. You don't have to believe something just because you always have or because everyone else does. Helping the individuals that come to you for support to see this as well is freeing.

- How do you best learn?
- How do you move yourself forward?
- Do you get ashamed or embarrassed that your thinking has changed? Or do you embrace it and are you happy to let go of previous mindsets?
- Are there times where you feel yourself being drawn away from your purpose in this work and toward the workplace or other "drama?" What would it be like for you to address concerns openly and directly rather than avoid them?

Living in environments where everyone has a sense of agency is unfortunately rare. For this reason, when it does happen, it is common to have both internal reactions and external pressure to shut it down, because it feels new and therefore unsafe. However, individual agency is needed for individual well-being. And your commitment to your own sense of agency, and promoting that of others, can serve as a catalyst for creating the types of synergistic environments needed for well-being everywhere.

The Myop: Making Past Wisdom Modern

From a position of agency, the Black Girl is able to challenge scientific short-sightedness when she encounters the Myop. Now confident in her own perspective, she overlooks his professional prestige and provides evidence of his failings, using her inner light. This failure illustrates, from an Indigenous African-centered perspective, the centrality of spirituality in psychological theory. Like the Black Girl, I reject the narrow scientification of knowledge and argue that the "myopic" image of helping as constructed by the West needs to be spiritualized in order to bring about individual and societal transformation. The case study presents encounters that highlight the issue of spiritual congruence as something which is not confined to a particular "doctrine," but involves how one lives one's life in connection with others and the environment.

Case Example: Indigenous Philosophy in Mental Health System Implementation

In 2014, I began working at a local college counseling center as an adjunct to my private practice. At this point of my career, I had enough knowledge of myself to practice in a way that I knew would actually provide effective helping (and in alignment with myself and an Indigenous African-centered philosophy) no matter where I was. I was committed to moving with a sense of ***agency*** and enjoying what it is that I do: Helping people live more satisfyingly. In systems where being healthy is still abnormal, and in a society that is driven by money, people who are healthy, empowered, and enjoying their work are rare. They tend to stand out, and others who share their values tend to gravitate toward them, leading to new opportunities. By 2015, I was asked to be an Associate Director at the center.

I've since been asked why I accepted the position, when my intention was simply to work there part-time. To be honest, this is not something I questioned. From an Indigenous African-centered philosophy, when you accept your responsibility, you cannot run away from it. Just like the members of the Nation of Islam who didn't pause to question if they *should* or *who* would get up to close the doors of the meeting hall when the wind flew them open (Chap. 5), I take my responsibility as a healer and an Elder seriously. This does not mean being sacrificial, as that would not be effective. While we have to be strategic and use discernment (as described in Chap. 6), for example, not wasting our breath when the evidence is clear that we will not be heard, when an opportunity to act in spiritual alignment arises, we must not turn away from it. Otherwise, what and who are we doing this work for?

However, ***contextualization*** is important to provide a full picture. The college I was working at faced a highly publicized suicide cluster amongst its students, and as with university counseling centers across the United States, it was clear that the demand for mental health services was significantly outweighing the resources available (as organized by the traditional Western mental health system). This resulted in long waitlists, a dangerous lack of access to immediate care, and increased acuity as students who could have been helped for lower-level concerns increased in severity by the time of their first intake appointments. Having taken the journey I did over so many years prior to expose myself to and internalize an Indigenous African-centered approach to helping, I knew that this system of care was highly inefficient, ineffective, and oppressive. However, it was not lost on me that the Western helping professions have always had access to Indigenous knowledge about more holistic, restorative, and effective systems of helping, and have not heeded this past wisdom—in part due to cultural supremacy, and in part due to the lack of financial advantage of such effective helping systems. However, at the university level, the crisis of mental health due to the ineffective systems of care *was,* most certainly, beginning to impact the wallets of the universities, which faced serious lawsuits from families. The financial motivation to try something new had finally come, and at that same time, I found my "Irishman."

At the Counseling Center Directors conference in the autumn of 2014, my director watched Dr. Peter Cornish on a panel speak for ten minutes about a new model to mental health services that might help to manage the resources-to-demand ratio at the counseling center. When he returned from the conference, we decided to reach out to Cornish and a group of five or six other counseling center directors to have a focus group on how everyone was managing the mental health supply-versus-demand crises at their institutions. Cornish's Stepped Care 2.0 (SC2.0) model (Cornish, 2020) was the one that stood out. It appealed to my director and our university as a way to reduce our long waitlist, and to ensure we were better able to see students in crisis and reduce our liability. Unbeknownst to my director, I felt the model resonated with me because it aligned with the Indigenous African-centered philosophy of helping, and what I had learned about helping from my own family. It appealed to me as a model based on the synergy strands of ***agency***, ***creativity***, and ***flexibility***, and was designed in such a way as to help redress historical harms. It was a model where individuals come and receive support when they are ready, know that they can always have immediate access to support but are informed that therapy is active and involves *work*, and have a range of options for how to work on their goals outside of weekly individual therapy. It encouraged staff clinicians to utilize their discernment and their strengths. My former director used to describe it as a "jazz symphony rather than an orchestra." Instead of viewing each individual student as our client, this model was one that reflected human interconnectedness in making the entire system of students our client. It meant viewing helping as a one-at-a-time process rather than a predetermined number of sessions that could not be offered equitably. It meant really seeing the individual in front of you and understanding *their* individual needs.

I did not at that time feel I needed to share my thoughts about how this model aligned with an Indigenous African-centered philosophy of helping; I had learned too many lessons along my journey to think that this would be valued or heard in this context. It was like watching the "tiny homes" movement—as if minimalism were a modern invention! Past wisdom will always eventually become modern, thus, like the once negatively perceived traditional roundavals in African villages, Alaskan igloos, or Native American teepees, recognition of their complimentary benefits to the environment are now evident. Instead, I saw it as my ***individual responsibility*** to help build the staff's inner resources to be able to implement such a paradigm shift, and to help all individuals live and work in better alignment with themselves through ***interpersonal responsibility*,** and interconnected with humanity as a part of a team. In other words, to build a sense of ***collective responsibility*** for wellness. Just as the Black Girl developed her own internal resources throughout her journey, those who were willing to think outside of the box of their Western training brought the technical strategy and the external tools to communicate the implementation process in a language that our university administration and counseling staff were familiar with. Such academic works (Katz, 2017, Cornish 2020) supported me, like the Black Girl who no longer needed the Bible and Knobkerry, to invest in keeping myself spiritually aligned and authentic while adapting and modifying my energy where needed. Why would I want to unlearn what I learned over such an intentional journey?

To the Reader: I often remind my students that, at the end of the day, they are a *professional*, and with that comes a way of being and a sense of responsibility. Once you learn to take ownership of your choices and understand what you enjoy about your work, you can then *do it*. Rather than feeling out of control, burdened, and without options, you'll instead be able to take back control when you accept your conscious choices.

When you accept that all past wisdom with any merit will someday be made modern, you can step out of the idea that the Western philosophical approach to mental health care is the only way. While my former director was drawn to the SC2.0 model for what *he* could take ownership of and be motivated by (reducing the center's waitlist, and a solution to the problem of demand outweighing resources), I encourage you to see such opportunities from an Indigenous perspective. From an Indigenous perspective, you seek to look at all things from a position of holism, and consider how your interventions or models of care will impact not only the "clients" but the entire community and the humans that work within it. When you are connected to the bigger picture and believe in human spiritual interconnectedness, you feel the accountability of being watched by your community, and responsibility for your actions will follow.

- What does it mean to you to be a professional helper in our society?
- How might you practice differently if you internalized the belief that you are spiritually connected to others and your environment?
- What would it mean to keep yourself spiritually aligned in the environments you find yourself in?
- How might you be able to adapt and modify your energy where needed without *losing yourself*?
- Are you taking ownership of your work and the strengths that you offer to helping?
- Are you taking ownership of your life?
- Why are you currently working at the job or the internship you are working at? Why did you choose the training program you are currently in? Why are you continuing to choose the program you are currently in?
- How can you see yourself as part of an interconnected whole, so that you consider your actions from the perspective of the greater good?

If you are reading this, you might be more than $70,000 in student loan debt, overwhelmed, possibly working several jobs in order to make ends meet. You may be thinking that a journey of personal development is not possible for you, given the constraints and limitations on you, your time, your resources, and the seemingly insurmountable systemic issues in the mental health care sphere. I want to remind you that no matter what, you will *always* have your internal guide and some degree of agency, even if very little. While keeping your head down and focusing on survival might feel like the safest option, working without a sense of agency and alignment has long-term emotional, physical, and spiritual costs. You have to be able to have congruence and a sense of wholeness to sustain yourself in this work.

The Cathedral Carriers: The Importance of Discernment

The Black Girl avoids the hypocrisy of the Cathedral Carriers and looks elsewhere for her God. The evidence in Chap. 6 presents an Indigenous African-centered perspective as being congruent with spirituality, which is conceptualized as a philosophy that guides a person in life. An Indigenous African-centered perspective on helping is understood to be a praxis that cannot be limited to the confines of *any* theoretical method or approach, but can only be understood and actualized as a holistic way of being.

Case Example: Indigenous Philosophy in Career Decision-Making

After I left southern Africa, the first job I had in the United States (the only job I could get) was at Social Services. Despite having fifteen years of experience as a licensed social worker and educator overseas, I did not yet have my United States professional license, so could not practice at the level I was qualified to practice at for some time. However, I was excited to finally be offered an interview with the Department of Social Services. When I arrived for the interview in the director's very big office, I noticed immediately that he was a commanding figure, a dominating character, a large white man with a beard. He told me to sit down and offered me a cup of coffee, which I welcomed as he told me about the job. I noticed that he did not ask me questions; not about myself, my experiences, my resume, or anything else. He just seemed interested in telling me about himself and the kind of "tight ship" he ran at Social Services. He appeared to merely feign interest in me. I also noticed that his desk was entirely cleared of all paperwork, which I found very unusual for an office in Social Services. The reality is that the work is overwhelming, and people in that department tend to have at least a few scattered papers on their desks, given the nature of the job. I noticed that he did not have any indications in his office about himself as a person: No artwork, no photos of family, no decorations. This gave me the impression that his focus was only about the work and not about the shared sense of humanity with others. Behind him was a corkboard that I noticed had every single pushpin symmetrically aligned. Though I only saw it briefly, the corkboard made a lasting impression on me. It gave off a feeling of control.

The final straw came at the end of the interview, when the director briefly gestured his head toward the cup that I was drinking and glanced from the mug to the kitchen. With this slightest of non-verbal expression, he expected me to automatically know what he was saying: Which I determined was that he expected me to return my cup to their kitchen, and that he certainly was not going to do that for me. I picked up on this all too familiar "unwritten curriculum" of the dominant culture that others are expected to just "know," as I have had the privilege of having mentors teach me their meaning and the potential consequences of how I'd be perceived if I did not pick up on them, despite the lack of reciprocity in attempting to understand my culture. Just like the Black Girl was able to look from a distance and see for herself that the Cathedral Carriers were arguing amongst themselves and she did not need to waste her time with them, I knew immediately that my needs as a learner were not going to be met there. I concluded that this manager prioritized control—it was his domain, and thus his rules. But I had a choice. I picked up the cup, brought it to the kitchen, chatted with the woman in the kitchen, and knew I would not accept the position to work there.

Shortly thereafter, I was able to obtain an interview with another county's Department of Social Services and had a completely different, warm, human, and enthusiastic interview experience with that county's director. In taking the ***individual responsibility*** to trust my gut in that initial interaction with my future director, I was able to work in an environment where I felt heard, appreciated, supported, received guidance, and was encouraged to be creative and expand upon my unique strengths. The flexibility and trust that I was provided helped me solidify my reputation in the local community and state level in my field, as I could better participate in our ***collective responsibility*** of empowerment in a synergistic environment. I was grateful that I trusted my internal guide and exercised discernment, as the Black Girl learned to do, to choose the job with the director who connected with me on a human level at my interview instead of the job with the interview experience that was rigid and cold. After my encounter with a similarly rigid and cold Fr. Kelly in Zambia, I did not want to learn the same lesson twice. I learned to more quickly recognize when someone else is and is not in alignment with themselves, and that this is an energy that I could *feel*. As an Elder, in addition to passing along the importance of listening to one's intuition, I also consider it an ***interpersonal responsibility*** to pass along my knowledge of the unfair "unwritten curriculum" used to pass judgment on those who are not in the dominant culture in "professional" spaces.

To the Reader: When you make the conscious choice to be a professional helper, from an Indigenous perspective, this is not a role you can choose to turn on and off; rather, it is a holistic way of being. Therefore, I encourage you to always practice your assessment skills as you make decisions based on interactions with others (as with most things, the more practice you get, the better you become). Part of being empowered means that you can exercise your own judgment. Many of us feel unable to do so because of internalized feelings of inferiority or imposter syndrome. Others struggle to do so because of previous experiences of safety in trusting in systems to have their best interest in mind. However, it is important that you learn to trust your intuition, and take the opportunity to reflect on the evidence in front of you. Hopefully, you have people in your life who challenge you to do so; however, if no one else does this for you, do it yourself. Ask yourself the hard questions, and be honest with yourself about the difficult things that you may not want to face (e.g. not accepting a job because of a brief encounter with the director, even though you are desperate for one). Learn to separate your intuition from your ego; when decisions are ego-driven, they are typically based in feelings of anxiety, guilt, or fear, and avoidance of them. But when we make decisions based on intuition, we make decisions based on the *evidence* of the entire picture, not just what we want to see.

- How do you distinguish between when your intuition is speaking to you versus your ego?
- How are you working to sharpen your conceptualization skills?
- Like me with Fr. Kelly and my potential new director, what is an example of a lesson you did not need to learn twice?
- How will you pass along information about unwritten curricula in "professional" environments?
- How can you distinguish between environments where you best learn and environments that will present barriers to your learning?

As an Elder, I share my own examples so that as you embark on your career as a professional helper, acknowledging that we are all interconnected, and hoping that you can find some benefit from my lessons about trusting your intuition and using discernment.

The Knobkerry, the Bible, and the Irishman: Finding Joy and Internal Alignment Despite One's Environment

An Indigenous philosophy is grounded in ***interconnectedness***; therefore, my value as an individual helper is less important than what I am able to pass along to others as they undertake their own journeys of discovery and go on to impact others. When I accepted the leadership role at the university counseling center, I knew it was time for me to accept my responsibility as an *Elder.* In Indigenous cultures, Elders are "Those who have shown wisdom and leadership in cultural, spiritual, and historical matters within their communities" (King et al., 2009, p. 82). While a few staff clinicians quickly resonated with the SC2.0 model's opportunity for empowerment and ***flexibility*** across all levels of the system, many staff members were scared and resistant to the shift. This was totally understandable in the context of decades of training in a particular approach to counseling. And though all could recognize this approach was no longer working to serve the needs of the student body, having been told repeatedly that this "gold standard" approach was the *universal* approach to professional helping (Chap. 2), it felt to them that anything different would be substandard. Many were also intimidated by the model's expectation that they develop their own discernment and clinical judgment, and exercise their unique strengths and creativity in clinical practice. Recall Jodorowsky's quote at the beginning of this book: "Birds born in a cage think flying is an illness."

After months of working with my team, we realized we had truly created a synergistic environment when I had a conflict where I was pulled in multiple directions of high importance at once. "Let me go and ask somebody," I thought, and realized I could go into *anyone*'s office and ask for support, no matter their title or their role in the center. And I could trust that staff would be honest with me if they were actually available to help or not. The fact that I didn't have to take everything on all on my own showed that we were an interdependent collective. That helped me realize we had cultivated an environment of empowerment, agency, honesty, and strength. I saw the transformation in our staff learning to be curious asking questions of one another in order to learn no matter their title or degrees, when interns were really starting to understand how to use their own clinical judgment, and when individuals who were otherwise used to being told exactly what to do found their unique voices and were able to evolve (Cornish & Berry, 2025).

By definition, part of the ***individual responsibility*** of being a good professional helper means collecting as much information as possible to fully understand and help individuals live more satisfyingly. Properly conceptualizing the sociopolitical culture surrounding an individual is crucial for constructing an appropriate plan of action to ***diplomatically disrupt*** (Cornish, 2023) the status quo. This, of course, happens on an ***interpersonal responsibility*** basis when working with clients and supervisees, but it can also be applied to an entire counseling center working together to come up with solutions to problems facing the entire community's wellness, and the barriers presented in the sociopolitical system. As an Elder, from an Indigenous African-centered philosophy, it is my job to *show you* so that you can figure it out rather than to *tell you*. Otherwise, how could I have trusted my team if I inevitably were out sick, took a vacation, or was otherwise unavailable for day-to-day problems? Leadership in an Indigenous philosophy is not sacrificial; it is ***growth-oriented*** in that one is constantly mentoring and training so that everyone around them feels more confident in their own discernment to create a ***collective responsibility*** to solving problems. Rather than simply tell staff what to do about big dilemmas, I would openly share with them the big picture of the sociopolitical issues facing the center. By holistically ***contextualizing*** the environment we provide services in, we can develop appropriate solutions; "Ye shall know the truth and the truth shall set you free." What I wanted our staff and our clients to internalize from an Indigenous philosophy is that despite what is going on in the world, you can still be yourself, you can still experience joy, and you can still do good work—though it might take some collective strategizing. I was always honest with them about any oppressive contextual factors that would have an impact on our work so that we could work together to construct creative solutions, as this is an essential component of ***truth and reconciliation*** in mental health care. It is possible to have well-being and wellness, and it is possible to exercise your unique strengths as a part of a collective whole, even when outside forces (such as racism, colonization, and other forms of oppression) are at play. By living out the values and principles that are rooted in nature, the joy we experienced was contagious with other teams in the university system.

To the Reader: While some may be disappointed to learn how the little Black Girl's journey ends, tending to a garden and having children with an Irishmen she coerced into marrying her, it's important to recognize that once she was able to internalize her faith and spirituality, she was able to make conscious choices to value her life. I did not anticipate staying at my part-time job very long, and did not imagine making a career out of working at a counseling center after having experienced the joy of private practice. However, making affirmative choices to do what I love each day, and taking responsibility for my actions, led me to my becoming part of creating a synergistic culture of wellness within the confines of our reality. And I was pleased to discover that my twice-a-week position had turned into five memorable years. It wasn't perfect, it wasn't glamorous, and it wasn't void of the many stressful realities of working in a high pressure, fast-paced mental health service environment within a capitalist society. However, by striving to value each day and encouraging others to do the same, we were able to enjoy the experience of affirmatively choosing to be where we were each day.

From a Western perspective, we have been led to believe that the life cycle is from the ages of 0–100 (if we are lucky). This perspective is that we live just one life, which places pressure on us to achieve all we can in that short amount of time. When you instead view the world from a holistic perspective, you see yourself as a part of a continuum. You are a part of the entire universe's life span: Those who came before you and impacted your life, those you cross paths with during your lifetime, and those who will go on to live and pass along your impact later. With this paradigm shift, we are not just responsible for our one life—rather, our actions have a ripple effect and live on. By considering that you are alive to contribute to the world in some way, and if you are doing what you need to do (wherever you are doing it, no matter what the external expectations on what your life should look like), you will shine. In my day-to-day experiences, whether going to the dentist or getting my coffee, I really only like to go to people who enjoy what they are doing. There is an energy that comes when you are living on purpose. You make the most of your life and your options. When you tap into doing what you are supposed to do, that authenticity is palpable and attractive.

- Why are you doing what you are doing?
- What conscious choices are you making to live currently?
- How can you exude an energy of authenticity in what you choose to do?
- Can you think of any examples of people in your day-to-day life that exude an energy of taking ownership of their lives and what they do?
- How can this philosophy impact your work with individuals who come to you for help who feel stuck and without options?
- How will you help individuals choose to live?
- What do you see as your responsibility to future generations?

You have a responsibility to create the life that you want, and I cannot tell you what that is—nobody can but you. It may involve being a professional helper, or it may not. Whatever it is, I want you to *choose* it and *live* it and to help others to do the same.

Conclusion

My hope in sharing these experiences is that they might exemplify the necessity for those like myself, who pursue careers in facilitating transformation in others, to be congruent with their professed beliefs. Many theorists use similar methods, which can be adapted by students of an Indigenous African-centered perspective on helping. This, to me, is not a new approach, but rather an adaptation of the holistic helping with which I was raised as a child, as many others around the world have been. It is these values that I now understand have been with me all along. By recognizing and giving them value, I can now see them for what they are: Culturally specific skills for enabling one to live more satisfyingly. It was my intention to be an effective helper, but my search for understanding has enabled me to conclude, as the Black Girl does in relation to her own quest, that it is more about personally living more satisfyingly and sharing this knowledge with others to promote their self-development.

In effect, this journey has been, like that of the Black Girl, a search for self-development. In the process, what has been revealed is a return to principles and practices that are well established in Indigenous communities around the world, as well as my own African traditions. The way forward is to concentrate not on the development of specific new models of helping, but to build people up with a concept of ***ubuntu*** (humanness), which can provide them with skills to help, support, and facilitate the development of the entire community (and harmonious relationships between communities), thereby enabling all to be able to live more satisfyingly. I am therefore attempting to communicate a concept of helping that focuses on an individual striving to become human. When one is able to be human, they respect humanity, and that is how harmony is restored.

Chapter 8
Marrying the Irishman: Cultivating the Garden

"God is at your elbow, and He has been there all the time; but in His divine mercy He has not revealed Himself to you lest too full a knowledge of Him should drive you mad. Make a little garden for yourself: dig and plant and weed and prune; and be content if He jogs your elbow when you are gardening unskillfully, and blesses you when you are gardening well."
(Shaw, 1932, p. 54)

Through the character of the Old Philosopher, Shaw suggests that evidence of the divine is woven into the very fabric of daily existence. With no definitive definition of the nature of God, the Black Girl reasons there was no longer a need to search for God. By simply tending to her own garden, she will be able to find God for herself. Guided by the fluid, dynamic interaction she has with the world, and trusting the internal and external inspiration that comes her way, she accepts the complementary purposeful relationship she has with the divine. Is it possible to capture and present such an Indigenous worldview on helping as a neatly packaged helping model of practice?

What has been described in this text may seem idealistic, and unrealistic for translation into day-to-day practice. My standard advice to "cultivate your own garden" is often met with the ethical and legal consequences for adopting such a response, in addition to claims of romanticizing this perspective, or being idealistic or unrealistic about what translating this perspective into current mental health systems could mean. Students and young professionals, in particular, often ask me to bring all of this theory to life.

I agree that there is no prescription or step-by-step guide for this sort of healing. The concept of the African forest is not a literal place, but rather a mindset that guides my therapeutic approach. Instead, ***synergy*** results from a reliance on the principles of an Indigenous African-centered philosophy, which I strive to apply in my own cultural context. It is by actively participating in the process of becoming human that I can share knowledge that is interwoven in the holistic, multidimensional, interconnectedness of daily life. I always find it easier to show students what I mean by having them join me, in my sessions and theirs, so they can see what it

G. Berry, *Helping?*, https://doi.org/10.1007/978-3-031-88586-0_8

really means to live congruently as a professional helper or Elder, from an Indigenous African-centered perspective, in a Western helping system. So, I wanted to leave you with a simple snapshot of what integrating such a perspective into my role as a clinical social worker in private practice looks like, with the caveat that no minute, hour, or day is the same.

Starting My Day

Around 8 a.m., after a workout at the local gym, instead of going straight to my office I take a detour to the coffee shop. I reluctantly avoid their vegan carrot muffin with my extra hot oat latte by reminding myself how good my body feels when I avoid too much unnecessary sugar. I then make my way to the commercially zoned, single-family home that I call my office. After viewing countless professional buildings, my frustrated but determined realtor suggested this out-of-the box option, and I express gratitude as I enter the building, as I have done every single day since getting the keys over a decade ago. I notice the dead plants at the entrance and take it as a reminder that I am not taking care of everything quite as I should, and make a mental note to do better.

I open up the building, making sure the trash bins are empty and the restrooms are presentable. I eat some granola for breakfast while taking a look at my schedule for the day. I prioritize what seems urgent, recognizing that there's an element of unpredictability to each day. I remain confident that I have the ***flexibility*** and ***creativity*** to handle whatever comes. I make some calls, pay off a speeding ticket, and then prepare for my first appointment at 9 am with Mr. H.

Mr. H is a client who was referred to me through Medicaid and has come a very long way in the eight years we have been working together. He is consistent, engaged, and really wants to do the work. He comes in these days mostly to maintain his sobriety and continue living the life he has worked so hard to be proud of over the past several years. In the beginning, he really stretched me clinically, because he didn't have much hope for his own life. He shared with me that he never had a space like this where he felt someone was really listening to him. There were and still are so many barriers in his way. He's told me about the homes he was raised in as a foster child, and how at his last home, local politicians in Washington, DC, were invited to visit by the foster parents, who would try to get the children to perform sexual acts for money. Because he refused, he felt as though high-power politicians were after him. He ran away and lived on the streets, where he naturally learned to wheel and deal to survive. He eventually got sixteen years jail time for selling crack cocaine during the epidemic in the 1980s. He described his self-esteem as being in the toilet. He struggled to see any wrong in how he was living, because he was doing what he always believed he needed to do just to survive. He didn't show care or pride in his appearance or in his actions toward himself and his family members, including his children. He used to carry around so much anger, which I felt was justified, given his life experiences.

As we talk about his next court appearance regarding child custody, I see how much his thinking has changed since that time. I spent years listening to, ***empathizing***, and validating his pain, and acknowledging the challenges he has faced to be able to slowly move to a place where he could understand that dealing with oppressive forces isn't about trying to win each individual battle, it is about the war. It isn't for me to reflect on how he got to this point, because he did the work. But did prioritizing his emotional distress above the wealth of necessary paperwork make a difference? Or did asking him for help to find my reading glasses inadvertently illustrate the give and take of the universe, reminding him as well as me that we are connected by virtue of our humanity? Perhaps being offered water or a cup of tea made him feel cared about. I'm not sure. Or was it the things I did behind the scene that made a difference—the accountability to my professional obligations, to the unseen force/God/ancestors who observe my work from a different dimension?

What I do know is that a ***growth-oriented*** perspective meant identifying what was within his control, recognizing the strengths he has relied on to navigate the prison system, and trying to identify the positives of his experiences, such as the discipline he learned to impose on himself. He learned to see value in the experiences that he has had so much that he wants to share and publish his life story in a book, so as to give it purpose. He realizes now that perception means everything: How we take care of and how we talk about ourselves matters. His current "war" is to regain custody rights with his children, and he's focused on that goal, despite the battles that continue to arise that would previously have derailed him.

Today, he expresses his gratitude for our work together. He says he appreciates that "when I'm wrong, you let me know I'm wrong. You keep me uplifted even when I can't lift myself." He also tells me that he appreciates knowing that "there's no hesitation when I call, you always answer." Which is technically not true: I answer when I can, and I let him know I'll get back to him when I can't. But I know his saying this is really about the sentiment he feels regarding our relationship: That I treat him like I would a family member, as I do with each of my clients. It was only when he knew he felt truly cared about that he was able to make his shifts in our work. He also knows that our work will come to an end at some point.

In the middle of my conversation with Mr. H, my daughter, who grew up working for the practice, knocks on our door. She only does so if there is some sort of client emergency, which she says there is now.

I excuse myself from Mr. H, who encourages me to "go take care of it, I'm good!" My daughter tells me a former client of mine, Ms. J, is having a manic episode and is in our waiting area. I calmly enter the room, greet her, and welcome her to the space. Because I can see she is in so much distress, I lower my voice and let her know that I am busy seeing someone at the moment and for another thirty minutes or so, but that my daughter will get her a cup of tea, and she can relax here until I can see her. She says that is okay with her, and she would like to wait in her car. My daughter makes her tea and brings it out to her in the parking space behind the office.

When I go to get Ms. J for the unscheduled crisis single session later on, she is much more relaxed. It has been over a year since I last met with her, and I have been unsure if I would ever see her again. The situation reminds me of Latisha. If this is the last time I am to meet with her, what would be meaningful for me to say? Should I say the things that will bring her immediate comfort, or should I say the things that she needs to hear—that she needs to pause more before she reacts, and recognize that the people in her life offering her consistent support need to be valued and cherished. Should we focus on the dominant presenting single issue, or the often-hidden underlying issues? We start the session with a breathing exercise, perhaps because I surmise it will help her hear things she may not want to hear. I ask her what made her decide she needed to see me so urgently. She shares that she found the address for my practice shortly after learning that I had left my last position, where she had been my client. And on this day, after knowing that she had not been doing well for a while, she decided, without calling or emailing, that she needed to drive directly to me. She says she remembers feeling seen and understood in our work together whenever she would arrive at the counseling center for a walk-in session. It brings to mind how, when I was younger, I would immediately feel a sense of calm when I was in distress and would head to one of my aunt's houses. I think this is what Ms. J felt she needed in her moment of crisis; a familiar face and energy.

I think to myself, how would I want to feel going to an aunt, or an Elder? After conducting a risk assessment to ensure she is not a danger to herself or others, I ask Ms. J what she is looking for and what she wants to achieve from our limited time together. In contrast to my traditional counseling training, which taught me to conduct a thorough, structured intake assessment at the first clinical encounter, I reverse the process by prioritizing what is presented by the client. I will then go back and complete the generic intake questions and demographics as they come up, or at the end of a session if relevant. In fact, my daughter is still preparing the intake forms when I retrieve her for our session, but that does not stop me from starting to work with her. Ms. J shares with me the stress she is going through. She is trying to do so much; a financial program, dealing with stuff at church, stuff at her job—she is clearly overwhelmed. It all came to a head with the pressure that she was under. From our previous work together, I know that Ms. J had grown up in foster care and really needed tender love and care during challenging times. We identify some goals: (1) to get her to forgive herself, (2) to understand her workaholic nature, (3) to help her find her passion in her life. Knowing that she knows she will always receive directness and clarification from me, I let her know upfront that I do not take the health insurance that she currently has. Ms. J lets me know that she is already aware, and that her friend has lent her some money to come and see me on a consistent basis. We determine a fee that works for both of us, and get her on the schedule for the following week.

Lunch Time

After wrapping up with Ms. J, I notice a missed call from one of my good friends, who is trying to finalize dinner plans with me for this evening. I call her back, chit chat for a bit, and plan to meet at around 8:00 p.m. at a new place she has found. We're on a mission to find our favorite Indian restaurant in the city, so are in the process of trying them all. I'm looking forward to it so much I have to hang up to grab my lunch to hold me over.

I normally walk to the local organic grocery store to grab my lunch mid-day, but because I decided to welcome Ms. J and meet with her, I drive the few blocks there instead today to save some time. As I'm there, I take a call from my brother, a local politician in England, who wants some feedback about two cases he plans to represent. The first has been in a twenty-five-year fight for justice after their sibling was beaten and killed in police custody, which was caught on video. After hearing the heart-breaking case, we feel publicity might be the next course of action (The Box Bundle, 2021). The other case involves a person who lost their job in a care home because one of the new residents felt uncomfortable being cared for by a person of color. The manager felt the resident's comfort was the priority, and happily shared this as the reason for her dismissal. But as the documented reason was the worker's inappropriate use of a cell phone during work hours, we conclude it will be a difficult case to prove. As I end this phone call, I think about all of the multiracial meetings I've been invited into after highly publicized racist incidents end up in the spotlight on the news. And I think about how shocked many people still are when these incidents happen, when these are the typical phone calls I have with my brother over my lunch break.

Another Unexpected Appointment

As I finish my meal, I am trying to get on with some paperwork, deal with Medicaid, prepare some letters I need to now write for the court for Mr. H, and do some last-minute preparations for a training I will lead in the afternoon, when I receive a phone call from a number I don't recognize. This is common, as my practice has a very general name, which means many people call it for all kinds of support thinking I am a larger social work agency. I typically answer if I have a moment, and try to help whomever is calling find what they need. Today, it is a father, Mr. O, an African immigrant who is calling about his thirty-five-year-old daughter who has been living in a shelter. He says he wants me to go to the shelter to make her come home, and he asks me not to tell her or anyone else that her parents sent me. While understanding his urgency and cultural context, I let him know that while I can't go and retrieve his adult daughter and make her do anything, what I can do is meet with him to give some insight about this family dynamic and offer some general support. I let him know I have about ten minutes to chat right now, and that if he'd like we can schedule some time in the next week to further work on what is going on for them. "I can talk to you and your family about your parenting style, your household, and what I can talk to your daughter about with her permission," I say. "I can't predict the system, can't force her to come home."

Mr. O begrudgingly agrees, and we schedule a time to work through the challenges his family has faced since arriving in the United States, which have left him in such a state of confusion about his grown daughter's decision to live in a shelter instead of his beautiful home. Once I get off the phone with Mr. O, I take a few moments to breathe in the fresh air on my porch before returning to work.

Afternoon

I have about thirty minutes before the start of the training session I'll be running, which is called *Seeing Things Differently: Social Work from an African-Centered Perspective*. I put some last minute preparations together and make sure all of my technology is working correctly as my daughter and I prepare the space for the participants.

As attendees arrive, my daughter signs them in, offers them tea and coffee, with the goal of making them as comfortable in the space as they would be in their own homes before we even get to the training content. In my experience with adult learning, small intimate classes are the best learning environments. About ten people can fit comfortably in my conference room in order to see the screen. One gentleman sits purposefully away from everyone else with his arms folded, appearing bored or disinterested, but other than that, everyone seems engaged.

I always make it clear to participants that this training is going to be different, but rarely do they anticipate how different it will be. I start with a mindfulness activity in which we put our feet into the earth to ground ourselves. The nature of this training requires that I pour a libation and call on my and the participants' ancestors to help us value our time together. My introduction includes acknowledging the context of the people who made me who I am, such as my ancestors, and I share some of my lived experiences across continents. I model my style based on a particular Elder, such as Harriet Tubman, to inform them and give them a choice as to whether or not they are open to this style. We talk about what it means to be uncomfortable. Similar to a personal trainer, we see where someone is and push them a bit further. This is very difficult in the context of training in our field, which conditions us to believe that we should not be pushed or made uncomfortable, but should simply be presented with information. To navigate this, I always ask how they learn, or what in my presentation I can do to aid their learning. The goal is for our time to be positive for all. We talk about cognitive dissonance, and empower participants to pay attention to how they are feeling. It's so important that I have their buy-in. I try to appeal to authority by presenting scholarly people talking about the importance of thinking differently. I always provide an example to display how easy it is not to be present, such as the Awareness Test (GlassworksVFX, 2010), which is one of my favorites. This is how I show that despite understanding a concept intellectually, we may not always follow through in our actions. Overall, my goal for these training sessions is to communicate information that is not new, but to do so clearly and memorably.

By the end of the training, we have done several case studies about what we would do differently coming from an Indigenous perspective. By the end of the training, they seem to have arrived at the place I love the most—discussing what they love about the work they do. Despite the challenges they raised at the beginning of the session, we seem to have arrived at a point where we are able to navigate the challenges we may face. The mood in the room has shifted, and even the skeptical gentleman in the back has opened up to the experience. Once the training is over, folks generally mingle for a while. But tonight I can't stay too long, as I have a community event I want to get to before dinner with my friend.

Evening

Once my daughter and I are able to send everyone off, I make my way across the city to Howard University to hear one of the founders of African Psychology. On this night, the audience is a mixture of students and the local community. There is a clear distinction between the two groups, with students attempting to ask critical and challenging questions of the founder, and community members attempting to engage the founder in more open dialogue. It seems many of the community members are more familiar with the topic of African Psychology and its impact, whereas the students are motivated by academic debate more than engagement—even as their questions reveal they have not studied much about the topic itself. I personally love to attend these events, because I acknowledge my naivety and I embrace that ongoing learning is a part of life.

When I think my work day is over, I stop at Walmart on my way to dinner to grab some printer paper, and take a call from a friend who is dealing with a personal issue. As is natural for me, I'm asking her questions and challenging her. Once I hang up the phone, the person in line behind me who had overheard our conversation taps me on the shoulder and asks me if I "could talk to her like that, because I could use some of that too!" We laugh and connect before I pay for my paper and leave the store.

I arrive on time at the Indian restaurant and meet my friend. We laugh and bond over things going on in both of our lives. We savor the experience of being together, and the food at this restaurant puts it at the top of our list so far. We commit to another dinner date the following month.

So, What Does It Mean to Help?

I return at the end of the day to sit on my porch and enjoy the quiet while I engage in my favorite mindfulness activity—completing a jigsaw puzzle. On my porch, I have pictures of my ancestors so I can feel their presence. They are still a part of my life, inspiring me on a day-by-day basis. What I do is not just about me alone, but an extension of what they have done. I think about the people I touched and who touched me throughout the day, and my mind wanders back to the first line of my application for social work school: "I want to help people."

Like the Black Girl, my search for understanding ends with me cultivating my garden. There is no doubt that my perspective has been shaped by the cultural expression I was surrounded by and shared with others. It was one which emphasized a connection to the world around me, and this African forest helped me see my role in it. I strive to make my days flow, like the river, and depending on the wind, the rain, the movements of the earth, I can be responsive to the needs of the clients. This means:

1. **Humanizing the Role of the Therapist**: Engage with the client from a place of mutual respect. For instance, ensure clients see me as a human being, not as a stereotypical image of a therapist. This might involve personal interactions, like asking a client to help find something in the room, subtly teaching them responsibility and connection.
2. **Healing Beyond Boundaries**: Take a holistic approach—it is not just about symptom management, but about teaching the client how to live a healthier, more connected life. And even in a single session, each client interaction holds the potential for transformation, not just problem-solving.
3. **Acknowledging Challenges**: Moments that may be construed as failures can be seen as necessary steps in helping clients confront difficult truths. This is a challenge to the client's way of thinking that may lead to eventual growth.
4. **Role of Eldership and Intuition**: In addition to professional obligations, there is an emphasis on the importance of intuition, spiritual guidance as well as inner wisdom, much like an elder guiding the younger generation. The goal is to connect to the idea of mentorship and consultation with trusted kin, a modified version of Rites of Passage, or the relationship with a mother or elder, to support someone navigating professional challenges.
5. **Tensions Between Professionalism and Authenticity**: It is not about ignoring the challenges between mainstream therapy and the more authentic, flexible practices in Indigenous perspective. Seeing relevance in some aspects of formulaic approaches, but also seeing how embracing intuition and flexibility may allow a helping practitioner to better serve clients.

At the time I wrote the application essay for my Masters of Social Work program, my starting point was honorable; I was committed, motivated, excited, and genuinely wanted to make a positive difference. As I look back on that today, I realize how naive that statement actually was—I genuinely entered the field thinking that they (the Western training program) would equip me with the knowledge of *how* to help. If I could learn and then follow the formula of my training, I felt that I would be making a positive difference. People are so invested in making this system work that they don't have time to reflect on it. We're so invested in wanting to "help," many of us don't stand back and think, "what can we do differently," because this is a system we have been taught to want to be a part of. It was only when I was confronted with very serious cases in which my training clearly did not work, such as that of Latisha, that I realized what I had been taught about helping did not sit well with me. This forced me to realize that I needed to think deeply about the existing system, and equip myself with the tools and experiences to remove the lens I had been given in order to see things differently. I needed to literally go on a journey outside of the existing system in order to learn other perspectives on helping to ground myself within. As a result of my journey I, like the little Black Girl in George Bernard Shaw's novella, actually learned *not* to help. I learned that helping is about healing.

What comes to mind is the quote from Rumi, the thirteenth-century Islamic poet:

> *Yesterday I was clever, so I wanted to change the world. Today I am wise, so I am changing myself.*

Conclusion

It was only when the [children] grew up and became independent of her, and the Irishman had become an unconscious habit of hers, as if he were a part of herself, that they ceased to take her away from herself and she was left once more with the leisure and loneliness that threw her back on such questions. And by that time her strengthened mind had taken her far beyond the stage at which there is any fun in smashing idols with knobkerries. (Shaw, 1932, p. 58)

Revisiting Latisha

As the Black Girl in Shaw's novella *The Adventures of the Black Girl in Her Search for God* reflected on her journey to find meaning, I, too, reflect on my first client, Latisha, and how our work together challenged me to reconsider my understanding of "professional helping." Much like Shaw's protagonist, I was forced to question dominant frameworks—particularly Western helping theories—and consider what it means to help through the lens of my own cultural and lived experience. This reflection highlighted the importance of reconnecting with Indigenous African-centered practices that honor the whole person and their unique context.

I do not claim to have definitive answers to the questions Latisha inspired. On the contrary, her story left me with more questions: What does it mean to truly help someone? How do we, as mental health professionals, balance our role as agents of healing while remaining authentic to ourselves and our histories? How do we create systems and spaces that honor interconnectedness and the multidimensionality of humanity? These questions continue to guide my professional helping practice, serving as reminders of the importance of curiosity, humility, and reflection.

What I have learned is that authentic helping begins with self-awareness—reflecting on who we are, the systems we operate within, and the cultural assumptions we bring to our work. For me, this meant returning to the teachings of my ancestors and embracing the Indigenous African-centered perspective that has

G. Berry, *Helping?*, https://doi.org/10.1007/978-3-031-88586-0

always been part of me. Helping is not about self-sacrifice or servitude but about fostering trust, empowerment, and mutual growth. It is a collaborative process that values connection over control.

Latisha taught me that healing is not about finding definitive answers—it is about embracing questions, valuing the journey, and committing to continuous growth. If I could work with Latisha today, I would help her contextualize her experiences. I would encourage her to see how systemic oppression shaped her reality without defining her worth or potential. I would aim to empower her to reclaim her agency and see the interconnectedness of her struggles with larger societal patterns.

Instead of focusing on accountability for systems that prioritize legality over humanity, my engagement with her would have been more authentic, less bound by rigid professional norms, and more rooted in empathy and cultural understanding. I would encourage her to connect with herself, with nature, and with the possibilities that extend beyond her immediate circumstances. This shift, I hope, would have allowed Latisha to see that there are more options available to her than the ones dictated by the system or her abusive partner.

For me, the lesson here is clear: Healing is not a one-directional act. It is a multidimensional process of connection, where both the helper and the helped learn and grow together. This requires moving away from hierarchical notions of "helper" and "helped" and embracing a collaborative, interconnected model of care. By adopting this perspective, we empower our clients to recognize their agency, their strengths, and their intrinsic connection to the world around them.

Reflection is essential to this process. It requires us to ask difficult questions: Who are we as helpers? What histories and assumptions do we carry into our work? Are we addressing our own needs as we help others? These questions are not just vital for our integrity as professionals but for the broader goal of fostering systemic and cultural change. Latisha's story reminds me of the profound impact of systems that fail to honor humanity and the importance of addressing structural inequities in our work.

Shaw's novella is particularly relevant because it captures the transformative power of questioning inherited narratives and systems. For me, it provided a framework to explore these questions in a culturally specific way. While other works also explore themes of self-discovery and transformation, it was Shaw's story that resonated most deeply with me. It spoke to my identity and experience in a way that these other works could not, offering a lens to examine the intersections of history, culture, and healing with relevance to my own journey.

My perspective is deeply informed by Indigenous African-centered practices, but it is important to recognize that values of interconnectedness, holism, and multidimensionality are not unique to one culture. These principles are shared across diverse traditions worldwide, expressed in unique and meaningful ways. The goal of sharing my experience is not to prescribe one approach to healing but to highlight the common humanity in these values and the potential for interconnected growth.

Ultimately, I now consider the work we do as mental health professionals as not being about fixing others. It is about fostering empowerment, authenticity, and shared growth. It is about modeling what it means to live in alignment with one's values and embracing the joy and purpose that come from interconnectedness. I see healing as a collaborative process that requires humility, reflection, and a commitment to the collective good.

As I reflect on Latisha's impact on my journey, I am filled with gratitude—not only for what she taught me about the complexities of helping but for how her story compelled me to reconsider the systems I was trained in and reconnect with the wisdom of my own heritage. There is no doubt in my mind that she helped me far more than I helped her, as I can now reimagine the concept of professional helping as an act of shared restoration, connection, and growth.

I'd hope that my work with Latisha now would focus on what she *can* do. How she can create a different reality for herself, which does not need to look like or be like what society says it should. She can have that sense of well-being even if the wider society does not validate her as a result of that. As a healer, my approach would be more about asking, "Who I am accountable to? What is my ethical responsibility?"

The scholars I have read along my journey who were willing to say things that did not fit into the norm have allowed me to engage in practices that enriched me. They were my Elders, and they were able to do the work they did because they had Elders of their own. Where did my grandfather learn his approach to healing? He must have learned it from people in his own family and community, and they in turn must have learned it from those who came before them. This is what being an Elder means to me: it is the responsibility I have, as a person trying to live in an authentic, synergistic, interconnected, and deeply holistic/spiritual way, to ensure that I leave something positive behind. In this book, I have sought to honor the wisdom that has been shared with me, and as I pass it along, I hope I have added to it the wisdom I have gained from my own experiences and adventures. Now, I share it with you, in the hopes that you will find it enriching, and that you, in turn, will share it with others.

Afterword

Embracing Synergy in Mental Health

Peter Cornish
Student Mental Health, University of California, Berkeley, CA, USA

Much like the Black Girl in Shaw's story, Gillian approaches the Western mental health system with a critical eye, examining its roots in colonialism, universalism, and secular ideologies. She asks many questions, questions that are meant not to provide definitive answers but to empower readers to ask questions of their own. She asks me in almost every conversation we have why I am thinking the way I do, but these seem less like challenges or criticisms than invitations. Years ago, she asked me when I was going to publish my work. Soon after co-authoring an article with her, she asked when I would write a book on the stepped-care model I had been formulating. I had no intention of writing about this work until Gillian raised the questions. I did not see it as significant, nor did I think myself capable of writing about it. I did not know that I could be a writer, but somehow Gillian did. And I soon discovered that writing is one of the greatest sources of joy and meaning in my life. She saw this in me.

Once, after listening for a few moments to a BIPOC colleague, she asked, "Why do you talk so much?" And then, reading between the lines of the colleague's long response, which touched on long-standing paternal pressures contributing to perfectionist traits, she asked, "When are you going to grow up?" As words on the page, these questions seem impertinent, almost abusive, but in the healing context, spirit, and love with which the words were delivered, this colleague received them with openness and humility. I observed Gillian's words as an unexpected gift from an Elder engaged in holistic healing practice. This colleague neither invited these questions nor did they ask for her wisdom, but Gillian understood that these questions were the right ones for the moment.

I was instructed early in my psychotherapy training never to ask "why" questions. "Why" questions would make those seeking help uncomfortable; they would challenge them to explain something they might not understand. Instead, my job was to be kind, listen actively, reflect back to what I was hearing, and be accepting of them as

G. Berry, *Helping?*, https://doi.org/10.1007/978-3-031-88586-0

they were at that moment. I did learn to do this, but it was a struggle. I was curious. I wanted to ask questions, and I wanted to challenge the status quo, but I was cautioned not to get too far ahead of those seeking help. I was urged to slow down. While this advice had some merit (it is indeed essential to match with the readiness of help seekers), until I met Gillian, I did not realize how bold questions coming from the heart can be experienced as an indication of faith in the capacity of the one being questioned to not only survive the discomfort but to grow and thrive as a result.

For me, this awareness meant knowing there had to be something more to offer, but I was not sure where to find it. And when I did find it, I didn't recognize its significance. Thankfully, Gillian did. She kindled a fire in me. She detected long-smoldering embers below the surface of my consciousness, and she fanned them into flames. I came to see and accept my true nature as a disruptor, a visionary of sorts, not a Rogerian client-centered therapist content with active listening and acceptance of the status quo. Through her persistent questions, Gillian helped me to see that I had succeeded in developing an innovative, more flexible approach to delivering mental health care, one that prioritizes self-management and resilience while improving access and efficiency. And through Gillian's mentorship, I discovered ways to integrate decolonizing principles into this work—recognizing that healing cannot be merely technical or symptom-based but must be rooted in cultural humility, authenticity, and respect for the individual's spiritual and community ties.

In reflecting on the collaborative nature of this book that you are reading right now, I am reminded of the intricate dynamic between Gillian and myself—one in which we each mentor and learn from the other. As a partner in this work, my role is, as Gillian suggests, akin to that of the white Irishman in George Bernard Shaw's *The Adventures of the Black Girl in Her Search for God*, a work that serves as the underlying literary device for this book. Shaw's Irishman, who encounters the Black Girl's search for truth with a mixture of caution and curiosity, is a figure who must navigate the discomfort of his position in the face of profound transformation. Similarly, I find myself in a role that is both reflective and active in the journey of mental health decolonization.

I have long felt dissatisfaction with practices sanctioned by the mental health professions. Most of my immediate family members have had significant mental health challenges throughout their lives, and the care they received has been lacking an appreciation of their strengths, gifts, and spirit. So much seemed to be missing in the available support. When I decided to study psychology, I did so with ambivalence. Something was missing there, too. The scientific method dominated the curriculum, and other epistemologies were at best barely tolerated, and at worst openly ridiculed. There appeared to be no humanity in the discipline. So, I looked elsewhere, taking a year off to study philosophy, history, and literature. Ever since, I have applied insights from outside the discipline to reconcile the harms perpetrated by the often rigid, biased, oppressive foundations of mental health practices.

After practicing for a while as a clinical psychologist, I was drawn to leadership roles where I could envision opportunities to disrupt the system by drawing on wisdom outside the discipline. I listened to activists, people with lived experience, and people doing healing work without "credentials." There was a lot of common sense creativity in places like rural Newfoundland and Labrador, where resilience, self-reliance, community efforts, respect for the harsh realities of the climate, and spiritual faith were highly valued components of well-being.

Over the past decade, through a lot of listening, I developed a framework for decolonizing and transforming mental health systems, which we call Stepped Care 2.0 (Cornish, 2020; Cornish & Berry, 2023; Cornish & Berry, 2025). The framework helps communities to broaden what constitutes healing resources, tap into existing community resources, and improve access to professional care. The idea that healing can be simple, and does not require sophisticated administrative structures, was captured by one participant in our innovation work: "Before Stepped Care 2.0, it was like waiting to get access to a backhoe when all you need is a shovel" (Mental Health Commission of Canada, 2019).

Gillian's decision to partner on this journey with me—a white male who, by conventional measures of power, might represent an authority figure in the Eurocentric system she critiques—is not without its risks. Much like Shaw himself (or his Irishman), who navigates the delicate balance between complicity and collaboration in a colonial context, I, too, must confront the complexities of my role as an ally in a system that has historically marginalized voices like hers. Yet, Gillian recognizes the potential for synergy in this partnership, just as the Black Girl in Shaw's novella ultimately engages with the Irishman despite the inherent contradictions. This partnership is not about relinquishing power but rather about co-creating new possibilities through mutual respect and shared purpose.

In mental health care, synergy means working together across divides, recognizing the strengths each brings to the table, and aligning our goals to create systems that are more inclusive, responsive, and culturally attuned. My work in developing Stepped Care 2.0 was a response to the inefficiencies and inequities I saw in traditional mental health systems—approaches that were too rigid and disconnected from the diverse needs of the population. Yet, this work was incomplete until it integrated the cultural insights and Indigenous healing practices that Gillian's perspective has brought to the forefront.

The Stepped Care 2.0 framework is centered on doing the questioning and listening work that Gillian focuses on in this book. It gets people closer to alternate ways of working, many of which draw on collective knowledge and wisdom passed down through the ages. It also encourages people to face the harsh reality of things that are truly broken in our society and to approach these boldly. It provides us with strategies to broach uncomfortable dynamics and topics directly, much like Gillian did when she asked a colleague in a paradoxically loving way, "Why do you talk so much?" and "When are you going to grow up?" The framework asks, much like the Black Girl, "Where is healing?" The answer is that it is everywhere, but perhaps not where you are looking.

In much the same way that Shaw's Irishman has an opportunity to adapt his worldview to accommodate the Black Girl's truths, I, too, received the invitation. By accepting, I acknowledge that the Stepped Care 2.0 model must not only be flexible in how we deliver care but also in how we engage with those who have been historically excluded from decision-making. By embracing the principles of decolonization—whether through a more inclusive mental health system or a more collaborative approach to care—we are not just making room for diverse perspectives; we are actively transforming the structure of mental health itself.

Gillian anticipates that some readers may criticize her choice to have two white men—Dick Katz and myself—bookend her work. Yet, like the Black Girl who challenges the Irishman, Gillian's choice is not about complicity but about recognizing the importance of working together in ways that transcend past divisions. As partners in this effort, our task is to dismantle the systems of exclusion while building something new and better in its place. We do this not by ignoring or denying our differences but by acknowledging them and using them to create something more powerful and effective.

This book is about genuinely helping, not following a script of half-measures. Gillian's synergistic approach to healing critically identifies the issues, explores options, identifies strategies, and constantly learns by investigating alternatives. In this same spirit of synergy, together Gillian and I and our colleagues have created a framework that is adaptive, responsive, and healing. Stepped Care 2.0 is not just a new way to reorganize mental health services, it is an invitation to rethink what it means to be in relationship with others, to listen deeply, and to collaborate across cultural and historical divides. Together, as allies and mentors, we can create a future where mental health care is more accessible, more holistic, and more inclusive.

As I conclude this afterword, I am reminded that our work together—like the search for God in Shaw's novella—is a journey, not a destination. We are not finished; we are only beginning. And in this beginning, we find the possibility for true transformation, one that comes not through individual effort but through the power of synergy.

Acknowledgements

Writing this book was not a task I initially embraced. For many years, I resisted the persistent inner voice urging me to complete this journey. It was only through the encouragement of those around me—whose belief in my abilities inspired confidence—that I finally committed to completing this work. While I cannot name all the voices of support (and some I never discovered), I am deeply grateful for the wealth of encouragement and contributions that made this part of my life journey possible.

I owe a debt of gratitude to the many scholars and thought leaders who shared their insights with me, whether in person, through their writings, or via social media platforms. Their contributions fueled my drive to understand and inspired me to persevere. To my colleagues across the globe—at the University of Botswana, the University of Zambia, the University of Birmingham (England), the University of Maryland, and The George Washington University—thank you for your encouragement, advice, and practical assistance. Your support has been invaluable.

I would like to extend special thanks to Dr. Richard Katz, Dr. Peter Cornish, Dr. Catie Greene, and André Forget for their invaluable guidance and mentorship. In England, my heartfelt gratitude goes to my colleagues at Birmingham Social Services Department, Perry Barr Sub Office. In Zambia, I am particularly indebted to the traditional healers who generously offered their counsel, as well as the Kara Counselling Centre, the University of Zambia Counselling Centre, and Chinamon Mental Hospital. I am deeply appreciative of Ms. Lillian Daka and the late Mr. Cyril Mwamba for their personal and translation assistance. Mr. Mwamba's faith in my work transcends his passing, and his confidence continues to inspire me. In the United States, my gratitude goes to the staff at the East Side Centre for Short Term Psychotherapy (New York), Sister Muhammad and her family (Los Angeles), and the Nation of Islam (Chicago). I am privileged to work with my colleagues at Stepped Care Solutions, (Canada) whose innovative approach to mental health delivery inspires me every day.

To all those who have attended my lectures, seminars, and training courses, or participated in one-on-one sessions with me—your questions, feedback, and

G. Berry, *Helping?*, https://doi.org/10.1007/978-3-031-88586-0

engagement have immeasurably shaped my journey. Thank you for contributing to this work in such meaningful ways.

I am profoundly thankful for the personal support I have received, that was so freely given and filled with so much love. My deepest thanks to my parents, who, though no longer with us, continue to guide me with their enduring love and wisdom. To my siblings who have joined them, I am grateful for the love and support we shared while you were here.

To the special people in my life who have made it so meaningful—my beloved daughter Shakira, and dear friends Patsy, Ralph, Almina, Sophia, and Jane—your unwavering faith in me has been a constant source of strength. Your encouragement gave me the confidence to see this project through to completion.

Above all, I am profoundly grateful to the force—the energy and power—that has sustained, encouraged, and guided me throughout this journey of understanding. This force has been my compass, and I am humbled by its guidance as I bring this work to life.

References

Abraham, K. C., & Mbuya-Beya, B. (1994). *Spirituality of the third world*. Orbis Books.
Afua, Q. (1992). *Heal thyself*. A&B Books.
Akbar, N. (1979). African roots of Black personality. In W. D. Smith et al. (Eds.), *Reflections on black psychology*. University Press of America.
Akbar, N. (1984). Afrocentric social sciences for human liberation. *Journal of Black Studies, 14*(4), 395–414.
Akbar, N. (1991). *The community of self (revised)*. Mind Productions & Associates.
Akbar, N. (1995). *Natural psychology and human transformation (revised)*. Mind Productions & Associates, Inc.
Akbar, N. (1996). *Breaking the chains of psychological slavery*. Mind Productions & Associates.
American Counseling Association. (2020, June 22). *Position statement*. American Counseling Association. https://www.counseling.org/about/values-statements/anti-racism-statement
American Psychiatric Association. (2021, January 18). *APA's apology to Black, Indigenous, and People of Color for its support of structural racism in psychiatry*. American Psychiatric Association. https://www.psychiatry.org/news-room/apa-apology-for-its-support-of-structural-racism
American Psychological Association. (2021, October 29). *Apology to People of Color for APA's role in promoting, perpetuating, and failing to challenge racism, racial discrimination, and human hierarchy in U.S.* American Psychological Association. https://www.apa.org/about/policy/racism-apology
Amokeodo, V. (1998, February/March). New hope on the horizon: The mental health system is failing Black people. *Black Perspective, 11*, 4–7.
Angers, M. E. (2011). How do we know? The question of science and psychoanalysis in the aftermath of "post-positivism". *Issues in Psychoanalytic Psychology, 33*, 13–31.
Ani, M., (aka Richards, D.) (2000). *Yurugu: An African-Centred critique of European cultural thought and behaviour* (10th ed.). Africa World Press Inc.
Appiah, K. (1992). *In my father's house: Africa in the philosophy of culture*. Oxford University Press.
Asante, M. (1988). *Afrocentricity*. Africa World Press Inc.
Asante, M. (1997). The Afrocentric metatheory and disciplinary implications. In M. Rogers (Ed.), *Multicultural experiences, multicultural theories*. The McGraw-Hill Companies Inc.
Asante, M. K. (2007). *An Afrocentric manifesto*. Polity.
Asante, M., & Asante, K. (Eds.). (1990). *African culture: The rhythms of unity*. Africa World Press Inc..
Association of Black Psychologists. (2021). *Statement*. Association of Black Psychologists. https://abpsi.org/wp-content/uploads/2021/11/ABPsi-Full-Statement.pdf
Azibo, D. A. (2015). Moving forward with the legitimization of the Azibo nosology II. *Journal of African American Studies, 19*, 298–313.

G. Berry, *Helping?*, https://doi.org/10.1007/978-3-031-88586-0

Azibo, D. (1994). The kindred fields of Black liberation theology and liberational psychology: A critical essay on their conceptual base and destiny. *Journal of Black Psychology, 20*(3), 334–356.

Baldwin, S. A., Wampold, B. E., & Imel, Z. E. (2007). Untangling the alliance-outcome correlation: Exploring the relative importance of therapist and patient variability in the alliance. *Journal of Consulting & Clinical Psychology, 75*(6), 842–852. https://doi.org/10.1037/0022-006X.75.6.842

Bar-on, A. (1999). Social work and the 'missionary zeal to whip the heathen along the path of righteousness'. *British Journal of Social Work, 29*, 5–26.

Bentley, E. (1967). *Bernard Shaw*. Methuen.

Berman, J. (1979). Counseling skills used by black and white male and female counselors. *Journal of Counseling Psychology, 26*(1), 81–86.

Boahen, A. A. (1987). *African perspectives on colonialism*. John Hopkins University Press.

Boahen, A. A. (Ed.). (1990). *General history of Africa: VII Africa under colonial domination 1880-1835*. James Curry United Nations Educational Scientific and Cultural Organisation (UNESCO).

Bolger, A. W. (Ed.). (1982). *Counselling in Britain*. Batsford Academic and Educational Ltd.

Branco, S., & Jones, C. (2021). Supporting Black, Indigenous, and People of Color counselors: Considerations for counselor skills training and practice. *Journal of Mental Health Counseling, 43*(4), 281–300. https://doi.org/10.17744/mehc.43.4.01

Brent, L. (1973). *Incidents in the life of a slave girl*. San Diego Harcourt Brace & Company.

Browder, A. (1992). *Nile Valley contributions to civilization*. The Institute of Karmic Guidance.

Brown, D., & Pedder, J. (1992). *An introduction to psychotherapy*. Routledge.

Brown, G. E. (1970). *George Bernard Shaw*. Evans Brothers.

Burkett, C. A. (2017). Obstructed use: Reconceptualizing the mental health (help-seeking) experiences of Black Americans. *Journal of Black Psychology, 43*(8), 813–835. https://doi.org/10.1177/0095798417691381

Cairns, H. (1965). *Prelude to imperialism: British Reactions to Central African Society*. Routledge & Kegan Paul.

Carlson, K. M., & Gonzalez-Prendes, A. A. (2016). Cognitive behavioral therapy with religious and spiritual clients: A critical perspective. *Journal of Spirituality in Mental Health, 18*(4), 253–282.

Césaire, A. (2017). *Journal of a Homecoming/Cahier d'un retour au pays natal,* (trans. N. Gregson Davis). Duke University Press (original work published 1956).

Charema, J., & Shizha, E. (2008). Counseling indigenous Shona people in Zimbabwe: Traditional practices versus western Eurocentric perspectives. *Alternative, 4*(2), 124–139.

Christian, M. (2019). A global critical race and racism framework: Racial entanglements and deep and malleable whiteness. *Sociology of Race and Ethnicity, 5*(2), 169–185. https://doi.org/10.1177/2332649218783220

Christie's. (1995, June 14). *Shaw, George Bernard: The adventures of a Black girl in her search* for God. https://www.christies.com/lot/shaw-george-bernard-the-adventures-of-324746/?intObjectID=324746&lid=1

Clark, C. X., McGee, D. P., Nobles, W. W., & Weems, L. X. (1975). Voodoo or IQ: An introduction to African psychology. *Journal of Black Psychology, 1*, 29–29.

Clarke, J. H. (1991). *World revolution: Africa at the crossroads*. Africa World Press.

Coetzee, P. H., & Roux, A. P. J. (Eds.). (1998). *Philosophy from Africa: A text with Readings*. International Thomson Publishing (Southern Africa) (Pty) Ltd.

Cornish, P. (2020). *Stepped care 2.0: A paradigm shift in mental health*. Springer.

Cornish, P., & Berry, G. (eds) (2023). *Stepped care 2.0: The power of conundrums*. Springer.

Cornish, P., & Berry, G. (Eds) (2025). *Synergy: The healing energy guiding Stepped Care 2.0*. Springer.

Dalal, F. (1988). The racism of Jung. *Race & Class, 29*(3), 1–22.

Davis, T. C. (1994). *George Bernard Shaw and the socialist theatre*. Greenwood Press.

Delaney, H. D., & DiClemente, C. C. (2005). Psychology's roots: A brief history of the influence of Judeo-Christian perspectives. In W. R. Miller & H. D. Delaney (Eds.), *Judeo-Christian perspectives on psychology: Human nature, motivation, and change* (pp. 31–54). American Psychological Association. https://doi.org/10.1037/10859-002

Delaney, H. D., Miller, W. R., & Bisono, A. M. (2013). Religiosity and spirituality among psychologists: A survey of clinician members of the American Psychological Association. *Spirituality in Clinical Practice, 1*, 95–106. https://doi.org/10.1037/2326.4500.1.S.95

Diop, C. A. (1974). *The African origin of civilization*. Chicago Review Press.

Diop, C. A. (1978). *The cultural unity of Black Africa*. Third World Press.

Dryden, W., Edwards, D., Woolfe, R. (1989). *Handbook of counselling in Britain*. Routledge. In Association with the British Association of Counselling.

Ellenberger, H. (1970). *The discovery of the unconscious: The history and evolution of dynamic psychiatry*. Basic Books.

Eysenck, H. J. (1952). The effects of psychotherapy: an evaluation. *Journal of Consulting Psychology, 16*(5), 319–324. https://doi.org/10.1037/h0063633

Eze, E. (1997). *Race and the enlightenment: A reader*. Blackwell Publishers.

Fanon, F. (1967). *Black skin, white masks*. Grove Press.

Fieldhouse, D. K. (1988). *Colonialism 1870-1945*. Macmillan.

Flick, H. (1981). Malcolm X: The destroyer and creator of myths. *Journal of Black Psychology, 12*(2), 166–181.

Fonlon, B. (1967). Idea of culture (II). in *ABBIA*. *Cameroon Cultural Review, 16*, 5–24.

Fuentes, M. A., Zelaya, D. G., & Madsen, J. W. (2020). Rethinking the course syllabus: Considerations for promoting equity, diversity, and inclusion. *Society for the Teaching of Psychology, 48*(1), 1–11. https://doi.org/10.1177/0098628320959979

Gail, M. (1976). *Dawn over Mount Hira*. George Ronald.

Gee, G., Dudgeon, P., Schultz, C., Hart, A., & Kelly, K. (2014). Aboriginal and Torres Strait Islander social and emotional wellbeing. In P. Dudgeon, H. Milroy, & R. Walker (Eds.), *Working together: Aboriginal and Torres Strait Islander Mental Health and Wellbeing Principles and Practice* (2nd ed., pp. 55–58). Commonwealth Government of Australia.

Genia, V. (1995). *Counseling and psychotherapy of religious clients: A developmental approach*. Praeger.

GlassworksVFX. (2010, July 23). *TFL Viral - Awareness Test (Moonwalking Bear)*. [Video]. YouTube. https://www.youtube.com/watch?v=xNSgmm9FX2s

Global Institute of Social Work (2022). *1860-1900: The friendly visitor*. Retrieved from: https://www.thegisw.org/copy-of-charity-organization-societ

Gordon, R. (1998). The rise of the Bushman penis: Germans, genitalia and genocide. *African Studies, 57*(1), 27–54. https://doi.org/10.1080/00020189808707884

Grayshield, L. (2010). Indigenous ways of knowing as a philosophical base for the promotion of peace and justice in counseling education and psychology. *Journal for Social Action in Counseling & Psychology, 2*(2), 1–16.

Guthrie, R. (1976). *Even the rat was white: A historical view of psychology*. Harper & Row.

Gyatso, T. (n.d.). *Compassion and the individual*. The Office of His Holiness the Dalai Lama. https://www.dalailama.com/messages/compassion-and-human-values/compassion

Hall, C. S. (1954). *A primer of Freudian psychology*. Mentor Books.

Halmos, P. (1967). *The faith of the counsellors* (2nd ed.). Constable.

Hlongwane, M. M., Govender, S., Makhubu, S. S., Makhonza, L. O., Kent, D., Ochiogu, S. N., Gumede, G. V., Nzima, D. R., & Edwards, S. D. (2018). African centered investigation into ways in which Ubuntu can promote social coherence. *Indilinga: African Journal of Indigenous Knowledge Systems, 17*(1), 53–66.

Holroyd, M. (1991). *Bernard Shaw: Volume III 1918-1950 the lure of fantasy*. Chatto & Windus.

Hountondji, P. (1983). *African philosophy: Myth and reality*. Hutchinson University Library for Africa.

Howe, S. (1998). *Afrocentrism: Mythical pasts and imagined homes*. Verso.

Jafari, K. (2016). Religion and spirituality within counselling/clinical psychology training programmes: A systematic review. *British Journal of Guidance & Counseling, 44*(*3*), 257–267. https://doi.org/10.1080/03069885.2016.1153038

Judy, R. A. (1991). Kant and the Negro. *Surfaces, 1*. https://doi.org/10.7202/1065256ar

Karenga, M. (1997). African culture and the ongoing quest for excellence: Dialog, principles, practice. *The Free Library*. Retrieved Jan. 28, 2025 from https://www.thefreelibrary.com/African+culture+and+the+ongoing+quest+for+excellence%3a+dialog%2c...-a019263785

Katz, R. (2017). *Indigenous healing psychology. Honoring the wisdom of the First Peoples.* Solar Power.

Katz, R., & Murphy-Shigematsu, S. (2012). *Synergy, healing, and empowerment: Insights from cultural diversity*. Brush Education.

Killingray, D. (1973). *A plague of Europeans: Westerners in Africa since the fifteenth century.* Middlesex Penguin Education.

King, M., Smith, A., & Gracey, M. (2009). Indigenous health part 2: The underlying causes of the health gap. *The Lancet, 374*(9683), 76–85. https://doi.org/10.1016/S0140-6736(09)60827-8

Kuhn, T. S. (2012). *The structure of scientific revolutions: 50th anniversary edition* (4th ed.). The University of Chicago Press.

Lartey, E., Nwachuku, D., & Kasonga, K. (Eds.). (1994). *The church and healing echoes from Africa*. Peter Lang.

Leahey, T. A. (1996). *History of psychology: Main currents in psychological thought* (4th ed.). Prentice Hall.

MalcolmShabazz. (2018, February 14). *Malcolm X: If you stick a knife in my back nine inches...* [Video]. YouTube. https://www.youtube.com/watch?v=DlfjmZw72bo

Mama, A. (1995). *Beyond the masks: Race, gender, and subjectivity*. Routledge.

Masson, J. (1988). *Against therapy*. Harper Collins.

Mato Nunpa, C. (2020). *The great evil (wosice tanka kin): Christianity, the Bible, and the Native American genocide*. See Sharp Press.

Mbiti, J. (1969). *African religions & philosophy*. Heinemann.

McCall, G. J., & Resick, P. A. (2003). A pilot study of PTSD symptoms among Kalahari Bushmen. *Journal of Trauma Stress, 16*(5), 445–450. https://doi.org/10.1023/A:1025702326392

McLeod, J. (2017). Science and psychotherapy: Developing research-based knowledge that enhances the effectiveness of practice. *Transactional Analysis Journal, 47*(2), 82–101.

Mental Health Commission of Canada. (2019). *Stepped care 2.0*. Health Canada. https://mentalhealthcommission.ca/what-we-do/access/stepped-care-2-0/

Messing, S. D., & MSS Information Corporation. (1972). *The target of health in Ethiopia : A holistic reader in applied anthropology*. MSS Information Corporation.

Miller, H. A. & Daniel Murray Pamphlet Collection. (1906). Some psychological considerations in the race problem. [Oberlin, Ohio?: s.n., ?]. Retrieved from the Library of Congress, https://www.loc.gov/item/91898230/

Mkhize, N. (2021). African/Afrikan-centered psychology. *South African Journal of Psychology, 51*(3), 422–429.

Montgomery, D., Fine, M., & James-Myers, L. (1990). The development and validation of an instrument to assess an optimal Afrocentric world view. *The Journal of Black Psychology, 17*(1), 37–54.

Morris, C., & Maistro, A. (1998). *Psychology: An introduction* (10th ed.). Prentice Hall.

Morris, G. T. (1992). International law and politics: Toward a right to self-determination for indigenous peoples. In M. Annette Jaimes (Ed.), *The state of native North America: Genocide, colonization, and resistance*. South End Press.

Mudimbe, A. (1988). *The invention of Africa gnosis, philosophy, and the order of knowledge*. London Indiana University Press James Currey.

Myers, L. (1993). *Understanding an Afrocentric world view: Introduction to optimal psychology* (2nd ed.). Kendall Hunt Publishing.

National Association of Social Workers. (2021). *NASW apologizes for racist practices in American social work*. National Association of Social Workers. https://www.socialworkers.org/News/News-Releases/ID/2331/NASW-apologizes-for-racist-practices-in-American-social-work

National Conference of Black Churchmen. (1999). "Black Power" statement, July 31, 1966, and "Black Theology" statement, June 13, 1969. In M. C. Sernett (Ed.), *African American religious history: A documentary witness* (pp. 555–566). Duke University Press. https://doi.org/10.2307/j.ctv11smnkh.62

National Joint Action Committee (n.d.). *What they did in slavery times.*. Port of Spain Information Department.

Ndlovu-Gatsheni, S. J. (2015). Decoloniality as the future of Africa. *History Compass, 13*(10), 485–496.

Nobles, W. (1980). African philosophy: Foundations for Black psychology. In R. L. Jones (Ed.), *Black psychology* (2nd ed.). Harper & Row.

Nobles, W. (1976). Extended self: Rethinking the so-called Negro self-concept. *Journal of Black Psychology, 2*(2), 15–24.

Nyamnjoh, F. B. (1999). African cultural studies, cultural studies in Africa: How to make a useful difference. *Journal of Critical Arts, 13*(1), 15–39.

Nyamnjoh, F. B. (2000). "For many are called but few are chosen": Globalisation and popular disenchantment in Africa. *African Sociological Review/Revue Africaine de Sociologie, 4*(2), 1–45. https://doi.org/10.4314/asr.v4i2.23225

Nyamnjoh, F. B. (2001). Delusions of development and the enrichment of witchcraft discourses in Cameroon. *Magical Interpretations, Material Realities*. Routledge.

O'Grady, K. A., & Slife, B. D. (2017). *The hidden worldviews of psychology's theory, research, and practice*. Routledge.

Omoregbe, J. I. (1998). African philosophy: Yesterday and today. In E. Eze (Ed.), *African philosophy: An anthology*. Blackwell Publishers.

Pargament, K. I., & Lomax, J. W. (2013). Understanding and addressing religion among people with mental illness. *World Psychiatry, 12*(1), 26–32.

Parham, T. A., Ajamu, A., & White, J. L. (2016). *The psychology of Blacks: Centering our perspectives in the African consciousness* (4th ed.). Routledge.

Paris, P. (1995). *The spirituality of African peoples: The search for a common moral discourse*. Fortress Press.

Parrott, L. (1997). *Counselling and psychotherapy*. McGraw-Hill Companies, Inc.

Parsons, N. (2000). *El Negro/El Negre of Banyoles: Bushman from Bechuanaland, or Bechuana from Bushmanland?* University of Botswana History Department Seminar Paper presented 30th March 2000.

Phillips, F. (1990). NTU psychotherapy: An Afrocentric approach. *The Journal of Black Psychology, 17*(1), 55–74.

Phillips, F. (1994). Notes on the Azibo theology-psychology comparison. *The Journal of Black Psychology, 20*(3), 357–359.

Plante, T. G., & Thoresen, C. E. (2012). Spirituality, religion, and psychological counseling. *The Oxford handbook of psychology and spirituality* (pp. 388–409).

Rabak, R. (2015). *The Négritude movement: W.E.B. DuBois, Leon Damas, Aimé Cesaire, Léopold Senghor, Frantz Fanon, and the evolution of an insurgent idea*. Rowman & Littlefield Publishers.

Ramsey, G. (1992). An Afro-centric perspective to social work training. *Journal of Training and Development in Social Work Practice, 2*(3), 47–50.

Richburg, K. (1997). *Out of America: A Black man confronts Africa*. Basic Books.

Robinson, L. (2009). *Psychology for social workers: Black perspectives on human development and behaviour*. Routledge.

Rodogno, D. (2020). Certainty, compassion and the ingrained arrogance of humanitarians. In *The red cross movement: Myths, practices, and turning points* (pp. 27–44). Manchester University Press.

Rogers, C. (1951). *Client-centred therapy*. Constable.

Rogers, C. (1957). The necessary and sufficient conditions of psychotherapeutic personality change. *Journal of Consulting Psychology, 21*, 95–103.

Rosmarin, D., Green, D., Pirutinsky, S., & Mckay, D. (2013). Attitudes toward spirituality/religion among members of the Association for behavioral and cognitive therapies. *Professional Psychology: Research & Practice, 44*(6), 424–433. https://doi.org/10.1037/a0035218

Sa'di. (2008). *The Gulistan (rose garden) of Sa'di: Bilingual English and Persian edition with vocabulary*. (trans. Wheeler M. Thackston). Ibex Publishers.

Sashidharan, S. (1997). *Schizophrenic—or just Black? Conference paper*. Black Mental Health Conference, the King's Fund, London, January 29, 1997.

Schiele, J. (2000). *Human services and the Afrocentric paradigm*. The Haworth Press.

Semaj, L. (1981). The Black self, identity, and models for a psychology of Black liberation. *The Western Journal of Black Studies, 5*(3), 158–171.

Semmes, C. E. (1997). Religion and the challenge of Afrocentric thought. In M. Rogers (Ed.), *Multicultural experiences, multicultural theories*. The McGraw-Hill Companies Inc.

Shaw, G. B. (1932). *The adventures of a Black girl in her search for God*. Constable.

Shostak, M. (1983). *Nisa: The life of a !Kung woman*. Penguin Books.

Spanierman, L. B., & Smith, L. (2017). Confronting white hegemony: A moral imperative for the helping professions. *The Counseling Psychologist, 45*(5), 727–736. https://doi.org/10.1177/0011000017719550

Sue, D. W., Alsaidi, S., Awad, M. N., Glaeser, E., Calle, C. Z., & Mendez, N. (2019a). Disarming racial microaggressions: Microintervention strategies for targets, white allies, and bystanders. *American Psychologist, 74*(1), 128–142. https://doi.org/10.1037/amp0000296

Sue, D. W., Sue, D., Neville, H. A., & Smith, L. (2019b). *Counseling the culturally diverse: Theory and practice* (8th ed.). Wiley.

Taiwo, O. (1998). Exorcising Hegel's ghost: Africa's challenge to philosophy. *African Studies Quarterly, 1*(4), 3–16.

Temples, P. (1959). *Bantu philosophy*. Presence Africaine Congo.

The Box Bundle. (2021, March 12). *Shine a Light on Darkness - Institutionalised Racism in Gloucestershire Fire & Rescue Services*. [Video]. YouTube. https://www.youtube.com/watch?v=4p7dpEulucg

Truax, C. B., & Carkhuff, R. R. (1967). *Toward effective counseling and psychotherapy: Training and practice*. Aldine Publishing Co..

Usher, C. H. (1989). Recognizing cultural bias in counseling theory and practice: The case of Rogers. *Journal of Multicultural Counseling and Development, 17*(2), 62–71.

Van Niekerk, M. (1998). Understanding trends in "African thinking": A critical discussion. In P. H. Coetzee & A. P. J. Roux (Eds.), *Philosophy from Africa: A text with readings*. Johannesburg International Thomson Publishing (Southern Africa) Ltd..

Waldron, I. (2010). The marginalization of African Indigenous healing traditions within Western Medicine: Reconciling ideological tensions and contractions along the epistemological terrain. *Women's Health & Urban Life, 9*(1), 50–68. https://hdl.handle.net/1807/24423

Wampold, B. E. (2010). The research evidence for the common factors models: A historically situated perspective. In B. L. Duncan, S. D. Miller, B. E. Wampold, & M. A. Hubble (Eds.), *The heart and soul of change: Delivering what works in therapy* (2nd ed., pp. 49–81). American Psychological Association. https://doi.org/10.1037/12075-002

Winston, A. S. (2020). Why mainstream research will not end scientific racism in psychology. *Theory & Psychology, 30*(3), 425–430. https://doi.org/10.1177/0959354320927086

World Health Organization & Joint United Nations Programme on HIV/AIDS. (2022, April 28). *Integration of mental health and HIV interventions: Key considerations*. World Health Organization Global HIV, Hepatitis and STIs Programmes (HHS). https://iris.who.int/bitstream/handle/10665/353571/9789240043176-eng.pdf?sequence=1

Index

G. Berry, *Helping?*, https://doi.org/10.1007/978-3-031-88586-0

S

T

U

The manufacturer's authorised representative in the EU is Springer Nature Customer Service Centre GmbH, Europaplatz 3, 69115 Heidelberg, Germany. If you have any concerns regarding our products, please contact ProductSafety@springernature.com

Printed and bound by CPI Group (UK) Ltd, Croydon, CR0 4YY
30/09/2026
02225608-0019